W9-ABV-454

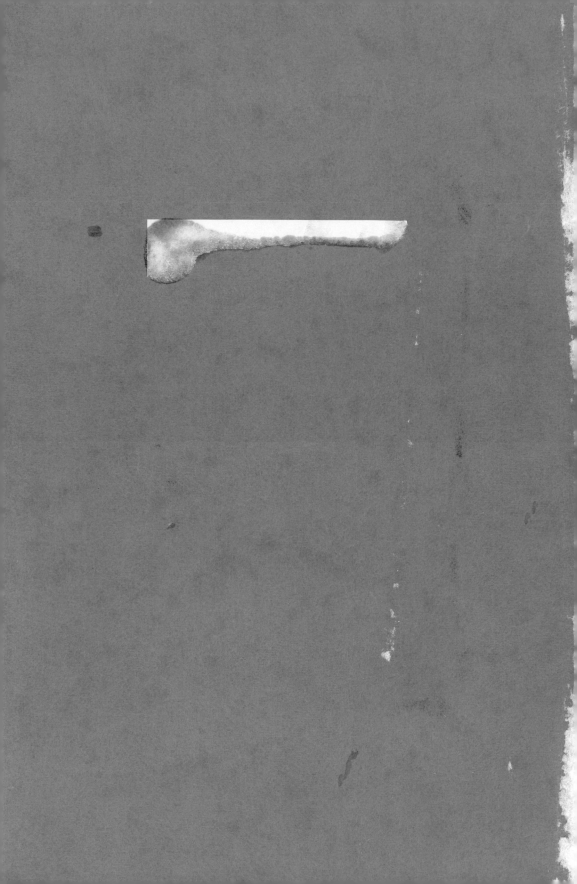

THE MIND'S BEST WORK

D.N. Perkins

The Mind's Best Work

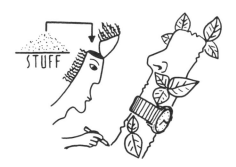

HARVARD　　　UNIVERSITY　　　PRESS
Cambridge, Massachusetts　London, England
1981

LIBRARY OF CONGRESS CATALOGING IN PUBLICATION DATA

Perkins, D. N., 1942–
    The mind's best work.

    Bibliography: p.
    Includes index.
    1. Creation (Literary, artistic, etc.)   2. Creative ability.   I. Title.
BF408.P387   153.3'5   81-4223
ISBN 0-674-57627-6   AACR2

To The Generations:
David and Leone Perkins
Ann Perkins
Ted, Alice, and Tom

ACKNOWLEDGMENTS

A finished book is a way for a writer to share ideas with others. But a book-in-the-making is an occasion for others to share their ideas with the writer. Many individuals have contributed in diverse ways to these pages, and here I gratefully acknowledge them. First of all, the research behind this book reflects the commitment and intelligence of several people who have worked with me over the past decade. Thanks go to Roy Rudenstine for helping with my early research using think-aloud methods; to Jerry Fisher for beginning the study of poets; to Fred Linsk especially for carrying out the larger part of that study; to Ann Troy for assistance in analyzing the data; to Mark Miller for investigating the solving of insight problems; to Bob Hodgman and Marshall Kirk for helping with several studies and library research on creativity; to David Grosof and Ashok Nimgade for library research on teaching thinking skills; to Mark Smith for investigating the role of analogies in inventive thinking; to Rick Allen and Jim Hafner for helping me to see this project through in many small ways; and to all the others who have assisted me on related projects.

I also want to thank those who helped in another way – the poets, artists, and other individuals who participated as subjects in my studies. They gracefully submitted to the strictures and intrusions of research. Much of what is said in these chapters could not have been said but for their willingness to venture.

Four of my colleagues wrote recommendations for a Guggenheim Fellowship I held for the year 1976–77 to write on the creative process. Their contribution goes beyond this welcome service. I want to thank Nelson Goodman for diverse insights about symbol use in human thought and artifacts; Paul Kolers for many lively conversations, several fruitful collaborations, and getting me started on my present course; Diana Korzenik for her educator's perspective and her artist's insights; and Israel Scheffler for his sound and humane logic applied to scholarly problems and his speaking out on numerous occasions in support of our work.

The research for this volume was done at Project Zero, a basic research program at the Harvard Graduate School of Education concerned with human symbolic processes and symbolic development. My thanks go to Howard Gardner, codirector of Project Zero with myself and colleague of many years, who commented discerningly on several chapters of the draft of this book. I am grateful for discussions with Vernon Howard that have clarified many points within these pages.

This book has been made a better one, and the finishing of it a pleasure, by individuals at the Harvard University Press. Editors Joyce Backman and Eric Wanner not only identified problems large and small but contributed some creative solutions. Gwen Frankfeldt matched form to subject matter by her inventiveness with the design of the book.

Let me express appreciation to the several agencies that have supported my research over the past decade: The National Institute of Education for funding investigations of inventive thinking, with particular gratitude to Martin Engel, our project officer, for his insight and encouragement; the National Science Foundation for funding investigations of problem solving and visual perception; the Spencer Foundation for underwriting research on everyday reasoning; and the Guggenheim Foundation for the year's fellowship during which I began the writing that evolved into this book. I add the customary disclaimer that the ideas presented here do not necessarily reflect the positions or policies of the supporting agencies.

Finally, my thanks go to my wife Ann for her astute criticisms and suggestions, our oldest son Ted for contributing a drawing as well as triggering several insights that have made their way into these pages, and to my whole family for their forbearance during the busy evenings and weekends behind the words collected here.

CONTENTS

THE MIND'S BEST WORK

 # A PARABLE

The Dutchman Roggeveen discovered Easter Island, a wink of land far from all the major island groups of the Pacific, on Easter Day 1722. Along with the island, he discovered a mystery. Scattered across the terrain were enormous stone faces with torsos, many tumbled down but, in Roggeveen's day, some few still standing on pedestals. The upright ones wore on their heads large topknots of a differently colored stone. In 1840, the last one to be toppled still looked over the treeless vista of the island. Perched on a wall the height of a man, its thirty-two-foot-tall body weighed about fifty tons. The topknot, weighing perhaps ten tons, had a volume of something like two hundred cubic feet. The main figure was two and a half miles from the quarry where it had been carved.

How were the figures transported? How were they erected? How were the enormous topknots raised thirty feet in the air and settled squarely on the heads of the idols? Such questions defined the enigma of Easter Island. Whatever skills lay behind this massive engineering effort seemed to have been lost. The archeological record showed that, in a social upheaval long before, the old faith had been denied and its symbols, the great faces, tumbled down one by one. Stone tools lay about the quarry, abandoned as though in the midst of work. Here it was clear enough how the job had been done. But as to the rest?

Easter Island posed not only a mystery but what might be called a "high mystery." The obscure religion, the great staring faces, the seeming physical and technological inadequacy of the inhabitants for feats of such magnitude, all conspired to suggest that something beyond human ken might be at work. Indeed, some have been quick to argue just this. In his notorious *Chariots of the Gods?* Erich von Dänikan devoted a short chapter to Easter Island. "Humanly impossible" was the gist of his conclusion. It might be, von Dänikan suggested, that ancient and alien astronauts visited our primitive planet, giving our ignorant forebears a genetic boost, starting civilization off, inspiring cults and lending a hand in the making of suitably respectful monuments.

A comparison with the way the mystery of creativity has been approached is not so farfetched. Creativity has often been taken as one of those "high mysteries." How a person has captured the insight and conjured the energy to paint a masterpiece, devise a revolutionary scientific theory, make music in a way that moves listeners down the ages, has been thought beyond the reach of human understanding, stubbornly inscrutable, essentially ineffable. Moreover, creativity has had its von Dänikans. Plato was one of them, putting into the mouth of Socrates a classic account of invention:

> For the poets tell us, don't they, that the melodies they bring us are gathered from rills that run with honey, out of glens and gardens of the Muses, and they bring them as the bees do honey, flying like the bees? And what they say is true, for a poet is a light and winged thing, and holy, and never able to compose until he has become inspired, and is beside himself and reason is no longer in him . . . for not by art do they utter these, but by power divine.

Now, to compare Plato with von Dänikan is downright scurrilous, not only because of Plato's profound philosophical accomplishments and cultural influence but because of von Dänikan's misrepresentations. When *Chariots of the Gods?* was first published in German in 1968, the solution to the mystery of Easter Island had been known for eleven years. The discoverer was the Norwegian student of Pacific cultures, Thor Heyerdahl, who published a popular account of his inquiries at Easter Island under the title *Aku-Aku*. This was the very source von Dänikan cited in his book. However, not once in the seven pages devoted to the island does von Dänikan mention how Heyerdahl persuaded the contemporary inhabitants to demonstrate the "impossible" feats of their ancestors.

So the parable continues. The shenanigans of von Dänikan will turn out to have their parallel, sorry to say, in some misleading descriptions of creating. But what about the mystery of Easter Island? Consider just a piece of it: the erection of the stone figures. After some thought, Thor Heyerdahl adopted a clever strategy. He told the mayor of the island, a descendant of the earlier inhabitants, that one hundred dollars would go to him when the largest of the old statues on a certain site was again upright on its pedestal. The mayor explained how, as a child, he had been drilled in an oral tradition of recipes for such matters until he could repeat them exactly. Why had he never disclosed the mystery before? No one had asked him, was the answer. Or perhaps no one had asked him so persuasively. The mayor and eleven other men, using three long stout wooden poles and a number of stones, raised the largest statue in eighteen days. More than twice the height of a man, the statue weighed about thirty tons.

The method was ingenious, First, the helpers worked together on the poles to lever up the statue slightly. Usually it seemed not to move at all, sometimes to budge just a little. Meanwhile the mayor was busy placing small stones under the edges of the fallen statue as his helpers heaved. Then the small stones were replaced with slightly larger stones. The process of levering plus building up continued, and at the end of the first day of work, the thirty-ton idol of Easter Island lay with its head on a mound of stones three feet above the surface of the ground, a feat of levitation as deft in its way as the work of magicians.

Speaking of creativity, some person or persons early in the island's history had been remarkably ingenious in evolving a way to shift monumental chunks of rock. Their invention had not been forgotten. By the tenth day, the statue lay prone on a pile of stones more than twelve feet high, and over the next days the figure was maneuvered gradually toward the pedestal, where in a few moments of carefully controlled climax it slid neatly into place.

There you have it, the mystery of Easter Island resolved by artful engineering. Now I want to point out something that easily could be overlooked: the clarity of this explanation. We can readily imagine how the eleven men could have pried up the statue slightly. We can envision the mayor placing the pebbles and larger rocks under the statue to preserve the millimeters of progress. We can appreciate how this cycle, repeated over and over, could erect the monument. Although the mayor's plan certainly was not obvious before he revealed it, once revealed its logic is plain. The puzzle of how the statues were erected reduces to common sense.

I hope for something like that clarity with the subject of this book. I want to make the strange familiar. I want to show how creating in the arts and sciences is a natural comprehensible extension and orchestration of ordinary everyday abilities of perception, understanding, memory, and so on, just as the erecting of the Easter Island statues was a comprehensible extension and orchestration of human muscle, the principle of the prop, and the principle of the lever. I want to argue that many significant insights can be explained as occuring in essentially the same way, by means of essentially the same psychological mechanisms, as the ordinary everyday act of understanding a Woody Allen joke. Many moments of discovery can be understood as exercising essentially the same phychological mechanisms that operate when we casually notice a dime on the street and pick it up. Many amazing scientific and artistic accomplishments can be understood as products of the kind of searching we do when we systematically pick lint off a sweater. In short, too often we have missed the connections between the marvelous and the mundane.

For this task, I will need the help of a number of ideas and experiments from contemporary psychology: the concept of pattern recognition, the concept of search through a space of alternatives, the concept of schema, findings on the role of fluency in creative thought, on the process of incubation in problem solving, and on efforts designed to teach problem-solving skills, to name just a few. Many pages will be spent reviewing and interpreting such studies.

But I will not go deeply into the technical theories designed to account for the details of such superficially simple acts as walking or talking or remembering. The concern is not to explain these everyday activities themselves, just as it was no business of the mayor of Easter Island, or Thor Heyerdahl either, to explain the psychology of how the natives saw with their eyes or moved their bodies in erecting the statue, or the physics of the levers they used. Such matters were taken for granted there. They functioned as givens in terms of which the accomplishment could be understood. The present strategy is similar. Often I will emphasize important "operating characteristics" of perception, understanding, and memory, some that have been prominent and some neglected in contemporary psychological inquiry. But I will not often examine accounts of how those mental processes do their work because this understanding simply is not necessary. The aim is to comprehend creating in terms of commonplace resources of mind and some of their familiar and less familiar operating characteristics, but not particularly to explain those resources themselves.

This should be a relief to the reader, and certainly has been a relief to me. In a way, the real challenge of psychological inquiry today is not so much to explain the marvelous, which with some thought and some investigation reduces readily enough to the mundane. The real challenge is to explain the mundane. It is a mission I will cheerfully sidestep for the length of this book.

The mystery of Easter Island posed a "how" question – how did the inhabitants accomplish their feats? The same emphasis applies here. This book is not about creativity. It is about creating. Most books that concern the inventive work of artists, scientists, or businesspeople are about creativity, a personal trait. "Creating," on the other hand, is a name for a process. It asks how the creative person *thinks*, not what the creative person *is*.

Moreover, this book is not about the felt experience of creating. After a look at certain of the following chapters, someone might well object "But that's not what it feels like!" I would often agree. That's not what it feels like – but that's how it works. Einstein is said to have said something of this sort: "The chemical analysis of a cup of soup should not be expected to taste like the soup."

But what is creating? I mean the process of producing outcomes that we normally judge to be creative. Then what is meant by "creative"? A familiar and often repeated definition will do well here: creative means original and of high quality. Thus a stereotyped product does not count as creative, however fine it may be. Likewise, a product with nothing else to recommend it does not count as creative, however original it may be. Such products are just superficially novel. With these definitions in mind, explaining creating means explaining how the originality and the quality "get into" or "get put into" the developing creative outcome during the making process.

The definitions of creating and creative are admittedly vague, but inevitably vague too. What we mean by "original" and what we mean by "quality" vary drastically from context to context. Also, they are often judged in tacit rather than explicit ways within a context. Thus a good-quality advertisement is good in virtue of different features than is a good-quality astronomical theory or a good-quality dance. An original advertisement is original in virtue of different features than is an original astronomical theory or an original dance. There is no way that an account of "creating" or "creative" can get explicit about the many partly tacit criteria of originality and quality that apply in different contexts, especially when invention often makes its own standards of quality, by leading people to discover kinds of quality they had little awareness of before. This is the way it is, and we will simply have to live with it.

Must creating involve a product? First it should be said that "product" or "outcome" can apply in a very general sense, including poems, paintings, scientific theories, puns, performances, gardens, conversations, dreams, desserts. A creative way of life need not be one that emphasizes the outcomes we conventionally think of as creative. However, I do think that some kind of product or outcome must be involved in creating. "To create" is a transitive verb. It is the fundamental nature of the concept that creating involves creating something, and to speak of creating when there is nothing understood as the thing created is not really intelligible.

The emphasis in this book will be on creating in the arts and the sciences, with products such as poems, paintings, scientific discoveries and theories. Also, there will be some attention to puzzles of various sorts because they provide a controlled way of investigating certain aspects of creativity. This choice does not imply that everything done within the arts and the sciences is creative. On the contrary, mediocre, unimaginative science and art are the rule more than the exception, just as mediocre and unimaginative work is in any area of human endeavor. However, the sciences and the arts are good choices for this discussion since many achievements in these domains count among the most creative accomplishments of humankind and since traditions of scholarship in the history and psychology of these areas can inform this book.

Finally, like Easter Island, this book has a few unusual features the traveler ought to know about in advance. First of all, I have found it helpful to organize most chapter sections around "propositions" and "revised propositions." A proposition, which usually occurs near the beginning of a section, is a concise statement of a familiar or plausible view about creating. The revised proposition, arriving near the end of a section, is another statement on the same issue, sometimes a direct contradiction of the original proposition and sometimes a qualification of it. The text of the sections is mostly a journey by way of evidence and argument from the original to the revised proposition. This device has helped me to keep the issues explicit and focal.

The second feature is the "personal experiments" that occur in most chapter sections. These are activities the reader can attempt, if he or she desires. They usually couple a task with some sort of introspection into the workings of the mind. Sometimes the task is a problem or puzzle to solve, although the real point is never the solution but the process of trying to reach it. These personal experiments are not meant for amusement, although most of them are fun. Neither are they presented as exercises, although I often have assigned them as exercises in classes. Their main function is something else entirely: they are part of the argument. Many of the points made in the following pages are most meaningful, best appreciated, and best considered critically, given some kind of direct personal experience of the phenomena.

Finally, there are my drawings. They appear mostly for fun, paper idols honoring some good and bad ideas about creating.

WITNESSES TO INVENTION

If we can believe it, a man on business from the town of Porlock scuttled one of the great poetic statements in the English language on a certain day in the summer of 1797. The story of this "one that got away" has a triple meaning in this book. First of all, Samuel Taylor Coleridge, describing how a fragment of his dream poem "Kubla Khan" came to be written down and the rest of it lost, offers us a compelling image of creation. Inventions appears almost as suddenly and completely as a jack-in-the-box comes out of its cubbyhole. Second, here also is a maker bearing witness to his own process. Coleridge's testimony demonstrates one of the few ways we can expect to learn about the workings of the mind during invention. Finally, a moral can be drawn from the unfortunate arrival of the man from Porlock. What he did unwittingly, any brash inquiry into the creative life might do with witless disregard for the delicacy of invention. We have to be circumspect. Otherwise, we would be nothing but a bumbling crowd of men and women from Porlock, destroying the very processes we want to disclose. That is, if we can believe it.

The story goes like this. In 1816, Samuel Taylor Coleridge published a curious poem entitled "Kubla Khan: Or, a Vision in a Dream." Introducing the poem itself was a brief preface in which Coleridge described how he had come to write the poem nearly twenty years before.

> In the summer of the year 1797, the Author, then in ill health, had retired to a lonely farm-house between Porlock and Linton, on the Exmoor confines of Somerset and Devonshire. In consequence of a slight indisposition, an anodyne had been prescribed, from the effects of which he fell asleep in his chair at the moment that he was reading the following sentence, or words of the same substance, in "Purchas's Pilgrimage": "Here the Khan Kubla commanded a palace to be built, and a stately garden thereunto. And thus ten miles of fertile ground were inclosed with a wall." The Author continued for about three hours in a profound sleep, at least of the external senses, during which time he has the most vivid confidence, that he could not have composed less than from two to three hundred lines; if that indeed can be called composition in which all the images rose up before him as *things*, with a parallel production of the correspondent expressions, without any sensation or consciousness of effort. On awaking he appeared to himself to have a distinct recollection of the whole, and taking his pen, ink, and paper, instantly and eagerly wrote down the lines that are here preserved. At this moment he was unfortunately called out by a person on business from Porlock, and detained by him above an hour, and on his return to his room, found, to his no small surprise and mortification, that though he still retained some vague and dim recollection of the general purport of the vision, yet, with the exception of some eight or ten scattered lines and images, all the rest had passed away.

In studying how people create, the most natural way in the world is to collect those writings where creative persons have tried to give an account of themselves. Then one can try to construct a theory to match what they report. Indeed, Coleridge's famous episode inspired a nearly as famous book, *The Road to Xanadu: A Study in the Ways of the Imagination*, published in 1927 by John Livingston Lowes. In his treatment of Coleridge's writing process and the Xanadu episode, Lowes argued that, far from receiving "Kubla Khan" out of the blue, Coleridge drew upon several sources from his extensive reading. These sources provided the images and sometimes the very phrases that made up the poem. It was not that Coleridge deliberately crafted the verses. Rather, his mind was so enriched by his readings as to be ready for this spontaneous rush of invention.

One trouble with such a biographical approach to creative process is that different people say different things. For example, there is hardly a statement about the creative process more opposed to the spirit and letter of Coleridge's experience than Edgar Allan Poe's 1846 essay "The Philosophy of Composition." In this article, Poe commented generally on the process of poetry writing and discussed in details his own creation of "The Raven," a work that had achieved an enormous literary success. A few quotes will show how uneasily Poe's account sits with Coleridge's, if we want to take them as reflecting some single way in which people create. On composition in general, Poe has this to say:

Most writers – poets in especial – prefer having it understood that they compose by a species of fine frenzy – an ecstatic intuition – and would positively shudder at letting the public take a peep behind the scenes at the elaborate and vacillating crudities of thought – at the true purposes seized only at the last moment – at the innumerable glimpses of idea that arrived not at the maturity of full view – at the fully matured fancies discarded in despair as unmanageable – at the cautious selections and rejections – at the painful erasures and interpolations – in a word, at the wheels and pinions – the tackle for scene-shifting – the step-ladders and demon-traps – the cock's feathers, the red paint and the black patches, which, in ninety-nine cases out of the hundred, constitute the properties of the literary *histrio*.

Concerning the creation of "The Raven," Poe takes pains to emphasize the logical, deductive character of the process. There is a strong reminder of Poe's great literary creation Monsieur C. Auguste Dupin, the sometimes detective who solved the mystery of "The Murders in the Rue Morgue" and the puzzle of "The Purloined Letter." Like Arthur Conan Doyle's Sherlock Holmes, Dupin was the cool creature of reason, calmly calculating his way to the resolution of problems where others would only bumble about. Poe too was a clever reasoner and solver of puzzles and liked others to know it. He addressed the problems of poetic creation with the same calculation, or so he said. For instance, Poe asserted about "The Raven," "It is my design to render it manifest that no one point in its composition is referable either to accident or intuition – that the work proceeded, step by step, to its completion with the precision and rigid consequence of a mathematical problem."

Poe backed up his generalization by describing how particular features of the poem were, well, deduced. He had this to say about the refrain word "nevermore" and the idea of the raven itself:

> The sound of the refrain being thus determined, it became necessary to select a word embodying this sound, and at the same time in the fullest possible keeping with that melancholy which I had predetermined as the tone of the poem. In such a search it would have been absolutely impossible to overlook the word "Nevermore." In fact, it was the very first which presented itself.
>
> The next *desideratum* was a pretext for the continuous use of the one word "Nevermore." In observing the difficulty which I at once found in inventing a sufficiently plausible reason for its continuous repetition, I did not fail to perceive that this difficulty arose solely from the pre-assumption that the word was to be so continuously or monotonously spoken by a *human* being – I did not fail to perceive, in short, that the difficulty lay in the reconciliation of this monotony with the exercise of reason on the part of the creature repeating the word. Here, then, immediately arose the idea of a *non-*

reasoning creature capable of speech; and, very naturally, a parrot, in the first instance, suggested itself, but was superseded forthwith by a Raven, as equally capable of speech, and infinitely more in keeping with the intended *tone*.

That "species of fine frenzy – an ecstatic intuition" that Poe so slanders seems to fit Coleridge very well. Poe's logical methodical progress with "The Raven" gives a very different picture of creative process than Coleridge's free and facile invention. Poe plays the tortoise to Coleridge's hare. The question is who wins the race, the race for the best account of the nature of human invention. Do we go with the hard-headed Poe? Or do we credit more the romantic image of invention presented by Coleridge, who of course does not argue that the "Kubla Khan" episode was typical but whose example has often been taken to be the quintessential example of creating? Or is some sort of duality or compromise or synthesis needed? Such problems as these come up whenever one tries to study the ways of the creative mind by relying on the after-the-fact testimonies of creative men and women.

But to ask those very questions is to get ahead of ourselves. There is a prior question that no lawyer worth his salt would overlook: Are these witnesses to invention trustworthy? If they are, such cases present dilemmas like the above. But if they are not, the dilemmas disappear, although other ways of investigating creating need to be found.

KUBLA KHAN AND THE RAVEN

Proposition: Samuel Taylor Coleridge, Edgar Allan Poe, and others who have reported episodes of creating can be trusted to have provided honest, careful, well-remembered accounts undistorted by preconceptions about the nature of creativity.

Simply putting this so baldly makes it sound unlikely. In fact, in the cases of Coleridge and Poe, the worst occurs. Neither man can be trusted.

The "Kubla Khan" episode inspired not only the classic work of Lowes but later and somewhat more critical studies. A fine example is a 1953 book by Elizabeth Schneider, *Coleridge, Opium and Kubla Khan*. Schneider presents a number of arguments which challenge the story of "Kubla Khan" as Coleridge originally told it. Perhaps most striking is this: In 1934, an alternative version of the poem and its history came to light. The undated manuscript was in Coleridge's own hand: "This fragment with a good deal more, not recoverable, composed in a sort of Reverie brought on by two grains of Opium, taken to check a dysentary, at a Farm House between Porlock and Linton, a quarter of a mile from Culbone Church, in the fall of the year 1797." Notice the contrasts between Coleridge's original public statement and this private version. The "profound sleep, at least of the external senses" of the public version was here a wakeful reverie, a very different thing. The "slight indisposition" was more specifically "a dysentary," the "anodyne" was "two grains of Opium." Although in the public account, Coleridge "wrote down the lines that are here preserved," the version of the poem discovered in 1934 differed in a number of minor ways from the published "Kubla Khan." In at least three cases, the variations lay closer to their sources in "Purchas's Pilgrimage" and also in *Paradise Lost*, suggesting that the newly discovered version was an earlier one.

Coleridge's story of the writing of "Kubla Khan" seems all the more doubtful for not appearing before 1816. Coleridge had a strong interest in dreams and mental processes generally and often discussed and wrote letters mentioning such matters. He reported dreaming four rather mundane lines of verse in an 1803 letter. He often recorded dreams and sentences from dreams in his notebooks. In 1803, he participated in a long discussion concerning dreams and poetry, a discussion later described by another participant. An 1811 or 1812 account of Coleridge's reciting "Kubla Khan" mentions the poem's concern with a dream palace and a consequent discussion of dreams. Yet not one of these sources mentions anything about "Kubla Khan"'s being created in a dream.

Finally, it has to be said that Coleridge often misrepresented the history of his compositions. Several of his contemporaries commented generally on his untrustworthiness. On a number of occasions he is known to have claimed a date of composition considerably earlier than the actual date. On one occasion, he implied a degree of fluency contrary to the facts. The subtitle of a four-hundred-line poem "Religious Musings" described it as "A Desultory Poem, written on the Christmas Eve of 1794." In fact, serious work on the poem had stretched over two years. If we extend the benefit of the doubt to Coleridge, and suppose that he wasn't deliberately misrepresenting the origins of "Kubla Khan," then in any case there would be problems of memory in his 1816 statement. Although Coleridge's own reported 1797 date of composition is in question, the poem is known to have been in existence by October 1800. Besides not being overscrupulous about correct reporting, Coleridge had sixteen years for his memory of the occasion to grow dim and plastic.

So the researches of Schneider and others suggest that slow-and-steady Poe may have won his race by default, the opposition disqualified. But in fact Poe's account also can be challenged. First of all, there is something close to an internal inconsistency. As Poe describes it, the process of composition involves much vacillation, selection and rejection, erasure and interpolation. Yet when Poe comes to "The Raven" things are different. Poe himself proceeded methodically from general considerations to infer the desired character of the poem and even some of its words. Only in admit-

ting that he thought of parrots before ravens does Poe acknowledge any trial and error at all. In short, Poe really offers two contrary visions of poetic process, one emphasizing trial and error, the other emphasizing systematic inference.

A number of historical sources cast doubt upon the latter. As

Poe describes it, "The Raven" sounds as if it were produced methodically in an afternoon, or at most a week. Poe labored over the poem for years. The poem appeared in several journals at once, early in 1845. However, a draft existed in the summer of 1842. Poe had shown it to someone, as he would continue to do through years of reworking. In the winter of 1843-44, Poe tried unsuccessfully to sell a version of the poem. In the spring of 1844, he read variations to friends and acquaintances in a tavern he frequented and elsewhere, trying this and that and requesting evaluations and suggestions. The poem was brought into its final form over the summer and fall of 1844, when Poe occupied a residence containing a bust of Pallas which, in the poem, provided a perch for the raven. In short, despite his claims in his "Philosophy of Composition," there is every sign that Poe worked very much in the trial-and-error manner he attributed to others.

There is also information about the origin of the raven and the refrain "nevermore." One perhaps dubious claim is that the raven was originally an owl. A more plausible source appears in a review of Charles Dickens' *Barnaby Rudge* that Poe published in 1841 and, in an extended version, in 1842. The novel's cast of characters included a raven named Grip, which Poe singled out for special comment. Poe saw opportunities in the bird that Dickens had not. "The raven, too, intensely amusing as it is, might have been made, more than we now see it, a portion of the conception of the fantastic Barnaby. Its croakings might have been *prophetically* heard in the course of the drama." Later, in "The Raven," the bird would be addressed as "Prophet! Thing of evil! – prophet still, if bird or devil!"

As for "nevermore," the work of other contemporary poets Poe is known to have seen probably gave Poe an assist. For example, there are these lines from Thomas Holly Chivers' "Lament on the Death of My Mother":

> Nor on the borders of the great deep sea,
> Wilt thou return again from heaven to me –
> No, nevermore!

And from Chivers' "To Allegra in Heaven":

Thy dear father will to-morrow lay thy body with deep sorrow,
In the grave which is so narrow, there to rest forevermore.

There would be no problem about these sources had Poe not told
the tale as he did in "The Philosophy of Composition." Poets do
have their sources. But Poe said he arrived at "nevermore" from
general considerations of sound and expression and then sought
a creature who reasonably could repeat the word. The sources
mentioned suggest somewhat less logic and somewhat more borrowing.

Finally, the cool, detached tone of Poe's method as he described it invites comment. Throughout the period of work on
"The Raven," Poe was under great stress. In January 1842 his
wife burst a blood vessel while singing. The case was quickly
diagnosed as one of advanced tuberculosis. Although his wife
hung on until well after the publication of "The Raven," her condition cycled through periods of some improvement and serious
relapse. At the same time, the Poes suffered great poverty, even
after Poe had attained considerable fame. Poe chronically fell into
bouts of drinking and other episodes of erratic behavior. There is
no doubt that, despite all this, Poe remained a skilled craftsman.
But clearly his agonized state of mind over his wife's declining
health found expression through the grim vision of "The Raven."
So Poe seems to have been very much slower and very much less
steady than his slow-and-steady portrait of himself.

None of this means that there is no truth at all in what Coleridge and Poe reported. The parts of Coleridge's story confirmed
by the handwritten note about "a sort of reverie" sound plausible
enough. Poe's general trial-and-error version of poetic composition matches his behavior, even if his image of Poe-as-Dupin-as-
poet does not. But surely, these cases stand as warning that one
can't uncritically credit the accounts notable figures in science and
art have given, voluntarily and much after the fact, about
episodes of invention.

There's no need to be paranoid about this. I'm not going to say
that autobiographical accounts should never be used in inquires
like this one. In fact, I'll use them myself a number of times in the
following chapters, sometimes critically and sometimes with ac-

ceptance. But, all in all, we need another method. We need one that will cut more deeply and cleanly through the snarl of accidental and calculated confusion surrounding creative process.

Revised proposition: After-the-fact accounts of episodes of invention have questionable validity and require careful critical scrutiny to make anything of them; there is too much opportunity for forgetting, faulty reconstruction, and even outright misrepresentation.

HARD EVIDENCE

There is another classic solution to the problem of studying creative process, one pursued by generations of scholars. The solution is to use the scratchwork and early drafts, the notebooks, sketches, and discarded versions that often exist along with a creative product of consequence. Like the footprints of shy night creatures, the physical trace of progress on a work of science or art may tell us more about its making than the maker could or would or did. There are various advantages that come with the use of such tracks. They often are all that we have, for one. For another, there is no investigative meddling of the sort discussed in the following section – the sort I finally will opt for. Finally, the problems of witnessing just discussed are worth remembering here. Unlike the testimony of the maker, the tracks cannot misconstrue, overgeneralize, conform to popular theories, promote a public image. Their very logical status makes this impossible. They are not claims about the work or its making, but physical pieces of the work's history. There is no need to get too smug about this, of course. The physical record might be incomplete, ambiguous, misleading, and coarse-grained. If it cannot misconstrue, certainly it can be misconstrued. Still, the real advantages shouldn't be overlooked. Let's be as optimistic as possible and say:

Proposition: A good physical record of an episode of invention provides an adequate basis for answering most of the questions we really want answered about creating.

A case in point. Under the title *Picasso's Guernica*, Rudolf Arnheim took advantage of a remarkable opportunity to follow the tracks of an episode of creation. Picasso himself gave Arnheim the chance by his own habits of record keeping. Picasso routinely numbered and dated his works. In the case of *Guernica*, he left sixty-one sketches and more complete works in various media which related to *Guernica*. The first forty-five apparently figured directly in *Guernica's* making. The others developed pictorial motifs from *Guernica* even after it was complete. In addition, seven photographs of the work were taken as it progressed. The richness of the visual record presented an ideal occasion for the hard-evidence approach.

However, I want to know much more about the creative process than Picasso's record tells us. But before explaining what's missing, let me acknowledge what's there. A mere glance at the sketches and the photographs reveals neither instant creation as in Coleridge's story of "Kubla Khan" nor methodical deduction as in Poe's story of "The Raven." Poe's trial-and-error view of creating seems closer to the mark. Picasso explored alternatives by means of numerous sketches, and *Guernica* evolved through several versions into its final form. But Arnheim's thoughtful scrutiny goes some way beyond that. For one general conclusion, he sees Picasso's process as a dialectic rather than a steady differentiation: "An interplay of interferences, modifications, restrictions, and compensations leads gradually to the unity and complexity of the total composition. Therefore the work of art cannot unfold straightforwardly from its seed, like an organism, but must grow in what looks like erratic leaps, forward and backward, from the whole to the part and vice versa". Arnheim also ponders the role of formal considerations. He notes that they lead to solutions that "are always more than formal." Always the broadened, deepened, and sharpened meaning of the work is a concern; merely compositional improvements would not do, at least not for Picasso.

So far so good. But now we ought to consider questions about creative process not so easily answered from Picasso's sketches and photographs. Consider an episode from the making of *Guernica*, the invention of the folded bull. In the final *Guernica*, a bull stands in the leftmost quarter of the work, his body facing inward, but his head looking leftward away from the carnage in the center. The flat cubist style makes the bull appear folded at the neck. But the bull wasn't always so. In the first three photographs, not only the bull's head but the bull's body faces leftward, the body sprawling back over nearly half of the painting. In the fourth state, the final disposition of the bull suddenly appears.

Arnheim praises the logic of this move. "The gain is remarkable . . . the bull now faces the scene, yet his head is turned away; the empty space at the left is filled with the eloquent tail; mother and child are enveloped and bolstered by the protective torso; the animal's hindquarters are removed from the center. Truly an ingenious invention." The change pays off also in letting Picasso lift the agonized head of the horse, earlier lost in the tangle of the center, up to scream at us. As Arnheim says, "the horse could not raise its head unless there was space in which to put it."

But now for those uncertainties. The first concerns Picasso's critical judgments. Arnheim offers us his analysis of why the folded bull makes sense, and Arnheim's conclusions sound reasonable to me. But he does not presume to tell us what Picasso had in mind at the time in keeping the folded bull. And what did he have in mind—all of these reasons, some of them, something else entirely? As Arnheim acknowledges in Chapter 2 of his book, hard evidence forces conjecture, which may miss the maker's actual reasons entirely. It requires the interpreter to model the maker's judgments upon his or her own, a risky enterprise (though one for which I would sooner trust Rudolf Arnheim than most people).

To underscore the point, let me mention another factor about the folded bull which might have pleased Picasso. The "body language" of the bull is radically changed by the fold. Before, head and body face decisively away from the carnage, and the bull might be said to be standing above and looking beyond the momentary disaster. Indeed, something like this is Arnheim's reading for the folded bull as well. The bull is a symbol of timeless Spain. "Guernica is not victory but defeat—sprawling chaos, shown as temporary by the dynamic appeal to the towering, timeless figure of the kingly beast. And "the bull's body faces the victims but his head is turned away from them, and his glance transcends the space of the scene entirely, focused as it is upon the infinite." To my eyes, though, the fold has made the bull both more dynamic and more ambiguous. Directing his body toward the center, the bull has turned his head aside. Instead of a *stance*, as in the earlier versions, there is now a *gesture*. What does this gesture express? It could be the transcendence Arnheim suggests. Or the bull could be averting his eyes from the dreadful scene; this perception is most dominant for me, although not constant. Also, the bull could be scanning the scene from side to side. Perhaps one of these latter readings was what Picasso saw and wanted to preserve. Or perhaps it was the very ambiguity he valued. After all, none of the three readings is incompatible with the painting's statement, and in that sense, as so often is the case in art, the ambiguity enriches rather than confuses.

So far, only judgment has been considered, the grounds for Picasso's liking and keeping the folded bull. The uncertainty of *aims* presents a second difficulty. It's too easy to conclude that if a change accomplishes a certain thing, the change was conceived with that end in mind. According to such a theory, advances are always treatments of the obvious ills of the work so far. But Arnheim see the ambiguity and hedges. In the prior version, the extreme left was empty, occupied only by an obvious filler. "Did the need for a filler suggest the turning about of the bull?" Arnheim asks. "This may well have been what logicians call the proximate cause, which, however, could hardly have brought about the action, had it not solved the problem of the bull's position." But so might the proximate cause have been the desire to get the bull's butt out of the center, the horse's head raised, a more ambiguous posture, or something else again. Which of these sparked the idea, and what others led Picasso to see the idea was a "keeper"? There seems no way of telling, but at issue here is the role of accident and intention, the balance of luck and foresight in creative process.

Uncertainty concerning alternatives is another problem. Picasso's record shows him exploring alternative designs for some features of *Guernica* – the head of the horse, for instance. But alternatives may also be conceived and reviewed in the mind of the artist. Arnheim notes, "there can be no real continuity in the sketches. Much thinking must have occurred that required no visible records." Was Picasso's placement of the bull in the fourth version the final choice of many alternatives or the immediate apprehension of the right thing to do in the circumstances? Again, there is no way of telling.

Moreover, if it is uncertain just what judgments, aims, and alternatives were involved, all the more uncertain are the processes yielding those judgments, aim, and alternatives. For example, whatever Picasso's aim was concerning the bull, how did it come to him – through hard pondering, sudden insight, the gradual consequence of living with the work? We shouldn't assume that the difficulties with the original bull were obvious. They may well appear obvious now only because we see them contrasted with the final product. Picasso no doubt had his reasons for first placing the bull as he did. We don't have to break away from that original concept because we don't know it.

The Illusion of Evidence

A while ago, someone put this riddle to a group I was in. As it happens no one got the riddle, and we all finally had to be told. It went like this: There is a man at home. The man is wearing a mask. There is a man coming home. What is happening here?

In a way, presenting the riddle in print is unfair because you can't ask questions of the riddler. To help just a little, let me answer some of the questions that might be asked. Is the man at his own home? No. Does the mask cover his whole face? Yes. Does the mask have something to do with his profession? Yes. Is the man a criminal of some sort? No. Is the man a repairman of some sort, like a welder? No. Does the man at home know that someone is coming? Yes. Does the man coming home know that someone is there? Yes.

Too bad if you solved this little puzzle (but congratulations) because the real point I want to make concerns how people *do not* get such puzzles rather than how they do. Probably upon reading the riddle, you immediately began to develop a concept of what was happening. Perhaps there was a mental image of a man standing in a living room, his face covered in some unclear way. Perhaps there was an image of another man on the bus, or walking along a sidewalk, heading home. The reason people have difficulty with riddles of this sort is that even such vague fillings in as that are premature. They make assumptions not really warranted by the situation as stated. A scene in a baseball game is what the riddle describes.

Picasso's tracks are like the riddle, only more so. They quickly lead us into an illusion not just of partial understanding but of fairly full understanding. They do this because the record reveals so well what could have happened. The bull's body could have seemed obviously awkward to Picasso. He could simply have noticed this and sought a solution; fairly soon, he could have thought of folding the bull, since this would move the undesirable part out of the way. Because we fill out such scenarios so readily and automatically given the evidence, the evidence seems to speak very definitely and fully about the episode. However, as in the case of the riddle, we may be making far too many assumptions far too quickly.

Stating the assumptions behind the above way of telling Picasso's story will make the danger evident: Problems are always obvious to the sensitive maker, recognized problems point directly to possible solutions, and candidate solutions are clearly appropriate or not. According to these premises, creativity boils down to sensitivity; everything else takes care of itself. Now certainly no creative effort would get far without sensitivity. But just as certainly to settle for that is to beg too many questions. Problems aren't always obvious, nor possible solutions clearly indicated, nor their appropriateness apparent at a glance.

I don't mean these words to be critical of Rudolf Arnheim's analysis. The quotes show him to be well aware of the uncertain-

ties; when Arnheim speculates, he lets us know about it. The conclusions he draws appear modest and well warranted by the data.
Furthermore, one would hardly refuse the gift Picasso offered to
our understanding simply because it did not tell us as much as we
might like to know. Nonetheless, the gaps in the data and the risk
of an illusory understanding must be recognized and respected
while we gather what insights we can.

Those gaps contain what might be called the texture of creative
process: the blow-by-blow progress of the developing product.
Describing that texture means generalizing about how ideas
emerge in the mind, how much trial and error contributes,
whether critical judgment occurs spontaneously or through
deliberate analytical attention to the work in progress, and so on.
If we are to learn about such matters, hard evidence won't be the
teacher.

Revised proposition: Even quite good physical traces of
episodes of invention disclose little about the judgments, aims,
and alternatives making up the process and the ways these
emerge in the mind of the maker.

A VOICE FOR THE MIND

In the words of a folksy metaphor, psychological inquiry into
creative process seems caught between the frying pan and the
fire. On the one hand, the after-the-fact testimony of creative
men and women presents many difficulties – problems of
misremembering, misrepresentation, and such. But when the
disgruntled investigator turns to hard evidence, gaps in the record
and ambiguities of interpretation keep back answers to some important questions, questions the creator might be able to answer
directly. So what are we to do?

From time to time over the past fifty years, psychologists have
tried yet another approach to the secrets of invention, an approach that revives the role of maker as witness and solicits
testimony in a radically intrusive way. Since the 1930s several
psychologists have asked people doing various tasks to think
aloud at the same time or to report their thoughts right after-

wards, not a day or fifteen years later. I have used such introspective methods to study the thinking of poets, artists, and others, and I'll discuss my own appraoch in the next section. The present business, however, concerns a natural objection to any such rummaging in the mind.

Proposition: Asking people to report their thoughts during or right after a mental activity disrupts the activity or yields a distorted description.

Disruption is the concern most people worry most about. We have some entrenched ideas about the nature of creative thinking, one of which says that invention is a delicate undertaking, a sort of night flower that promptly withers under the flashlight of inspection. To put this in other words, I can hardly do better than to steal a remark of Paul Valéry's quoted in *Picasso's Guernica:*

> there are functions that prefer the shadow to the light, or at least the twilight – that is, that minimum of conscious awareness which is necessary and sufficient to make these acts come about or to bait them. If failure or blocking is to be avoided, the cycle of sensation and motor activity must take its course without observations or interruptions, from origin to the physiological limit of the performed act. This jealousy, this kind of modesty of our automisms, is quite remarkable. One could derive a complete philosophy from it, which I would summarize by saying: Sometimes I think, and sometimes I am.

Here, of course, Valéry plays on Descartes' *Cogito, ergo sum* by suggesting just the opposite. But even supposing that at least sometimes thinking and being get along together, there remains another problem: accurate reporting. The person thinking aloud or reporting right after the fact must still try to give an undistorted account. Can this be taken for granted? In a 1953 essay on introspection, Edwin Boring emphasized a crucial point. The notion that introspective reports reflect some kind of direct unmediated access to mental events should be left behind with Wundt and the other so-called introspectionist psychologists of the late nineteenth and early twentieth centuries. Introspective reports are observations subject to the same kinds of distortions that affect observations of external events – problems of memory loss, bias, unwarranted filling in of gaps in plausible ways, and so on. Studies of eyewitness testimony have demonstrated how serious such distortions can get. For one striking example, subjects in an investigation reported by Gordon Allport were briefly shown a drawing of several people on a subway train, including a seated black man and a standing white man holding a razor. Fifty percent of the subjects later reported that the black man held the razor. Findings of this sort are more the rule than the exception.

Such results give as much reason for suspicion as the tall tales Coleridge and Poe told long after the fact. But what about reports gathered on the spot? More cause for alarm comes from a 1977 article by Richard Nisbett and Timothy Wilson, one of the few articles directly concerned with problems of introspection. The authors reviewed a number of experiments, conducted by themselves and others, in which subjects were asked to explain the thoughts behind their decisions or actions. In the experiments conducted by others, this request for explanation usually was incidental to the main method of the study, but Nisbett and Wilson were able to take advantage of its presence. Again and again, such experiments revealed that the subjects had little awareness of the real influences on their actions. Though most of the experiments did not concern creative or problem-solving behavior of the sort discussed here, I'll describe two experiments that come close to my concerns.

In one, conducted by Nisbett and Wilson themselves, subjects were asked to choose from four pairs of stockings, laid in a row, the best-quality pair. The statistics revealed a strong and surprising position effect. Although in fact the stockings were identical, the rightmost pair was preferred over the leftmost by a factor of almost four to one. But when asked about reasons directly, no subject ever mentioned position as a factor. Furthermore, when position was suggested an an influence, almost all the subjects denied the possibility.

The other example is Norman Maier's classic two-string problem, first reported in 1931. Two strings were hung from the ceiling in a cluttered laboratory. The task was simply to tie the two ends of the strings together, but there was a catch: while holding onto one string, a person couldn't reach the other. The subjects were supposed to solve the problem in several ways, some of them easy to find. One, though, evaded most of the participants. This was to tie a weight to one of the cords, swing it, and catch the end on the upswing while holding the other cord. Maier also determined that the typical subject would get this solution if Maier dropped a hint seemingly by accident. He would brush past one of the strings and set it swinging. Soon the pendulum solution would be discovered. However, Maier established that, on questioning, only about a third of the subjects could report the swinging string as a clue. Moreover, Maier was able to trick some subjects into thinking that another clue entirely had been important. For some subjects, before brushing the string, he twirled a weight on a cord. These subjects always reported that the latter was the tip-off. Yet Maier was able to show by giving this clue by itself that in fact it didn't help at all. In general, Nisbett and Wilson concluded that people really had little access to their mental processes. Instead, people simply reported how they thought they must have done something.

Despite these causes for concern, since the 1930s a number of investigators have made major use of introspective methods to examine the work of the mind during creative and problem-solving activities. In the thirties, Catherine Patrick asked poets and artists to think aloud while developing works, recorded their remarks in shorthand, and analyzed the transcripts, seeking signs of certain stages of thought that Graham Wallas had proposed in 1926. Around 1940, A. D. de Groot started to study chess playing by gathering transcripts from competent amateur and master-level players as they considered a next move. Allen Newell, Herbert Simon, and their associates began to collect think-aloud reports concerning human problem solving around 1956. Their work came to include studies of chess playing, and solving cryparithmetic and symbolic logic problems, and in 1972 yielded their *Human Problem Solving*, surely one of the major statements on the topic. Such techniques have been applied in recent studies of the process of medical diagnosis. Since 1971, I have used introspective methods in several studies of poets and artists at work and in studies of metaphor making, achieving personal insights, and solving so-called insight problems. I will say more about my approach to such work in the next section. Here I list these investigations simply to affirm that a number of individuals have taken introspective methods very seriously and used them with apparent success, in the sense of producing writings acceptable for publication in professional journals. Can it really be that such methods are so misleading?

Let me begin with the supposed problem of disruption. Likely as this problem sounds, I want to argue that the risks of disruption are largely a cultural myth, something so plausible-seeming and so often repeated that people take it as fact even though there is hardly any evidence for it. Indeed, there is evidence against it.

     The Game of Centipede

A personal experiment makes a good beginning. We have all heard the dangers of disruption expressed in a metaphor to this effect: if a centipede thought about how it walked, it would get into a tangle. This is a simple enough claim to test, if one can test it on people instead of centipedes.

To begin with, just walk across the room.

Now walk across the room deliberately trying to control every muscle. Probably this will seem very slow and awkward.

Now walk across the room letting your legs do what they want to do. However, pay attention to what they do. Notice the action of the foot, the ankle, the knee. Ask yourself: What contribution do the toes make? What if there were no toes, what difference would there be? Most people find that thinking about what they are doing in this way doesn't disrupt their walking.

The moral of this simple demonstration is just as simple: everything depends on what "thinking about" means. If it means trying to seize control of a physical activity muscle by muscle, that certainly will be disruptive. But if "thinking about" just means observing, that need not be disruptive at all. "Thinking about" might mean other things too – the kind of self-consciousness, say, where there is not only attention to but some kind of anxiety concerning the activity. Even so, it's worth noting that self-consciousness usually doesn't disrupt an activity drastically, although it may well "take the edge off." Still another sense of "thinking about" might be pondering while doing. Certainly, if you attempt to ponder a course of thought underway, you will bring to a halt the original course of thought. However, "pondering while doing" is not what psychologists using introspective techniques ask subjects to attempt. Subjects are supposed simply to express their thoughts while engaging in an activity, not to think about their thinking.

In addition, experimental evidence suggests that disruption is no great problem. *The coherence of reports:* Subjects' reports typically describe a fairly coherent course of thought. There are often gaps or changes of direction, but on the whole one can follow more or less what a subject was doing, and typically the reports show progress on the task at hand. If introspection disrupted the process, there should be, instead, complaints of confusion and frustration and little progress on the task. *Objective comparison of outcomes:* Comparisons of outcomes when people are introspecting and not have shown few effects of introspection. Catherine Patrick in her studies of poets and artists reported that the products done for her were in much the same style and of much the same quality as the participants' usual work. A 1953 dissertation by David Karpf involved a study of hypothesis testing and used a think-aloud method. Karpf found no differences in the success of groups thinking aloud and silently. *Objective comparison of process:* Sometimes overt symptoms of a process can be used to compare people introspecting and not. A very simple symptom is time spent. An investigation of mental arithmetic revealed that those thinking aloud arrived at solutions just as quickly as those working silently. Scratchwork is another source of information. Newell and Simon studied students who instructed an experimenter what written manipulations to try on a blackboard in a formal task. Some thought aloud and some silently, but their scratchwork, carried out for them on the blackboard, provided a way of comparing their procedures. Both groups apparently explored alternatives in much the same way. *Subjects' impressions:* People can be debriefed concerning the introspective experience and whether they felt it influenced their procedures and progress. Patrick reported that her poets and artists reacted favorably, indicating little disruption and more or less normal progress. In my own studies, participants characteristically have mentioned *slightly* slower than normal progress, slightly greater tension, and no other disruption, although in a very few cases both unusually good and unusually disappointing experiences were reported.

To my mind, the above demonstration and arguments show that disruption is not a serious problem. But there remain the ominous findings of Nisbett and Wilson about distortion in introspective reports. Here some welcome help comes from an article by Eliot Smith and Frederick Miller which criticized the position of Nisbett and Wilson. Smith and Miller acknowledged that the earlier article had some telling points to make, but they also saw a need for qualifications. For one thing, they showed that Nisbett and Wilson were mistaken in their analysis of certain experiments, although not the ones I described earlier. For another, most of Nisbett's and Wilson's examples concerned activities that people don't normally engage in very consciously, activities such as forming an impression of another's personality.

The stockings experiment smacks more of deliberate problem solving than many of the results Nisbett and Wilson reported. So it helps to find that Smith and Miller had some special bones to pick with it, reservations that might apply to some other cases as well. Smith and Miller were unimpressed by the subjects' failure to report rightmost position as a reason for their choice. Suppose, they argued, the subjects were following a procedure something like this. A subject would begin on the left, compare adjacent sets of stockings, and if the next appeared at least as good as the first, go on. Such a procedure would lead to the rightmost pair being chosen. But of course subjects would deny that this was the *reason* for their choice. It was not a reason in the usual sense – a quality in virtue of which stockings should be selected; the position effect was an accidental result of the comparison procedure. Of course, Smith and Miller do not claim to know what the subjects really did, but their point is an important one. In general, not everything correlated with a decision is a "cause of" or "reason for" the decision in the usual way of speaking. When asked about such reasons, no wonder people often don't acknowledge them, or even know about them.

Another point ought to be mentioned. Not even the most ardent introspectionist expects introspective reports to reveal everything, certainly not the firing of neurons in the nervous system but not even necessarily such things as what clue triggered an insight. In fact, a little experience with think-aloud techniques quickly teaches that people simply do not have time to report everything that happens consciously if they are to get on with the task. So, in the Maier string experiment, it is of no great concern that two thirds of the subjects couldn't report the clue of the swinging string. More worrisome is the way Maier misled subjects into believing that another clue was what had helped when in fact it had not. But here again there is something very important to be said. When investigators deliberately insert factors designed to distract and fool, of course they often will succeed, just as magicians routinely succeed in fooling audiences of thousands. But neither the tricks of magicians nor the tricks of such investigators demonstrate that, in general, we seriously misapprehend.

In fact, if the question were put to Maier's problem solvers in the right way, they might not have been fooled at all. When people are asked to explain what led to a decision or an insight, how do they understand the query? My own experience with think-aloud and retrospective methods tells me that people often assume an explanation is wanted – their best reconstruction of what happened. So that's what they try to provide. However, if subjects are instructed not to try to explain but just to report what they remember, something quite different occurs. They start making distinctions between what they actually remember and what appears plausible. This doesn't mean that they succeed in sorting the one from the other perfectly, but it is clear that they are doing something in that direction. Maier's subjects might have done better had they been warned against explaining and urged just to remember.

In summary, there are many reasons why the cases Nisbett and Wilson review aren't that much of a threat to introspective methods. In some cases, there are mistaken analyses, in others odd notions of cause or reason. Nisbett and Wilson don't for the most part address challenging intellectual activities. Proper introspective techniques differ from the kind of "please explain" reports that Nisbett and Wilson discuss, and differ in a direction that ought to help with accuracy. And so on. None of these points proves that the effects Nisbett and Wilson worry about could not possibly occur. Of course they could, and occasionally probably do. But there is no reason to believe on present evidence that they seriously confound the accuracy of introspective reports used as described.

Revised proposition: Asking people to think aloud or report their thoughts immediately after episodes of invention does not substantially disrupt the activity or yield substantially distorted accounts.

THE ART OF INTROSPECTION

Is introspection easy? One might draw that conclusion from reading the research reports of most investigators who have used introspective methods. Usually, little is said about how the participants were instructed to manage so rare a performance. So perhaps there's nothing to it.

Proposition: Satisfactory introspective reports can be had simply be asking someone to think aloud.

I'm not even going to defend that before denying it. There is an art to helping people to share their minds with an investigator, and I want to devote a few paragraphs to describing that art.

When a person is merely asked to think aloud, one of two things often goes wrong. Either the person will overexplain, interrupting the activity to give not a report of the thinking but a speculative analysis of it, or if that doesn't happen, often the person will comment sparsely. Especially as the task becomes involving, a person may sometimes let thirty seconds or more elapse without a word. In addition, other more minor snags occur regularly. Such experiences when I first began to use introspective methods led me to try to develop a better way. There may be other "better ways," too, as well as ways to improve this one. But in any case, here it is.

The method begins with instructions organized into six principles. The first three promote a complete record and the second three discourage overexplanation.

1. Say whatever's on your mind. Don't hold back hunches, guesses, wild ideas, images, intentions.
2. Speak as continuously as possible. Say something at least once every five seconds, even if only, "I'm drawing a blank."
3. Speak audibly. Watch out for your voice dropping as you become involved.
4. Speak as telegraphically as you please. Don't worry about complete sentences and eloquence.
5. Don't overexplain or justify. Analyze no more than you would normally.
6. Don't elaborate past events. Get into the pattern of saying what you're thinking now, not of thinking for a while and then describing your thoughts.

Simply informing people of these six principles helps considerably. It's also useful to provide five minutes or so of practice on some light task unrelated to the experiment. People can be reassured by telling them about the strong warm-up effect that almost always occurs. While the first minute or two of thinking aloud may feel awkward, as one becomes used to the speaking and absorbed in the activity, the reporting becomes more and more fluent.

In the best of all possible worlds, participants in such experiments would follow the six principles faithfully and produce perfect data. In actuality, it's usually necessary to encourage people a little. The researcher should sit unobtrusively to one side but not behind the participant, at some distance, and prompt about rules 2, 3, and 5 if he or she falters. Rule 2, especially, requires attention, and a simple "What are you thinking now?" is an adequate reminder. It's natural to worry that constant prodding would distract a participant. Surprisingly, experience teaches that this isn't so. After a few prompts, people learn to maintain continuous reporting and so further reminders are rarely needed. However, if the researcher refrains from prompting, many people will relax into the patterns of behavior that the six rules are designed to discourage.

A person's remarks are tape-recorded for later transcription and analysis. An audio recording plus preservation of any scratchwork suffices for activities such as solving puzzles or writing poetry, activities that don't involve much overt physical expression. In contrast, for activities like painting, a videotape record is important. Here the reported thoughts are often meaningless without the visual record. I am often asked if painters, in contrast to poets, can put into words what they are thinking about. The answer is that they can – providing the words can have reference to the image. Their remarks do not so much fully package their concerns as point to where their concerns appear visually in the work in progress.

An example will make clearer the sort of material this method obtains. The following is an episode from an actual session. The sample comes from a poet who had completed several lines of a poem begun during the session. The excerpt commences just as she had completed the words, *If the chaos of the night becomes forboding we can* . . . Her aim was to finish the *we can* in a way that would connect back to the motif of rain which was to continue throughout the poem. Thinking aloud, she reported:

Oh, I can get back into the rain, somehow. Reads: *if the night becomes forboding / we can* (pause). Writes: *slide* – I'll use *slip* again. Writes: *into the dancing of the rain*. I'm not sure *dancing* is the right motion. It's too up and down, and rain only comes down. Reads: *we can slide into the* (pause) – not *falling*, because that's too hopeless (pause). Reads: *if the chaos of the night becomes forboding / we can slide into* – well, make it *comfort*. Reads: *into the*. Writes: *comfort*. Reads: *of the rain*. Um (pause), I'll copy this whole thing over, as far as I've gotten, see if I can feel continuity to it.

This excerpt illustrates nicely what thinking aloud ought to be. The poet is plainly getting on with her job and at the same time telling us a bit about it. She mentions a general aim, invents a phrase, *into the dancing of the rain,* to fulfill her aim, finds *dancing* unsuitable, then, while preserving the rest of the phrase, conceives and rejects *falling,* and finally settles on *comfort.* We see where she began, where she ended up, and how she traveled from one place to the other. I don't mean to imply that the poet has expressed every thought consciously accessible to her during this episode of invention. She may well have considered fleetingly another option or had in mind definite reasons for accepting *comfort* which she didn't relate. Also, much mental processing is inaccessible. Nonetheless, such records as this clearly inform us about some of the ways and byways of invention.

  Speaking Your Mind

More perspective on the think-aloud technique discussed here comes from the personal experiment of trying the technique for yourself. The instructions have already been given, principles one through six above. The only other requirements are a tape recorder and a problem to address. Before I provide a problem, the tape recorder should be set up and turned on to record.

Now here is the problem, not the sort one might expect. Try to remember what you were doing on this same date one year ago today. Does this seem impossible? It isn't. Often people can pinpoint just what they were doing and, if not that, then get a general idea. Begin now, starting to think aloud. Remember to try to say something every five seconds at least. Make an effort to maintain a fairly continuous flow of speech.

After doing the best you can with the problem, rewind the tape recorder and listen to the verbal record of your thinking. What patterns of thought become apparent? What gaps are there? Were the six principles followed? Judging from the tape and the remembered experience, was it difficult? If so, in what ways? Not infrequently, perhaps a quarter or a fifth of the time, people do encounter some difficulties with the think-aloud technique when attempting it without the help of an experienced investigator. Usually this is because one of the six principles has been neglected or not rightly understood. With an investigator to help, such problems seldom arise. In my experience, perhaps only one out of fifteen subjects has special difficulty with the think-aloud method, enough difficulty to warrant giving up.

If there were no such problems, the tape recording should tell quite a tale about how the mind can recover and assemble information. This problem often is used to demonstrate the deliberate and constructive character of some kinds of remembering, where a person must reason from partial recollections in order to reach a conclusion.

I have mentioned a couple of times that the mind works somewhat faster than the mouth. In fact, during moments of insight, a person often arrives at a conclusion much too quickly to give an adequate account "on the fly," as the think-aloud method requires. For probing such moments, there is a better way: a retrospective report. Usually, after-the-fact reports have been used as a coarser-grained substitute for thinking aloud, to avoid burdening people during the activity. But a few investigators have used retrospective reports as a finer-grained improvement over thinking aloud, one designed to collect a more detailed account of the last minute or so of thinking. The opportunity to do this arises from a remarkable circumstances: people can remember a great deal about the last few moments of thinking if they stop and take the time to review.

Of course, requests for retrospection have to be infrequent or one would constantly interrupt the activity. A good way to handle this is to ask people to think aloud and occasionally, when their speech indicates an insight, to request a retrospection. Another way is to set problems that are worked on silently, especially problems that tend to be solved in a flash after laboring for a while, and to ask for a retrospection immediately after an answer occurs.

A request for retrospection can be phrased something like this: "Can you tell me (or write down) what thought led to the next over the last several seconds up to the point you just arrived at? Try to indicate what happened step by step. But only report what you actually remember now, not what you think might plausibly have happened." After collecting a response to this, the investigator can refine it with further queries. Going over the events mentioned, the investigator might ask questions like "How sure are you that you actually remember this – rate yourself on a five-point scale ranging from very unsure to very sure," or, "Do you remember any mental images associated with this event," or "Do you now remember any thoughts coming after this, but before the next event you mentioned?" Whether and what questions to ask varies with the circumstances.

I won't quote an example of a retrospective report or give an exercise in producing one since both occur as part of the next chapter, which explores the nature of moments of insight. Let me just emphasize how the instructions and follow-up questions for a retrospective report encourage remembering rather than reconstruction. With retrospectives much more than with thinking aloud, people tend to offer plausible explanations, explanations that weave together their bits of memory to provide a fully coherent and motivated account of what happened. But making sense of the record is the business of the investigator, not the subject.

Revised proposition: Satisfactory introspective reports are most reliably obtained only with the help of good tactics, including careful instructions that warn against explaining or filling in, but encourage as continuous a report as memory and other factors permit.

CREATION AND CONSCIOUSNESS

It is standard lore that the business of creation is the business of the unconscious mind. Whatever conscious thoughts there might be are as irrelevant as the ripples on the surface of a pond, or so the story goes. The introspective methods discussed in this chapter seem to challenge this familiar idea. They reveal that makers of things or theories can say much more about their activities than people usually suppose. Perhaps creating is not so unconscious after all. But perhaps it is. In one way or another, I will have to return to this question several times over the following chapters.

Earlier, in the discussion of whether introspection disrupted an activity, it was important to sort out some different meanings of "thinking about" what one was doing. I want to do some more sorting here. A person can be conscious of an action in different senses. Suppose, for instance, I'm feeling like Don Rickles one day and I deliver an insult. Maybe it is fully premeditated. Both well before and as I say it, I know just what I'm doing. But maybe instead it is an opportunity suddenly seen and seized; I grow aware of, and have time to quash, the impulse, although it tends to flow toward its conclusion. Or maybe the putdown is wholly spontaneous; in the very saying, I recognize the sting and even regret it. Or then again, this same reaction might come not with but just after the remark. Or I may say something insulting without meaning to at all, and recognize it after the fact because of the victim's reaction, or never. Why this parade of possibilities? Simply to make the point that, introspective methods aside, awareness of the same superficial action can vary drastically in the natural course of events.

Deliberate introspection brings into awareness mental events which normally proceed without attention. As with the game of centipede, one can become conscious of automatic behavior like walking which does not need the support of consciousness to follow its familiar pattern. But while in such personal experiments attention may only watch and not lend a hand, attention of a somewhat different kind sometimes cuts in because it can and must help out. We walk down a summer sidewalk with no need for special attention, but an icy and rutted winter sidewalk captures our full awareness. We place our feet with conscious precision. Thus the border between the conscious and the unconscious shifts with need and circumstance, whether the needs and circumstances are those of the investigator of a slippery topic or the walker on a slippery road.

None of this means that the boundary of consciousness is wholly elastic. That walker on ice may control exquisitely where he places his feet, but he doesn't do so by guiding his muscles individually. Any effort to do this, or even to achieve a passive awareness of precisely which muscles are doing what, is very difficult. Simple acts of remembering provide another example. We all can remember our telephone numbers. They surface in our minds as dutifully as trained seals. But when we try to introspect how we search out that information, nothing comes. Whatever the mind does to look up such information in whatever sort of directory it has, the process is wholly covert.

So what about the issue we started with: Is creating unconscious or not? Even the above off-the-cuff examples warn that we need to be wary of glib answers. If creating is supposed to be unconscious, does this mean that the course of thought behind the achievement was not deliberately carried out, or not in fact conscious at the time, or never conscious even afterwards, or closed in principle to awareness? What people usually seem to have in mind is that the creative process is wholly closed to awareness. But plainly the effectiveness of introspective methods contradicts that. People *do* reveal significant things about things about their inventive thinking. A more reasonable sense in which the creative process is unconscious might be this: not surprisingly, makers are not routinely conscious of how they proceed. They attend to their work, not to the thought processes that are getting the work done. The success of introspective methods measures not what creators are usually aware of, but what they can be aware of without too much trouble.

But what about what they can't be aware of? What about mental processes like remembering your telephone number which hide wholly from consciousness? Maybe there, exactly there, is where most of the action occurs in creative thinking. In a sense, this has to be so. Not only creative thinking, but everything we do including taking out the garbage and polishing our shoes requires the support of hundreds of covert mental processes. What we are aware of, and even what we can be aware of, are only fragments of the ensemble. The unconscious is always where most of the action is, for anything.

But such an answer is somewhat beside the point, the present point at least. I have emphasized that my aim was not to explain the mundane miracles of human behavior, achievements like speaking or walking that we take for granted. Instead, I would hope to say something about how some things we usually recognize as marvelous, like the writing of a fine poem or the devising of a revolutionary scientific theory, can be understood in terms of those mundane miracles. That same philosophy applies here. The real question is not whether introspective reports explain everything about the course of thought. Certainly they don't. The real question is whether introspective reports reveal enough to reduce those marvelous accomplishments of the inventive mind to everyday if nonetheless mysterious mechanisms.

One clarification before I leave this topic. The following chapters call on many methods besides introspective ones, including cheerful thievery, with due acknowledgment, from whatever prior writers have said that is helpful. Probably not even a quarter of what I will have to say relies on introspective methods. Yet I wanted to take the time in this chapter to lay out what they were, how they worked, and what they were good for. All that with a simple enough motive: this is no doubt the most controversial source of information I will use.

2

CREATIVE MOMENTS

One of the most intriguing creative moments I know was described by the French mathematician Henri Poincaré. Poincaré had been developing a theory of a group of mathematical functions he came to call the Fuchsian functions. Among several moments of insight Poincaré related in connection with this work, the following especially fascinates:

> Just at this time I left Caen, where I was then living, to go on a geologic excursion under the auspices of the school of mines. The changes of travel made me forget my mathematical work. Having reached Coutances, we entered an omnibus to go some place or other. At the moment when I put my foot on the step the idea came to me, without anything in my former thoughts seeming to have paved the way for it, that the transformations I had used to define the Fuchsian functions were identical with those of non-Euclidean geometry. I did not verify the idea; I should not have had time, as upon taking my seat in the omnibus, I went on with a conversation already commenced, but I felt a perfect certainty. On my return to Caen, for conscience' sake I verified the result at my leisure.

There are many well-known moments of insight in the history of science. This is one of the most spare. Stepping onto the bus, Poincaré got his idea and that was all there was to it.

It's interesting to compare this with some other famous moments of creation – Charles Darwin's for instance. Darwin in

1838 had been convinced for some time that evolution occurred, but he had no explanation. What was it that caused animals and plants to evolve? Darwin puzzled over this problem for months, a course of thought I will return to later. His creative moment finally came with a prompt from a seemingly unrelated source. As Darwin recorded in his notebooks, he happened to be reading Malthus' *An Essay on the Principle of Population,* which discussed human population pressures and the struggle for existence. All at once, Darwin saw that the competition among living things would lead to a selection process. Favorable variations would survive and unfavorable ones perish, the favorable variations passing on their characteristics to their offspring. Thus, generation after generation, species would become more adapted to their circumstances. Darwin had his explanation for evolution.

The great grandfather of all such tales is the probably apocryphal story of Archimedes in his bath. Hiero, new ruler of Syracuse, had commissioned a golden crown, meaning to dedicate it to the gods in thanks for his success. Hiero had provided the craftsmen with an exact amount of gold by weight. The finished crown weighed the same. However, a charge was made that some of the gold had been stolen and the weight made up with mere silver. How to be sure? Hiero sought an answer from Archimedes. Silver has more volume than gold for the same weight, so an adulterated crown would be larger than one of pure gold. But the crown was so irregularly shaped that there was no ready way to compare it by volume with the same weight of gold. Worrying over this, Archimedes chanced to go to the public bath. On getting into a tub, he noticed that the deeper he settled, the more the water overflowed. All at once he had it: his body was displacing the water in the tub. Likewise, the volume of the crown could be measured by immersing it in a full tub of water and measuring the overflow. Archimedes, so the story goes, sprang from the tub and ran naked through the streets of Syracuse shouting "Eureka!" which means in Greek "I have found it!"

In a way, these insights of Darwin and, supposedly, Archimedes are more dramatic than Poincaré's. One has a vivid sense of the mind leaping from a situation that barely hinted at a solution directly to the solution. Poincaré merely stepped onto the bus. But just that makes Poincaré's experience more difficult to explain. Malthus for Darwin, the water overflowing the tub for Archimedes – these happened to have something about them related to the problems. Poincaré reported no such stimulation. If we can trust his story, his insight truly was out of the blue.

Any serious exploration of creating ought to offer an account of such creative moments. Just what is special about the mental activity leading to sudden discovery in cases like those of Darwin, Archimedes, and, most of all, Poincaré?

MENTAL LEAPS

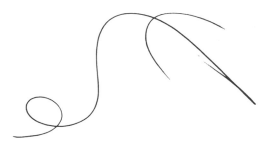

We might begin on an answer by comparing some psychological theories with the stories about mental leaps that creative individuals have told. The theory that matched the stories best would be the explanation for sudden insight. Or would it? Expecting that it would assumes that the stories are true. However, if the stories are not, the chosen theory would explain something that did not even occur. The misrepresentations of Poe and Coleridge should come to mind here, but of even more concern that such flagrantly misleading accounts are the risks of being honestly mistaken in after-the-fact reports about the delicate course of events during invention. Perhaps before much time is spent comparing stories and theories, there ought to be a more cautious look at the stories. One thing is assured. The tales of Poincaré, Darwin, and Archimedes are typical. Dozens more could be listed just as easily. If these reports can be taken at face value, mental leaps fit the following general formula.

Proposition: Mental leaps usually (1) achieve an insight quickly, without conscious thought; (2) achieve an insight toward which there has been no apparent progress; (3) achieve an insight that otherwise would seem to require considerable ordinary conscious thinking, if ordinary thinking would help at all.

Even something as sketchy as this has implications for the art of problem solving. Insight, it seems, is something that happens apart from anything you might do deliberately. Insight experiences point to a powerful mental process which can't be commanded by conscious tactics. If you want to take advantage of this process, you can only involve yourself in a problem and then await an idea. Problem solving becomes a kind of gambling where people bet on their intuition to find a way.

However, are (1), (2), and (3) above really so? For some years, I've been investigating mental leaps. I've examined mental leaps that occurred in the study of poets thinking aloud, as well as puzzled over episodes described by Poincaré, Darwin, and others. I've conducted a small experiment in which people solved insight problems and described their experiences. Immediately after some insights of my own, I've written down what I could remember of my mental processes, and I've asked others to do the same. I've had to conclude that the above proposition about mental leaps needs some revision.

     Look After You Leap

Insight problems are puzzles that often, although not always, are solved in sudden moments of insight. Certainly the solutions to such puzzles have no great significance. In this sense, such an experience is a very minor version of the grand insights of potent thinkers like Poincaré. However, the feeling of the experience seems much the same, and, I will argue later, much the same psychological mechanisms appear to be at work. Accordingly, insight problems provide a way of manufacturing in the laboratory experiences of insight for study. The method is the retrospective report.

Before giving the problem, let me spell out how the retrospective report should be made in this case. Upon solving the problem, write down step by step any thoughts that you can remember leading up to a solution. Try to recall some thought a minute or so before and then follow the thinking forward. Read over the list of steps. Cross out anything not definitely remembered, even if it seems to be plausible. After each remembered step, ask: Were there any visual or other sensory images associated with the step? Describe those. After each step, ask: Can I remember anything else that occurred between this step and the next? Write that down. All this needs to be done immediately after the insight because details are soon forgotten, so have pencil and paper ready.

What if no answer comes to mind? Probably that will not happen, since I know from experience that most people solve this problem. However, if it does, there are opportunities to try similar experiments later. Sometimes the easiest problems become the hardest if one doesn't happen to consider them in just the right way.

Here is the problem: A stranger approached a museum curator and offered him an ancient bronze coin. The coin had an authentic appearance and was marked with the date 544 B.C. The curator had happily made acquisitions from suspicious sources before, but this time he promptly called the police and had the stranger arrested. Why?

If an answer was reached, any thoughts leading up to it should now be noted before reading on.

The eight participants in the insight experiment attempted a very similar task. Each one worked on insight problems until he or she had solved four, and after each success reported the course of thought. Then the experimenter posed questions about each step: Was the person sure of remembering it? Could anything else be added? Did any mental imagery accompany a step?

Three of the participants tried and answered the B.C. problem. Here are reports from two whom I'll call Abbott and Binet, slightly paraphrased for clarity. Abbott said he:

1. Couldn't figure out what was wrong after reading through once.
2. Decided to read problem over again.
3. Asked himself, do archeologists dig up coins? Decided yes.
4. Asked himself, could the problem have something to do with bronze? Decided no.
5. Saw the word "marked." This was suspicious. Marked could mean many different things.
6. Decided to see what followed in the text.
7. Saw 544 B.C. (Imagined grungy coin in the dirt; had an impression of ancient times.)
8. Immediately realized – "it snapped" – that B.C. was the flaw.

Binet said he:

1. Thought perhaps they didn't mark coins with the date then.
2. Thought they didn't date at all – too early for calendar. (Image of backwards man hammering 544 on each little bronze coin.)
3. Focused on 544 B.C.
4. Looked at B.C.
5. Realized "B.C. – that means Before Christ."
6. Rationalized that it couldn't be before Christ since Christ wasn't born yet.
7. Saw no possible way to anticipate when Christ was going to be born.
8. Concluded "Fake!"

Those who attempted the personal experiment have a chance here to compare their experiences with Abbott's and Binet's. Were solutions reached as abruptly as in Abbott's case or in the roundabout way of Binet, or something between? What were the crucial steps and what suggested them?

I'd like to emphasize two commonalities and one difference

between Abbott's and Binet's reports. For the first, in neither case was there a leap directly from reading the problem to the solution. Both Abbott and Binet tried various approaches before finding one that led to a solution. Second, both Abbott and Binet focused on the date 544 B.C. before understanding how it resolved the problem. The date was the only very specific information in the problem statement. It attracted Binet's attention from the first, plausibly because it appeared out of place and therefore something that might be important. Often, although not always, insight problems contain "give away" phrases such as that, phrases that seem out of place because they are somewhat too specific, too vague, or awkward. They are clues to the solution, and, if you notice them or seek them out, much of the work is done.

The difference between Abbott and Binet is clear. Abbott focused on the date and then solved the problem in one more step – "it snapped." Binet reported several steps between focusing on the date and settling on a solution. Yet in a sense, Abbott and Binet had to do the same thing. Solving the problem requires using several facts. Abbott and Binet both had to understand that B.C. means before Christ. They had to use the knowledge that the date on a coin refers to the period when the coin was made and that the date was stamped on the coin then. They had to realize that craftsmen working before Christ's birth would not know of him. All this is implicit in understanding the difficulty with the date. While Binet reported some of this logic explicitly, Abbot did not. What Binet overtly reasoned out fell into place for Abbott, without any conscious thoughts that Abbott could remember.

How does all this concern mental leaps? Abbott's experience seems very much like a mental leap, certainly much more so that Binet's. However, as a mental leap, is Abbott's experience really all that it should be? A good way to explore this question is to ask yet another: Just what is the leap in Abbott's report? Obviously one would not want to call the whole process the leap. This would not conform to the proposition stated earlier. However rapidly and spontaneously Abbott may have had his several thoughts, he thought them and reported them nonetheless. Starting from his reading of the problem, his solution certainly did not occur "quickly, without conscious thought."

More plausibly, the leap appears only as part of Abbott's report, the last part from focusing on the date to discerning the solution, where Abbott described no intervening steps. But this also does not match the proposition. In focusing on the date, Abbott selected the crucial clue. Indeed, if Abbott had not attended to the date, it is hard to imagine how he could have solved the problem at all. The focusing on the date was important progress prior to the supposed leap. Abbott did not "achieve an insight toward which there had been no apparent progress." Finally, did Abbott really "achieve an insight that otherwise would seem to require considerable ordinary thinking?" Presumably, Binet was the ordinary thinker. His more piecemeal progress is the measure of the distance Abbott leaped. However, Binet's few extra steps do not amount to all that much more ordinary thinking. Abbott's supposed leap was more of a hop.

We've been looking at just two examples. What did the insight experiment disclose in general? Episodes with the limited leaplike qualities of Abbott's were not common, even though the problems were chosen to be the sort presumably solved in such ways. Of the thirty-two reports I gathered, only seven or so seemed somewhat like Abbott's. No subject ever solved a problem without some kind of focusing or narrowing down. Each problem sometimes was solved by more straightforward thinking, without any sense of a leap at all, and these reports were not on the average longer than those that contained seeming leaps.

However, something more like an ideal mental leap can occur. Recently I gave the B.C. problem to a class of sixteen students. They wrote down their steps just as described earlier. One student reported an experience that was as leaplike as anyone could wish. This person noticed the catch in 544 B.C. before he had even finished reading the problem. Other persons reported experiences more like Abbott's or Binet's. Yet another did not solve the problem at all. Therefore, the results do not suggest that ideal mental leaps never occur. They do suggest that experiences which subjectively feel like mental leaps aren't usually examined as carefully as they might be. When they are, usually they appear less leaplike than might have been thought.

Revised proposition: Experiences that feel like mental leaps usually (1) achieve an insight quickly, but with a few discernible steps; (2) achieve an insight toward which the steps progress; (3) achieve an insight that might be reached by only a few more steps starting from the same point, without any suggestion of a mental leap.

This revised proposition is important for at least two reasons. It implies that what we call mental leaps are less mysterious and more explainable than they are usually taken to be. Also, it implies that we have more access to our minds than we might have thought. With that greater access might come greater opportunity to tinker.

What about Poincaré? He did not report any mental steps, nor did he describe an experience like that of the person mentioned above who discovered the catch in 544 B.C. at once. That person at least responded to a physical clue, the B.C., as Darwin did reading his Malthus and Archimedes easing into his tub. However, Poincaré reported no such clue in his situation. The circumstances discussed here therefore are not wholly parallel to Poincaré's, certainly not in the significance of the problem solved but also not in the availability of an external clue, or so one would conclude from Poincaré's statement. However, my examples also highlight the risk of incomplete observation. The mental steps revealed by a retrospective examination would never be recognized unless one took the trouble to think back and, perhaps, knew something about how to do so. The Poincaré episode might be a case of faulty observation rather than out-of-the-blue insight.

THE STILL-WATERS THEORY

Henri Poincaré not only had a number of remarkable experiences of insight but also a theory about them. Although the theory included several details, its basic claim was the following: "Most striking at first is this appearance of sudden illumination, a manifest sign of long, unconscious work. The role of this unconscious work in mathematical invention appears to me incontestable." With this remark, Poincaré left off describing and began to explain. We need to do the same, especially since I've just discussed how mental leaps ought to be described, not how they ought to be explained.

Poincaré's suggestion articulates one of our most cherished ideas about creative thinking. Inheritors of Freud, we find easy a belief in the unconscious as a place where mysterious things happen. Poincaré's suggestion might be called a still-waters theory of mental leaps. "Still waters run deep," so goes the saying. A still-waters theory of mental leaps asserts that thinking runs deep even though quiet on the surface, or quiet at least as far as the problem of interest is concerned. Active thinking, much as a person might do consciously, proceeds unconsciously for a considerable period while the person rests or attends to other matters.

★

Proposition: Mental leaps depend on extended unconscious thinking. During the experience we call a mental leap, the results of that thinking suddenly become conscious.

The usual evidence for extended unconscious thinking is a phenomenon called incubation. By definition, incubation occurs when time away from a problem helps to solve the problem. We often have the impression that this has happened when we set a stubborn problem aside and then think of a solution out of the blue, or immediately upon returning to the problem. It's important in considering incubation to keep separate the phenomenon and the explanations for it. The word incubation itself suggests that something is gradually developing, and sometimes people use the word as though it *meant* extended unconscious thinking. However, I want to emphasize that, as used in psychology, incubation means only that time away from a problem helped, no matter how.

With all this in mind, what evidence do we need to be sure that extended unconscious thinking occurs? First of all, it's necessary to be convinced that incubation does occur. Second, it's necessary to exclude other possible explanations of incubation besides extended unconscious thinking. Let me examine those issues one at a time.

As for being convinced that incubation occurs, certainly there is ample opportunity for people to fool themselves. Although time away from a problem may seem to help, this may be because people in fact turn to an absorbing problem briefly at odd moments, while riding the bus or mowing the lawn. The "time away" is time away from the desk and concerted effort, but not really time away from the problem. Work at odd moments is easily forgotten when people finally achieve a solution and accept extended unconscious thinking as an explanation. Simple accident also can be misleading. Sometimes a person, although seemingly stymied, may leave a problem on the verge of being solved. Returning to the problem, the person may solve it readily and form the impression that incubation has occurred. Such deceptive accidents would not be common, of course, but they would be striking and striking events tend to be remembered.

None of this shows that incubation does not occur, but merely describes how we could misjudge the matter by informal observation. In fact, there have been several psychological studies of incubation which have sought to remedy the weaknesses of informal observation. The findings are annoyingly inconsistent. Sometimes, time away from a problem has helped, and sometimes it has not. Moreover, where time away did help, efforts to replicate the results often have failed.

Let me describe one particularly naturalistic study. The psychologist Robert Olton carefully created circumstances where incubation would be expected. A number of chess buffs volunteered to try to solve a chess puzzle. Some worked continuously on the puzzle, while others took two-hour breaks after about an hour of effort, at times of their choosing. They were asked not to work deliberately on the puzzle during their breaks. Most browsed and snacked in a nearby student center. The participants apparently were very interested and involved in the puzzle, and most said they had benefited from incubation before in connection with chess. One subject even discovered the solution spontaneously during his break – like Poincaré stepping onto the bus. However, despite the ideal circumstances, about the same percentage of people in the incubation group and in the continuous group solved the problem.

I am not convinced by such experiments that incubation never occurs, for reasons to be explained later. However, the negative findings in these experiments do seem to be a fairly persuasive argument against the still-waters theory, against extended unconscious thinking. Presumably, in extended unconscious thinking, the mind goes through much the same logical steps as it might consciously, perhaps with even more effectiveness. If people are capable of this, incubation experiments ought to show decisively positive results, especially naturalistic experiments such as Olton's. Since positive results do not appear, extended unconscious thinking probably does not occur.

Let me set aside these findings now and turn to the second concern, whether explanations for incubation besides extended unconscious thinking can be excluded. The first point to recognize is that other explanations are plentiful. There are many reasons why time away from a problem might help. For instance, you may return to a task physically refreshed and with a new will. You may forget the details of an approach or understanding or attitude concerning the problem and recover a kind of distance and openness to new possibilities. Even if a prior approach is remembered, the emotional commitment to it – the feeling of "I've invested so much time this way, I've got to make it work" – may have lessened, making other approaches emotionally acceptable. Finally, people often notice clues to the solution in supposedly irrelevant contexts while doing something else altogether. This certainly seems to have happened to Darwin and Archimedes.

What kind of evidence could exclude these other explanations for incubation, if indeed incubation occurs, leaving extended unconscious thinking as the preferred explanation? The amount of thinking required by a problem seems to be the crucial factor. Physical refreshment, forgetting details, finding new approaches, or noticing clues in unexpected circumstances would not accomplish extensive mental work. If a great deal of thinking somehow had to get done without conscious attention, extended unconscious thinking would be the only explanation left. The quest to demonstrate a still-waters theory of insight becomes a quest to find cases of incubation which clearly must have required extensive thinking, and therefore extensive unconscious thinking.

In groups I have spoken to about the nature of incubation, people often offer personal anecdotes taken as demonstrating extended unconscious thinking. Always, in my experience, their examples fail to meet this standard. The insight achieved simply is not that remote in number of mental steps (or amount of thought required however one wants to measure it) from the person's starting point. This does not mean, of course, that such insights are easy to achieve. The need to think in just the right direction often makes problems difficult even when the solution is not remote from the starting point.

The insight experiment I discussed earlier also discouraged a still-waters theory of mental leaps. One of the findings was that those who solved the B.C. and other problems without any leap did not require significantly more mental steps than those who experienced a leap. Sudden insight wasn't a symptom of a long unconscious train of thought. However, such artificial problems might mislead us about truly significant insights. So a look at more authentic examples is in order. For one certainly significant insight, I will return to the discovery of the principle of natural selection. Unfortunately, Darwin gave only the briefest description of this crucial moment in science:

> In October 1838, that is, fifteen months after I had begun my systematic enquiry, I happened to read for amusement "Malthus on Population," and being well prepared to appreciate the struggle for existence which everywhere goes on from long-continued observation of the habits of animals and plants, it at once struck me that under these circumstances favourable variations would tend to be preserved, and unfavorable ones to be destroyed.

However, an accident of history has provided another, more detailed account. Darwin delayed publishing his theory for a number of years, and in 1858 Alfred Russell Wallace conceived the same theory of natural selection independently, also commencing with Malthus:

One day something brought to my recollection Malthus' "Principles of Population," which I had read about twelve years before. I thought of his clear exposition of "the positive checks to increase" – disease, accidents, war, famine – which keep down the population of savage races to so much lower an average than that of more civilized peoples. It then occurred to me that these causes or their equivalents are continually acting in the case of animals also; and as animals usually breed much more rapidly than does mankind, the destruction every year from these causes must be enormous in order to keep down the numbers of each species, since they evidently do not increase regularly from year to year, as otherwise the world would long ago have been densely crowded with those that breed most quickly. Vaguely thinking over the enormous and constant destruction which this implied, it occurred to me to ask the question, Why do some die and some live? And the answer was clearly, that on the whole the best fitted live. From the effects of disease the most healthy escaped; from enemies, the strongest, the swiftest, or the most cunning; from famine, the best hunters or those with the best digestion; and so on. Then it suddenly flashed upon me that this self-acting process would necessarily *improve the race*, because in every generation the inferior would inevitably be killed off and the superior would remain – that is, the *fittest would survive*.

Just how much of a mental leap was Wallace's experience as he described it? Certainly there was a critical moment – "Then it suddenly flashed upon me," much as with Darwin's "It all at once struck me." However, with Wallace, the insight hardly came all at once. In fact, the following progression toward the idea of natural selection appears in Wallace's account:

1. Malthus and the positive checks to human increase.
2. The same causes act in the case of animals (Wallace's interest as a naturalist appears).
3. Since animals breed faster, this implies constant and enormous destruction (here the means of selection – destruction – appears).

4. Why do some die and some live? (The lucky question – prompted perhaps by the habit of the scientific thinker to seek causes.)
5. The best fitted live (the obvious answer).
6. The race is improved (Wallace recognizes the best fitted as the most adapted and realizes he has an explanation for how species become adapted).

Not only does Wallace relate a fairly continuous sequence of thought, each step leading sensibly to the next, but to my mind that last step is no less continuous, no more of a leap, than the others. Yes, it is the crucial step, but it is rather like that last step of the first man to climb Mount Everest – a step supremely significant in its accomplishment but, in its mechanism, just one more like all the others.

In short, we have here a comparison between Darwin and Wallace rather like the comparison between Abbott and Binet. Darwin may have had a more abrupt experience of insight than Wallace, but even Wallace's train of thought did not continue that long. There was no need for extended unconscious thinking here, simply because there was no need for extended thinking of any sort. This point, of course, does not diminish the accomplishment of Darwin and Wallace. These able thinkers, saturated in the problem, discerned a significance in Malthus another would have missed. Indeed, later I will discuss how Darwin, over many months, evolved an understanding of evolution which made the ultimate insight possible. Nonetheless, the final chain of thought was not a long one.

 Personal Insights

This is the sort of question you can test on yourself as well. The requirements are simple: a couple of days of patience and a notepad and pencil kept handy. Minor insights are fairly frequent experiences for most people. The aim is simply to stay alert for one, especially one concerning something not attended to at the time, and to write down the thoughts leading to the insight just as for the B.C. puzzle. Remember the importance of recording whatever can be recalled immediately after the experience, before memories have a chance to fade. This is the reason for carrying a notepad and pencil around.

After an insight has occurred and notes have been made, some crucial questions can be asked. *Were* there steps to write down, or just an abrupt insight? If there were steps, were any of them of a "falling into place" character, as with Abbott on the B.C. problem? Was there anything in the situation – something seen or thought about – that prompted the insight? Were there very many steps? Would the insight have required very extensive straightforward thinking (starting with the same observation if any)?

I cannot predict exactly what will happen with those who try this personal experiment. However, I've collected a number of reports from people asked to attempt it. I've also kept track of some of my own moments of insight in the same way. Finally, I've examined cases such as Darwin's and Wallace's where I could find them. In contrast with the puzzle problems of the previous section, such cases have an intrinsic claim to authenticity. Moreover, their general characteristics do not appear to differ much from the episodes of thinking found in the insight experiment. Here, as there, true mental leaps in the sense defined previously were rare, much rarer than subjective experiences of having a mental leap. Almost always some focusing in on a significant clue or other stepwise progression occurred before a solution. Furthermore, I have never, not once, encountered a case of out-of-the-blue insight that clearly required extended thought, thought that therefore might have occurred unconsciously over a considerable period.

This argues strongly against the still-waters theory. First of all, because insight experiences apparently don't require extended thought, there are no grounds for excluding the alternative explanations for incubation. Moreover, although extended unconscious thinking remains a logical possibility, it becomes a pointless one. There simply is not that much thinking to account for in cases of insight, so why defend an extended unconscious process that has nothing to do?

None of this means that incubation doesn't occur. I think it does – but in ways other than extended unconscious thinking. I believe this because I've observed those specific ways in my own and others' experience. Physical refreshment, fruitful forgetting, losing commitment to an ineffective approach, and noticing clues in the environment all are events that sometimes happen and sometimes clearly help. A very reliable sort of incubation is the sort that occurs when one sets a product aside for a while and then returns to it with a fresh eye for strengths and weaknesses.

It remains to explain why the laboratory studies have not demonstrated incubation. I suspect the answer to that lies in the hit-or-miss character of incubation, which helps only on certain occasions with certain problems. In my experience, incubation proves most reliable in complex situations where one needs to recover distance and good judgment. However, these are not the sorts of problems that have been examined in the laboratory studies. Also, a person is more likely to notice clues relevant to a concern while not attending to it if the concern is a complex, many-sided one. Under such conditions, present circumstances can match up to various parts of the concern in various ways, and opportunities for chance contributing to the course of thought are increased. Again, however, such conditions aren't typically created in the laboratory studies.

Revised proposition: Extended unconscious thinking does not occur. Deferring a troublesome problem and returning to it later occasionally helps for reasons that have nothing to do with extended unconscious thinking.

One further note: This conclusion does not at all imply that unconscious processes have no role in thinking. On the contrary, most of the mental operations that mediate thought occur unconsciously, a point that will become more and more obvious as this book proceeds. However, the moment-to-moment work of unconscious processes in support of the thinker's current activities is one thing, and extended unconscious thinking while the person attends to something else is quite another. The latter is the only victim of the above arguments.

THE BLITZKRIEG THEORY

The informal theories that pervade everyday thinking about sudden insight all try to explain the mental work that insights accomplish. The still-waters theory proposed that the work gets done unconsciously over a long period. Another theory takes a different view of this. The mental work gets done very rapidly, although still mostly unconsciously, during the experience of insight itself. Dreams, some people say, occur in the few seconds before waking even though they seem to last for hours. Poincaré, Darwin, and Archimedes were hardly dreaming, but perhaps some special accelerated process explains how they could achieve so much so suddenly. I will name this notion the blitzkrieg theory, after the German word for lightning war.

Proposition: Mental leaps are explained by an accelerated thought process special to insight which compresses considerable normal mental effort into a couple of seconds.

This proposition fits our subjective experience of mental leaps, but, as emphasized earlier, the impression that mental leaps require considerable thinking somehow accomplished is simply false. In the cases reviewed, there was no evidence whatsoever for a process that did the work of hours in seconds. The acceleration proposed by the blitzkrieg theory seems unneeded.

This point is important to recognize, but I do not think it is the crucial one. Some version of a blitzkrieg theory still might make sense. First of all, nothing in the proposition specifies just how much more rapidly thought occurred. Working on the B.C. puzzle, Abbott took a single step combining several steps of Binet's. A student given the problem discovered the catch in the date while reading the problem. Darwin's description of arriving at the theory of natural selection suggested an abrupt insight, while Wallace's description suggested a progression of thought. Certainly something seems to happen faster on some occasions and slower on others. If it is only two or three times faster, still that deftness deserves attention.

Furthermore, sometimes mental work can be done very much faster in one way than in another. A nice example concerns perceiving an artist's style. When you are not too familiar with an artist and want to sort the artist's works from some rather similar ones, an analytical approach is natural. You might examine a work feature by feature, looking for nuances of texture, line, and so forth. However, if you have examined the artist's work often, matters are very different. The artist's products come to have a "look" to them, recognizable in an instant. With experience, acts of recognition take over from acts of analytical identification, a dramatic gain in efficiency.

However, this plea for the reality of rapid mental processes raises other reservations about the blitzkrieg theory. First of all, the blitzkrieg theory refers to accelerated thinking, as though what normally happened in a plodding way sometimes occurred much faster. However, recognition, in contrast with identification by more roundabout means, seems not just faster but qualitatively different. The blitzkrieg notion of a kind of mental "high gear" where everything happens in the same way only faster is too simplistic to take seriously. Second, while the blitzkrieg theory speaks of a process special to insight, nothing could be more mundane than recognition. Whatever role recognizing plays in insight, recognizing occurs constantly in our everyday activities. We recognize friends on the street, words in a book, typographical errors, or the way to work. If recognition is important to insight, it certainly isn't special to insight.

Let's explore the notion that recognition and related concepts account wholly or in part for experiences of insight in terms of ordinary acts of mind. The B.C. problem provides an "in part" example. For both Abbott and Binet, focusing on the date was a crucial event. This apparently depended on spontaneously recognizing the date as suspiciously specific. Although someone might approach a problem by scrutinizing each phrase for a clue, Abbott and Binet seemed simply and quickly to have noticed the clue without analytically seeking one.

It's also plausible that recognition contributed to Darwin's and Archimedes' experiences. Both were confronting real physical situations. In each case, there was a kind of pattern to the situation that related to the problem. For example, Darwin had been seeking some kind of *selection* mechanism already, an idea suggested to him by his observations of deliberate selection in stock breeding. If Darwin happened to recognize the struggle for existence Malthus wrote of as a selective process, because some survive and some don't, only a few more steps would have taken him to the idea that such selection would result in evolution. Darwin would have recognized the selectionlike nature of the situation Malthus described as potentially relevant, much as Abbott and Binet recognized the suspiciously specific phrase 544 B.C. as potentially relevant. Such speculations can't show what actually happened in Darwin's mind, of course, but they show that recognition easily could have helped.

However, to explain insight at all adequately, I think we have to consider processes more general than recognition. Recall again the B.C. riddle and that deft step of Abbott. In realizing that an authentic coin couldn't say B.C., Abbott had to depend on facts about the way coins were made, the impossibility of foreknowledge, and so on. No doubt Abbott had encountered anachronisms before, but probably not this particular inconsistency. One wouldn't want to say he simply was recognizing the same catch, as one might if he had seen the same puzzle or a very similar one before.

Perhaps instead of *recognizing*, we should say *realizing*. Just as when we speak of recognizing something we usually have in mind a quick spontaneous act, we also do when we speak of realizing something. As recognizing is a word for abrupt identification, realizing is a word for abrupt understanding. We simply realize what we instead might have had to work out. Of course, to speak of realizing is not to explain how realizing occurs. Realizing is only a name to go with the fact that some mental work can occur quickly and largely unconsciously to result in understanding. Realizing is a shorter label for "things falling into place."

Like recognizing, realizing operates all the time. Consider understanding sentences, for example. We do not merely recognize them or their meanings, since we probably haven't seen those very same sentences before. However, we realize their meanings for the most part: we simply hear and understand. Also, we realize the significance of everyday situations, like the car bearing down as you start to cross the street. As with recognizing, there is nothing specific to insight about realizing.

What I am saying here may seem a little odd. I am suggesting that catching on to the b.c. problem, or even catching on to the possibility of natural selection, is not such a very different process from understanding an ordinary situation or statement. There are seeming contrasts. However, perhaps these are illusory. The simplest one to ponder concerns literalness in everyday understanding. Although a sentence may say what it means directly, the b.c. riddle has a hidden flaw to detect. Its "I am a lie" message is not stated. This may seem like a fundamental difference between understanding ordinary matters and catching on to subtle patterns, but it is not. Though some routine sentences say what they mean, most do otherwise. Typically, sentences imply much more than they state. We understand many of those implications with no effort at all, as part of the normal realizing process. Recent research on understanding stories has emphasized again and again how much the listener fills in.

Consider the b.c. riddle. Apart from the solution, merely to read and understand the problem one has to read between the lines. Did the story say a man offered to sell an ancient coin to the curator? No. It only said "A stranger approached a museum curator and offered him an ancient bronze coin." With nothing mentioned about selling or buying, selling was understood. If the context had been a little different, "offered" would have been taken in quite a different way. Consider for instance: "The rich collector of antiquities J. Anderson Anderson approached a museum curator and offered him an ancient coin." In that sentence "offered" sounds more like "offered as a gift" than "offered for sale." Such examples emphasize that one doesn't just understand what a sentence states. One fills in what the sentence plausibly means.

Hardly limited to sentence understanding, this talent for filling in is a pervasive characteristic of human thought and perception. In Jerome Bruner's felicitous phrase, the human creature is an expert at "going beyond the information given." In an article of the same name, Bruner maps many ways in which this occurs. Bridging the gap in the b.c. problem is only a special case of a general and often effortless act of mind.

But just what sort of a special case is it? One realizes what the catch in 544 b.c. is by frustrated filling in. The little historical tale implicit in 544 B.C. – men stamping the date onto the coins centuries before Christ – doesn't make sense, as a crooked witness' story might not. When the anomaly is suddenly discovered, that automatic process of filling in, going about its work, has encountered and reported an inconsistency. Of course, the anomaly in 544 B.C. itself is not an anomaly at all in the riddle as a whole. On the contrary, it answers the riddle by explaining why the stranger was arrested. A complicated two-level process of realizing occurs; the failure to realize sense in 544 B.C. leads to success in realizing the sense of the whole riddle.

I've argued that the filling in aspect of insight is well represented in ordinary acts of understanding. However, another contrast between insight and ordinary understanding demands attention. The subjective experiences of the two are utterly different. In routine understanding, there is none of the heady sense of discovery that has earned mental leaps the name of Aha! or Eureka! Could this be a sign that, in the case of insight, the mind is working in a fundamentally different way? I don't think so. I suggest that the special feel of insight should be attributed to what the person achieves rather than how the person achieves it. In particular, insights usually have some special significance for the person, even if only the satisfaction of solving a puzzle. Insights most typically make sense of something that has resisted understanding, or make sense of something in a new way, displacing an old construal of it. Although rapid understanding occurs all the time without any great sense of insight, understanding with those additional features occurs much less often and carries with it a quality of significant discovery that colors the experience.

   Getting the Point

The phenomenon of humor provides an argument that the affective quality of insight has more to do with mental product than mental process. Understanding humor has many parallels with discovering something, an idea Arthur

Koestler has discussed at length in *The Act of Creation*. The experience of humor is a sort of "missing link" between insight and routine moments of understanding. As to insight, humor has more of the feel of insight – the sudden shock of sense. As to routine understanding, we ordinarily do consider appreciating humor to be a matter of understanding. We speak of understanding the joke or "getting the point." If the feel of humor is due to unexpected sense made by the usual processes of understanding, why not the feel of insight too?

A case in point: I'm going to tell a joke. The only requirement for this personal experiment is to pay attention to the quality of the experience as the joke proceeds to its conclusion. This story concerns a Jew who was disturbed to find that his son, back from college, had converted to Christianity. He went to a friend and explained his problem.

"Funny you should mention it!" the friend said. "Why, only last week I found a New Testament hidden under my boy's mattress."

"We must bring this matter to the attention of the Rabbi," they decided.

"Funny you should mention it!" the Rabbi responded. "Why, my own son has joined the YMCA."

There was only one thing left: an appeal to God. So the three prayed, "What shall we do? All our sons are converting to Christianity!"

The clouds parted, a beam of brilliant light shone down from above, and a soft voice slowly and thoughtfully began, "Funny you should mention it . . ."

People getting the point of this joke often experience an emotional and intellectual reaction very much like insight. They experience the falling into place of a new, more comprehensive pattern. All the human fathers have the same problem, but the pattern is unexpectedly extended. No one would imagine the heavenly father to have the problem too and yet, so goes the joke, he does. His son too has "converted to Christianity" – as

Christ himself. Remarkable here as with the B.C. problem is the variation from person to person in speed of comprehension. I gave this exercise to the same group that attempted the B.C. puzzle. Most understood the joke fairly quickly. Some people, however, had to puzzle over the joke before understanding it. One person anticipated the punchline before reading it, simply from the earlier lines. This recalls the person who noticed the catch in 544 B.C. before reading the whole problem.

The question remains why we do not call the point of a joke an insight, even though the audience achieves a sudden unexpected understanding. What distinguishes this sort of realizing from the sort that fully warrants the label insight? The answer seems to be that we speak of insight only when a person achieves an understanding that might well have been missed. Jokes are designed to lead people to get the point, and so, even though getting the point involves an intellectual and affective reaction characteristic of insight, the person does not receive credit for any achievement. In the case of the B.C. puzzle, which is designed to challenge the audience a little, it makes somewhat more sense to speak of insight. In those cases where a person anticipated the anomaly in the B.C. problem or the punchline of the above joke, insight seems just the right word.

Insight, in short, involves doing more with less. Insight differs not qualitatively but quantitatively from its near relative of understanding humor, where sudden understanding of an unexpected sort emerges from plentiful information. In insight, the person's own mind provides what in more ordinary circumstances would be supplied from without. However, the "doing more" of insight does not mean that any special process is at work. Remember, ordinary understanding of sentences required going beyond the information given. Indeed, the punchline of the above joke demands considerable filling in. The punch line only has God say, "Funny you should mention it . . . ", the rest remaining for the reader to interpret, as the reader almost always does. Insight involves filling in just as with ordinary acts of understanding, only filling in more than would be expected.

Revised proposition: Many mental leaps are explained by the ordinary mental processes of recognizing and realizing, processes that do, however, accomplish quickly what one might attempt more consciously and deliberately over a somewhat longer period. Recognizing and realizing routinely involve filling in, but we reserve the names mental leap and insight for those occasions when (1) the pattern or understanding arrived at makes significant sense of previously less organized or differently organized information; and (2) the person fills in more than would ordinarily be expected.

THE BETTER-MOUSETRAP THEORY

My remarks so far sound as if they were meant to settle the question of insight, but now I want to unsettle it once again by taking up one more perspective. The concern is the role of reasoning in insight. The common attitude toward this again aims to explain how the work of insight gets done. Reasoning, so it's said, is the normal manner of thought, a manner that ill fits the flight of the mind during mental leaps. Therefore, mental leaps involve some special mental process that shortcuts normal rational thinking to attain a solution more directly. Whereas the theory that insight occurs in a special place, the unconscious, received the name still-waters theory, and the theory that insight occurred at a special rapid pace received the name blitzkrieg theory, the idea that insight requires a distinctively nonlogical process will be called a better-mousetrap theory because it posits a better mousetrap for catching ideas.

The literature on creativity includes a number of better-mouse-trap theories. The names of these concepts and their efforts to express something of the mind's extraordinary powers are provocative in themselves. For example, there is Arthur Koestler's bisociation, Silvano Arieti's paleologic, Edward de Bono's lateral thinking, Albert Rothenberg's Janusian thinking and homospatial thinking. Whatever the labels, and granting some important differences, all these notions are to some degree better-mousetrap theories. They all at least suggest that insight is not a matter of reasoning.

Proposition: Insight depends on some special mental activity that shortcuts reasoning.

The relationship between this proposition and what has already been said about insight is a little complicated. On the one hand, I've argued that nothing special marks the mental processes involved in insight. They are the same processes of recognizing and realizing which mediate ordinary acts of quick identification and understanding. Therefore, the better-mousetrap theory's claim for a special process won't do. On the other hand, nothing said so far has addressed the role of reasoning in mental leaps or in ordinary acts of rapid understanding. And the very rapidity of these acts of mind seems to remove them from the realm of reasoning as we usually think of it. Is this impression sound? Just how does reasoning relate to insight?

It's easy to underestimate what everyday reasoning can accomplish. Very often insight can come about just exactly through reasoning. Something of a case for this has been made already. Although one may solve the B.C. problem with a sense of insight, the process involves a form of reasoning. Realizing the solution requires detecting a logical inconsistency in the date that explains the logic of the riddle as a whole. Whether that occurs more or less quickly and spontaneously – Abbott versus Binet again – it would seem to be reasoning of a sort. Furthermore, a more natural example is available. Here is another report of an insight experience, one with some compelling features. This example concerns not an artificial problem but a problem during the actual writing of a poem. It concerns not a trivial puzzle but something very significant for the person. It concerns not a problem with an obviously logical character but one much more personal and aesthetic. For all that, reasoning seems remarkably apparent.

The poet was one of the twenty who helped me with the thinking-aloud studies described earlier. The poet, a professional, came in for a session where she would try to draft a poem, starting perhaps with an idea but nothing already on paper. The poet did bring an idea. She had the notion that "the day proceeds like an air raid drill, because I've been thinking about the way my children sound." This was the seed of her poem.

She started by writing *My babies are wailing like those air raid drills / I remember.* She then worked steadily, producing a number of lines about air raid drills when she was a child, what they were like and the anxiety they created. None of this referred directly to her babies. Finishing this part, she faced a problem she had mentioned even at the beginning. So far, the metaphor between babies and air raid drills was too superficial – just a matter of sound and alarm. To complete the poem, she wanted to deepen the metaphor. The poet thought about this without making much progress. Then she read the poem through from the start, ending with the lines *I am still fighting that cold war / alone. The wailing babies . . . "*

Then she said, still thinking aloud, "Aha! It has to do with . . . preserving your own life first. I think that's what this has to do with actually. Maybe I'll call this poem 'self-preservation.' " She had found her deeper metaphor. From the first, the wailing of the babies, like the sirens, had been frightening, but now the babies, like the sirens, had a specific message: preserve yourself. The poet went on to conclude the poem with this theme.

How little thinking aloud sometimes reveals. One moment the poet finished reading her draft, then it was "Aha!" and the answer. No information appeared about the poet's process. However, retrospective reporting sometimes can provide more information. Before the poet continued, immediately after her "Aha!" and another sentence or two, she was asked to try to remember the thoughts leading up to her insight. Here is what she said:

Well, I was thinking, (reads) *and I am still fighting that cold war / alone. The wailing babies* – what did they signal me to do? What is it a signal for me to do? And actually, (pause) why do you hide? It's because you're trying to preserve yourself, and that's what the babies are signaling me to do too, because basically I can't, I don't tolerate them very well, and it does me in so much that I have to leave them and go into silence, someplace that's silent so I can preserve myself.

Let me describe what I think is happening here. There is a choice about how many steps to suggest. The six below could be four or eight, but they clarify the poet's thinking.

1. What do the wailing babies signal me to do?
2. Well, what does the siren signal me to do?
3. The siren signals me to hide.
4. Why do I hide on hearing the sirens?
5. To preserve myself from the air raid.
6. The babies signal me to preserve myself too.

This abstract relates to the poet's report as follows. Step 1 comes straightforwardly from "What did they signal me to do?" Step 2, "Well What does the siren signal me to do?", corresponds to the poet's "What is it a signal for me to do?" – the "it," considering the following sentence, indicates a shift of attention from babies to air raid siren. The poet's "And actually, why do you hide?" clearly refers to the air raid and implies steps 3 and 4. Steps 5 and 6 come from "It's because you're trying to preserve yourself, and that's what the babies are signaling me to do too."

This outline displays the poet's logic. An apparently spontaneous chain of thoughts led the poet to an important insight but, spontaneous or not, the steps were reasonable. Wanting a more profound metaphor relating babies and sirens, a more meaningful property common to both, the poet considered what the siren signaled her to do until she found something that, in a sense, her babies signaled her to do too.

Could the poet be rationalizing her report? Was the real process more haphazard? There's no way of determining for sure. All that can be said is that the poet reported as she did, and her report gives a plausible explanation of her insight. All in all, I'm inclined to take what she said seriously. Examples like this are no comfort to ideas like Koestler's bisociation and Arieti's paleologic. Metaphor making supposedly needs to be explained by processes that leap over logical limits, but here logic itself does the leaping.

 Squaring Off

We can explore this question further with the sorts of insight problems discussed before. I'm going to describe another such problem. Again, those wanting to try this personal experiment should be prepared to write down any thoughts leading up to a solution immediately after reaching it. Below are four dots in a square. How can just two dots be moved to make a new square with twice the area of the original one?

One subject in the insight experiment – I'll call him Costa – found a solution by moving dots around until something fell into place. Finally shifting the upper right dot upward, he noticed that that dot, together with the upper left and lower right dots, made two sides of a square tilted diagonally, as below. Then he moved the lower left dot to complete the square.

A subject I'll call Dill took a very different approach. He asked himself what the longest distance between two dots was. After all, if two dots were moved, two would be left behind, and those two would have to be part of a larger square. He decided that the two dots left behind needed to be diagonally opposite and checked whether the length of such a side would double the area. Finding that it would, he had his solution.

How do Costa and Dill compare? Costa proceeded more or less by trial and error until he recognized the partial tilted square. Pattern recognition explained his insight. Dill worked with logic. He reasoned that the conditions of the problem implied that the dots left behind had to be on a diagonal. Both these subjects took longer than three minutes. When I first saw this problem, I did it Dill's way, but it only took me five or ten seconds. I mention this facile solution (there are plenty I've had trouble with) only because I need to make a point about reasoning. Where Dill explored the problem in other ways before beginning his reasoning, and then plodded through it, in my case the same logic began at once and continued very quickly and spontaneously.

Here are some conclusions about reasoning and insight. Reasoning is a perfectly good way to achieve an insight. Reasoning may proceed slowly and deliberately or very quickly and spontaneously as in "realizing." Reasoning may be a better approach than trial and error for some insight problems, because then the conditions of the problem will force one toward a solution. Reasoning may help in avoiding the traps that some problems have. Many insight problems are difficult because people tend to make unnecessary assumptions. In the four-dots 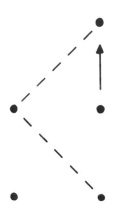 problem, for instance, people tend to suppose at first that a side-by-side pair of dots should be moved. By logic, one can reject this at once, without trial and error. The alternative to reasoning need not be one of those better mousetraps, some exotic mode of thinking. It can be an ordinary act of mind. In the four-dots problem, Costa's little leap was simply a recognition.

I've used the terms realizing and reasoning many times. Something ought to be said about the relationship of the two. In brief, some but not all cases of reasoning are cases of realizing or recognizing, and some but not all cases of realizing or recognizing are cases of reasoning. The example of the poet shows that conscious reasoning can be very like realizing. Certainly the poet's sequence of thought resembled realizing much more than it did puzzling out. Of course, the poet reported too much about her thoughts for this to be considered an extreme case of realizing, a true mental leap. However, there are cases of realizing that one might want to call cases of unconscious reasoning, for example Abbott's solution of the B.C. puzzle. A kind of reasoning process, unconscious or conscious, appears to be the only way to achieve the solution.

Still, not all cases of realizing ought to be called reasoning. If I realize I have forgotten my umbrella, I might do so by a rapid chain of associations not at all like a sequence of logical steps. Moreover, not all cases of reasoning ought to be called realizing. Reasoning can be painfully slow and deliberate, but by definition this isn't so of realizing. In fact, reasoning and realizing are different ways of characterizing a mental process. Reasoning occurs when each thought can be considered an inference from prior thoughts. That is, reasoning has to do with the pattern or structure of thought, regardless of pace. But realizing refers to rather rapid mental activity. Realizing has to do with the pace of thought regardless of its pattern. Thus reasoning can appear in various modes of thinking – sometimes in realizing, sometimes in the slow application of formal rules, and perhaps in other ways, but it's all reasoning and always there is the potential of reasoning your way from the conditions of the problem to a necessary or likely solution.

The better-mousetrap theories propose various extraordinary mental processes that avoid ponderous reasoning. Not only is reasoning not necessarily ponderous, but it's not necessarily ordinary in one sense. Much of the time, we don't think to reason about problems. We ignore chances to discover how the conditions of a problem force a solution. Instead, we work by trial and error and hope that something will fall into place. Sometimes this is fruitful, but sometimes it isn't and we might have used a very powerful kind of thinking to solve the problem.

Revised proposition: Far from being contrary to insight, reasoning is an important means to insight, and often a neglected one. Reasoning is a better mousetrap.

NOTHING SPECIAL

The question has been: What is special about the mental processes that explain sudden insight? The answer seems to be: very little. To review the circumstances, there was no evidence that extended unconscious thinking occurred – the still-waters theory. There was no evidence that the mind accomplished a great amount of work in very brief periods by means of some special process – the blitzkrieg theory. True, the mind did function more quickly sometimes than others, but this could be explained by workaday processes of recognition and realizing. There was no evidence that insight required some special mental process that avoided reasoning – the better-mousetrap theory. On the contrary, reasoning itself was an important means to insight, the better mousetrap that we sometimes need. None of this implies that moments of creation are not special. However, the special thing about them has to do more with what they accomplish than with how they accomplish it.

Now, what about Poincaré? Have we considered any processes that could explain his experience as he described it? Recognition could not. Poincaré did not describe any clue in his surroundings – nothing like Darwin's Malthus or Archimedes' bathwater – nor did he describe anything he might have been thinking about at the time, in which he recognized something significant. The same objection applies to realizing. Both recognizing and realizing start with something and continue from it, and Poincaré reported nothing to start with. Indeed, apparently Poincaré had not even been seeking the discovery he made. It simply occurred to him as he stepped onto the bus. The decision has to be that Poincaré's experience as he told it can't be explained.

My conclusion is that he didn't tell it rightly. I have never heard of a completely out-of-the-blue insight when the person had reviewed the thinking immediately afterward. Furthermore, it is easy to imagine how Poincaré might not have done so. Surprised by his discovery, resuming his conversation on an unrelated matter, he probably didn't review what had happened as he stepped onto the bus. That effort to remember is important. The examples in this chapter show that often insights fall into place rapidly, and only considerable care ensures recalling just what occurred. Indeed, Poincaré's discovery might have been a recognition – about the fastest thing that can happen. Poincaré said he discerned that "the transformations I had used to define the Fuchsian functions were identical with those of non-Euclidean geometry." Clearly identification was involved. Identifications often are accomplished by recognition, and some pattern or feature common to the transformation for the Fuchsian functions and non-Euclidean geometry might well have allowed Poincaré, familiar with both, to recognize one in the other. He would only have had to be thinking briefly of one or the other as he stepped onto the bus.

WAYS OF THE MIND

Proposition: There must be something special about the mental processes that lead to discovery.

The conclusion of the last chapter is hard to take. Extraordinary outcomes like moments of discovery ought to involve extraordinary means. More than a critique of the still-waters, blitzkrieg, and better-mousetrap theories will be needed to challenge this proposition. There is need to show not only that "special" theories of insight lack evidence, but also that a "nonspecial" theory of insight makes sense. I began that job by emphasizing recognition, realizing, and reasoning. Now I want to explore more fully how ordinary acts of mind accomplish invention.

DIRECTED REMEMBERING

If we were to name various everyday mental functions in order of

their inventiveness, surely remembering would fall near the bottom of the list. Remembering has a bad image, suggesting the names and dates that came unstuck during the Modern European History exam or the vocabulary with which we did battle in learning French. Anyone would acknowledge that remembering has a necessary role to play in creating, just as remembering has a necessary role in any human activity. However, it is not immediately obvious that remembering makes a particularly inventive contribution. Does remembering ever "do the inventing"? Curiously enough, it does. This notion makes the best sense if developed through several steps of a personal experiment.

 Remembering as Inventing

1. Remember and list ten or so white things. Try to recall objects like chalk that are characteristically white, not objects like cars or shoes that are only occasionally white.

This is quite easy to do – items come readily to mind. There may be a subjective sense of reaching or groping, but probably no experience of conscious problem solving. Also, rarely do you need to reject a word that suggests itself but doesn't meet the criterion. A condition harder to satisfy would produce more strain and overt problem solving.

2. Remember and list several things that are characteristically white, and soft and edible.

I acknowledged that a condition harder to satisfy would require more overt effort. However, what might appear to be harder does not necessarily turn out that way. Listing things white, soft, and edible seems nearly as easy as listing only white things: again, appropriate items simply come to mind. It's important to notice how much your mental apparatus is doing for you here. Imagine what the task would be like if several conditions couldn't be combined to direct a single act of recall. You would have to recollect objects satisfying a single condition – say white – and screen the results for items satisfying the other two. In fact, a list of white things is available from task 1, but how many of those white things are also soft and edible? Probably none. It would be a formidable job to accumulate a list of white, soft, and edible items by listing white items and screening. Fortunately, our memories are organized to allow recall according to multiple constraints.

Tasks 1 and 2 depended on conditions about the things remembered. White, soft, and edible are properties of spaghetti, for instance, and certainly not properties of the word "spaghetti." In contrast, "starts with the letter s" is a property not of spaghetti but of the word that names it. A remarkable testimony to the flexibility of recall is that we can combine conditions that refer to the thing and to its name.

3. Remember and list vegetables whose names start with the letter c.

Even this is not so difficult. Again, items suggest themselves without much overt problem solving. Yet notice the mixed mode: it is corn that is a vegetable, to mention one item that would fit on the list, but the word "corn" that starts with the c. The two conditions don't refer to the same entity but to two closely related entities – the thing and its name.

Certainly all this identifies some interesting capacities, but what do they have to do with creating? Simply that in creating one often has to think of things satisfying several conditions, and, furthermore, the conditions frequently lie on both sides of that boundary between thing and name. The poet may want a word with a certain meaning – a matter of what it refers to – and a certain rhyme or alliteration – a matter of how the word is said. True, poets devise and screen alternatives, but not as much as you might think. I'll discuss later how a poet in one or two tries usually finds a word acceptable at least for the moment. This is remembering, but not merely remembering. It is remembering that invents parts of the poem.

4. List some familiar cities; then list some unusual cities.

Again, the performances can be managed readily. Multiple constraints are involved: in the first, cities plus familiarity;

in the second, cities plus unusualness. As with the previous task, there is a peculiar crossbreeding of properties. Familiarity is not a property of the physical city, not even a property of the physical name of the city. Rather, familiarity has to do with how often we encounter that name, another example of the mind's indifference to exactly what thing properties are properties of, and another symptom of the flexibility of recall.

Where creating is concerned, another especially interesting feature of this example merits attention. Very often, creating involves the seeking of something unusual. For example, depending on the style, a poet may want to include less familiar rather than more familiar near-synonyms in a poem for the sake of their added freshness. Therefore, it's especially handy that such abstract properties as familiarity and unfamiliarity can direct remembering. This easily might not be the case. Familiarity and unfamiliarity might well influence strongly the ease with which we remember something. Unfamiliar cities might be much much harder to remember than familiar ones. No doubt they are a little harder, but this informal experiment suggests a less than drastic difference. It's profoundly important that you can ask your mind for something – even when unusualness is a desired property – and, at least some of the time, expect to get it.

I don't mean to say that any of the inventing done by memory in the above personal experiments is inventing of a high order. However, these are merely examples without the supportive context of an ongoing work to lend direction and substance to recollections. As is most obvious in the case of the poet, the recollection of a single right word can be a significant creative act. This can be just as much so in other contexts too – for instance, as the philosopher or psychologist puzzles over a phenomenon. Recollecting just the right word to characterize the phenomenon may disclose its nature much better than a less apt term, leading on to a rich development of consequences. Even so simple and everyday an act as remembering a word should not be scoffed at where the work of creating is concerned.

In the examples of directed remembering above, the constraints guiding recollection always were explicit. However, that is unnecessary. To a great extent, tacit constraints govern what word a poet reaches for or what technique a physicist invokes in approaching a problem. In fact, some data I will discuss later suggest that most often there is at least one conscious "focal" constraint, supported by a penumbra of tacit constraints reflecting the maker's sense of the context. The way people direct their remembering – and thinking in general – involves a curious mix of the explicit and the tacit.

NOTICING

Another way of the mind I want to discuss has a convenient everyday name: noticing. Consider what we mean when we speak of noticing something. Suppose I go out to my garage and happen to observe that my left front tire is flat. I might say that I noticed the tire was flat. Now suppose I went out intending to inspect the tires. I wouldn't remark, "I checked each tire to see whether it was flat and noticed that one was." That usage sounds odd. We say "notice" only when we're not looking directly *for* or *at* whatever we find.

Noticing is a kind of pattern recognition, but one that differs from recognition as we often think of it and recognition as it is often studied in the psychological laboratory. We usually consider recognizing to be a matter of looking at something in order to recognize it, and succeeding. Likewise, psychological experiments on recognition characteristically direct subjects to scrutinize a stimulus and try to recognize it as a certain sort of thing. I celebrate the familiar word "notice" here to emphasize that often recognition occurs with much less attention and intention. When this happens, recognition is that much more of an accomplishment. Something has been recognized that might well have been overlooked.

How does all this concern creating? Creative activity often involves unfocused attention, where makers do not check for what they seek point by point. The same can be said of much uncreative activity too, of course. After examining the phenomenon of noticing more carefully through some personal experiments, I'll comment further on the fole of noticing in creating.

 Noticing and Visual Search

1. The assignment here is simply to *notice* each time the word "probably" or variants of it like "probable" occur over the next few paragraphs. This shouldn't be done by keeping the task constantly in mind. Rather, the objective is to set yourself to notice "probablies" when they occur and then to continue reading, without concentrating on the task.

2. With task 1 continuing in the background, here is another. You need a watch to time yourself in seconds, a pencil, and paper. The aim is simply to scan the array of letters below fairly quickly, counting the number of *x*'s. Check the time and proceed.

```
q  w  x  r  t  y  x  x  x  p  x  s  d  f  g  h  j  k  l  z  a  c
v  b  n  m  e  x  s  z  x  q  c  d  x  v  f  r  b  g  t  n  h  y
m  j  x  k  x  l  x  p  p  x  x  x  y  t  r  x  w  q  l  k  j  h
g  f  d  s  x  m  n  b  v  c  i  z  v  b  c  n  o  m  z  g  h  f
j  d  k  s  l  x  u  x  t  x  r  x  x  p  w  q  l  k  j  h  g  f
d  s  x  p  x  x  x  u  t  r  x  w  q  m  n  b  v  c  u  z  k  l
```

Now write down the number of seconds and the number of *x*'s found. You probably experienced the array in a curious way: the *x*'s seemed to stand out from the background of other letters, which weren't individually and distinctively seen. Although to do the task you have to look for the *x*'s, you don't have to examine each letter individually to decide whether it's an x. Instead, you notice the *x*'s wherever they occur. (By the way, there was a "probably" earlier in the paragraph.)

3. Suppose there were multiple target letters instead of a single one. Would the search take that many times longer? Below appears another array, and now the task is to search for any of the letters r, x, v, s, w, and to count how many times they occur in total. This should be done not by scanning the array once for each letter but by scanning the array a single time, keeping in mind all five letters. Note the time and proceed.

```
q  w  e  r  t  y  u  i  o  p  a  s  d  f  g  h  j  k  l  z  x  c
v  b  n  m  x  s  w  z  a  q  c  d  e  v  f  r  b  g  t  n  h  y
m  j  u  k  i  l  o  p  p  o  i  u  y  t  r  e  w  q  l  k  j  h
g  f  d  s  a  m  n  v  b  c  x  z  v  b  c  n  x  m  z  g  h  f
j  d  k  s  l  a  y  u  t  i  r  o  e  p  w  q  l  k  j  h  g  f
d  s  a  p  o  i  u  y  t  r  e  w  q  m  n  b  v  c  x  z  k  l
```

The experience here somewhat resembles that with task 2 and the x's. Again, the target letters probably stood out from the background of the other letters, which were hardly seen as such. People do usually find that this task takes considerably longer than the prior one – considerably longer, but not five times as long. Somehow, one can monitor the array for any one of the five target letters without checking for each of them as a completely separate step. Such efficiency needn't have occurred, but the mind and eye are so constructed that it does.

4. The target set, r, x, v, s, w, was an arbitrary one. What would happen with a more familiar set? Return to the array above, but this time let the target letters be a, e, i, o, and u – the vowels discounting y. As before, count the number of target letters. Note the time and proceed.

People usually find that task 4 requires more time than task 2 with x's, but substantially less time than task 3 with r, x, v, s, w. Occasionally, people do the vowels just as fast as the x's. Why? Not because the vowels resemble one another visually any more than do r, x, v, s, w. So far as shape is concerned, they seem just as arbitrary. Apparently, the efficiency derives just from the familiarity of the set.

Tasks 2-4 demonstrate a well-known perceptual phenomenon called visual search. One of the important laboratory findings is that, with experience, people can learn to scan for a large number of targets about as efficiently as they can scan for a single one. In fact, just by being a familiar set, the vowels seem to be on their way to that kind of efficiency. The gain in efficiency may be due in part to "parallel processing": the mind learns to check for all the targets separately but simultaneously. Research has shown, though, that matters are probably more complicated than this. To some extent, the mind extracts features common to the target set as a way to detect target letters; then the viewer does not check for each letter in parallel so much as check for those features that distinguish the target letters collectively from other letters. Moreover, the viewer may learn things about the texture of the nontarget letters and in effect scan for breaks in that texture. It may not always be possible to scan *quite* as efficiently for a large number of targets as for one, even with considerable practice. Nonetheless, the essential effect remains: with familiarity of the target set, and much more so with practice, scanning for multiple targets becomes highly efficient. Incidentally, in tasks 2-4, the correct number of targets was always 25. Finding that exact number, however, is less to the point than appreciating how one can detect most of the targets very efficiently by noticing.

These tasks and task 1 (which still continues) demonstrate in a formal way a mental ability that functions constantly in creating. For instance, when poets and artists examine their works critically, my think-aloud studies suggest that they typically notice difficulties rather than examine their work piecemeal for particular sorts of difficulties. In doing so, they are scanning for multiple targets at once, as in tasks 3 and 4, and probably without even reminding themselves of the targets at the outset. Many difficulties can occur in a poem, say problems of obscurity, metric strain or tedium, clichés, inconsistency. The skill of the poet in part consists in being able to read the poem and notice whatever is wrong. Another feature of making art is the "dialogue with the work." Many writers have observed that an artist does not simply execute a preconceived plan. The work in progress suggests ways to proceed. One could say that the maker notices *opportunities* in the work so far.

Noticing in such cases is supported by the context: the maker notices things relevant to the activity underway. However, the most remarkable cases of noticing occur out of context. Working on problems, we become sensitized to them and often notice clues to their solutions in seemingly irrelevant circumstances. This is one of the ways incubation works. Something like this apparently happened to Archimedes in the bathtub, to Darwin reading Malthus, and to many other figures in the history of science. In discussing Archimedes, for instance, I used the term "notice" but didn't particularly emphasize it because my point there was somewhat different. I was arguing that insights did not occur complete but in consequence of brief sequences of thought. Here I want to emphasize the remarkable character of those out-of-place recognitions that sometimes initiate such sequences of thought.

In fact, we miss the full importance of noticing and recognition in general if we only consider recognizing things in the world. Our thoughts, too, are events of a sort and we can notice in them patterns and concepts leading to insights about other contexts. Recall the case of Alfred Wallace, for example. Where Darwin discovered the principle of natural selection while reading Malthus, Wallace merely happened to be thinking of Malthus' views. The lack of an overt physical stimulus didn't prevent Wallace's thoughts about Malthus from stimulating him to make a connection with the seemingly remote problem of evolution.

Besides yielding insights, of course, noticing contributes in mundane ways to everyday perception and cognition. Probably not a minute goes by but what we do some noticing. We notice an old friend on the street or an arresting headline in the newspaper. We browse in a bookstore not looking for any particular thing but noticing what interests us, or notice and correct spelling errors in something we're writing. Without noticing, many prosaic activities would be drastically less efficient. We would have to look explicitly *for* what we wanted and *at* those places where it could be found, a tedious business indeed.

A final note on noticing those "probablies." Task 1 is not very easy. When I've spoken to groups about some these ideas, I've asked people to raise their hands on hearing each "probably." Usually, only two or three people detect the first target word. Gradually the number increases. However, even after fifteen or twenty minutes and a number of targets have passed by, many people still miss each one. The words fit so inconspicuously into the ongoing speech that it's difficult to form an instant habit of noticing them without attending explicitly to the task.

CONTRARY RECOGNITION

Polonius: My Lord, the queen would speak with you, and presently.

Hamlet: Do you see yonder cloud that's almost in shape of a camel?

Polonius: By the mass, and 'tis like a camel, indeed.

Hamlet: Methinks it is like a weasel.

Polonius: It is backed like a weasel.

Hamlet   Or like a whale?

Polonius: Very like a whale.

(*Hamlet*, III.ii)

Hamlet is teasing Polonius with an experience we've all had: recognizing creatures in clouds. I call this sort of experience *contrary recognition*. Things usually are recognized for what they are but, in contrary recognition, things are recognized for what they are not, and indeed obviously are not. The cloud obviously isn't a camel, but we find the camel in it. Although normally we perceive things as they are, that ability in fact has a remarkable amount of stretch to it. Deliberately or accidentally, it can function in a less strict way to reveal patterns in the world that otherwise would be missed.

Wittgenstein and others have referred to seeing camels in clouds and similar experiences with the phrase "seeing as": the cloud is "seen as" a camel. "Seeing as" is closely related to but not quite the same as contrary recognition. By the latter, I mean the process of coming to "see as," that act of mind and eye by which we discover counterfactual appearances. Contrary recognition is one way of devising metaphors and analogies. A poet in my think-aloud studies reported a blatant example of this. He'd been strolling down a street earlier that day, had observed some irises, and had noticed that the pistils resembled tongues. Later, he used that comparison in a poem he wrote during the experiment.

Observe the use of the word "notice" in this example. Noticing and contrary recognition overlap. Some cases of contrary recognition are cases of noticing as well – the person notices the contrary identity. However, not all cases of contrary recognition are cases of noticing, since a person may deliberately try to apprehend a contrary identity. Likewise, not all cases of noticing are cases of contrary recognition, since often noticing involves recognizing something as what it literally is. Noticing and contrary recognition are two ways that recognition can diverge from directly inspecting an object to identify it for what it is. Recognition can differ from that case in one of these ways, the other, or both at once.

Contrary recognition has potential significance beyond the literary arts, wherever metaphor and analogy are important. For instance, sometimes people speak of visual metaphor. A fine example of this is a caricature by David Levine portraying Samuel Beckett as a buzzard. Beckett's large nose and glaring eyes become the buzzard's hooked beak and predatory gaze. Levine might will have discovered his caricature by regarding a picture of Beckett and recognizing it in a contrary way. In any case, his caricature teaches us to do just that. Once you have seen Levine's Beckett-as-buzzard, you tend to recognize the buzzard in Beckett whenever you encounter his photograph.

The cases I've considered so far all have involved actual physical stimuli. In the normal course of thought and action, we encounter not only things in the world but things in our minds as well – images, ideas, sounds. These, too, can be objects of contrary recognition, just as they can be objects of noticing. One case in point is the well-known experience of the chemist Friedrich August von Kekulé. It's been remarked many times that scientific and technological discovery often involves metaphorical thinking. In 1865 Kekulé had been attempting with little success to discover the chemical structure of benzene. The molecule consists of a ring of atoms, but at that time ring structures were unknown. Saturated with the problem, Kekulé had a dream in which the molecules appeared as strings of atoms. They twined and twisted in a way that reminded Kekulé of snakes. Suddenly one of the snakes curled around and seized its own tail, and this suggested to Kekulé the ring structure of benzene.

Under the name *synectics,* William Gordon and others in the 1940s began to develop a group-discussion procedure to solve product design and other business-oriented problems. Analogies of various sorts were the principal strategies for devising ideas. One problem involved the design of a compact jack. Contained in a box no more than four inches on a side, the jack should crank out three feet and support a weight of up to four tons. Imagining what this would be like, one member of the group compared the jack to the Indian rope trick, where the soft rope, charmed, became rigid. Pursuing the idea of how to make something soft rigid, the group eventually devised a solution. Two chains, each flexible in only one direction like bicycle chains, met as they unrolled from the box to form a single rigid column.

To my mind, such examples sound not only like metaphor but metaphor achieved by contrary recognition, although I am less sure of this than I would be if detailed think-aloud accounts were available. In any case, the ease with which the mind performs contrary recognition can be explored directly.

 Perverse Perceiving

1. The meaningless scrawl below is just that, a meaningless scrawl. Nevertheless, look at it and try to recognize it as something. List several things it might be.

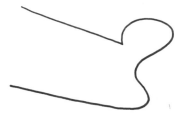

2. Like a Rorschach inkblot or a summer cloud, such a scrawl invites "reading in." It presents no strong meaningful structure of its own to compete with whatever you might imagine. However, does a rival structure pose that much of a problem? Select an object in the room – a chair, a pillow, a shoe. Look at it, refuse to accept its conventional identity, and insist on recognizing it as something else. List several things it might be.

3. You can do that fairly easily. But could this be because the object is physically present? After all, we are discussing recognition and recognition as usually thought of means recognizing real things. Nonetheless, neither Kekulé nor the synectics group dealt with things literally present. Therefore, imagine something – an open black umbrella – make it vivid in your mind, and then recognize that image as something else, not an umbrella. Recognize it as several other things.

That we can do this is rather remarkable. One might think that a mental image would depend entirely on the concept that generated it. Yes, a real umbrella might be recognized in many counterfactual ways, but the imagined umbrella is imagined *as* an umbrella and, lacking any independent physical existence, that's what it might have to be. Informal experiment shows that, although reasonable, this simply is false. It is as if the mental image had an independent existence, so that one could rerecognize it in the mind's eye as something else.

4. The contrary recognitions so far have probably cut across everyday object categories. The umbrella might have

been recognized as a bat or a parachute, but probably not as another kind of umbrella. Would contrary recognition function within rather than across such categories? Attempt a somewhat more difficult task. Look at a familiar face – someone you know or a public figure in a newspaper or magazine – and try to recognize that person as someone else. Often people find slight resemblances they never noticed before. Such contrary recognitions depend on the subtleties that distinguish one individual from another rather than the grosser differences between object categories.

5. In task 4, you choose not only the thing to be looked at but the kind of contrary result, trying to recognize the face as another face rather than as just anything. The kind of result can be controlled even more finely than that. Try this variant of recognizing people for who they aren't. Walk down a street and examine the passers-by, first attempting to recognize them as public figures. Jimmy Carters or Bob Hopes may appear. Now attempt instead to recognize the pedestrians as personal acquaintances. Likenesses of friends and neighbors may appear.

Besides demonstrating the flexibilities of contrary recognition, these tasks also remind us that contrary recognition functions in mundane circumstances. In many respects, the tasks ask you to attempt what often occurs spontaneously. We not infrequently recognize likenesses of things in clouds or wood grain or likenesses of celebrities in a crowd. We recognize likenesses of one object to another – the fronts of Edsels look like faces or, as any child knows, pens look like rockets. The English language acknowledges a number of contrary recognitions in words and phrases such as eye of a needle or of a potato or of a hurricane. In everyday discourse, we forget about these metaphorical meanings, but originally they must have been fresh and vivid. Reminded of them now, we *see* what they mean.

There are two additions I want to make to this general picture of contrary recognition. The first broadens the range of its contribu-

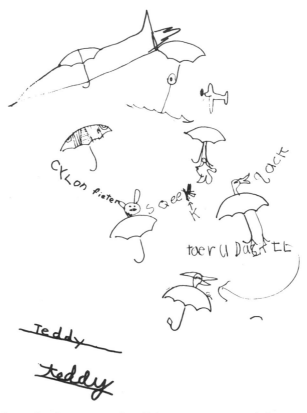

tion. Although the examples I have mentioned have all concerned visual perception – either with the physical eye or the
mind's eye – recognition as a mental operation encompasses
much more than the visual. Most simply, there are the other
senses. For example, popping corn can sound like a typewriter, a
steam engine like a sneeze. Moreover, metaphor often involves
matters not straightforwardly connected with one of the senses. In
Shakespeare's line, "summer's lease hath all too short a date,"
sensory likenesses figure meagerly. Yet the abstract relationships
that make up a situation of leasing can be recognized literally, and
therefore it's reasonable to suppose they can be recognized in a
contrary way too. Perhaps Shakespeare arrived at his trope in
that very manner, by recognizing the "leaselike" quality of summer, and of course perhaps he did not. We cannot know how

Shakespeare conceived the metaphor, but we can expect that contrary recognition functions with abstractions in much the same way that it functions in sensory domains.

My second addition concerns the role of metaphor in discovery generally, whether it is metaphor arrived at by contrary recognition or other means. There can be little question about the importance of metaphor to the literary arts. It's equally clear that metaphor occasionally figures in scientific discovery and in insights of other sorts. Kekulé's discovery of the benzene ring through his dream of snakes or the familiar metaphor of the atom as a miniature solar system might be recalled here. Arthur Koestler, in *The Act of Creation,* gives a number of examples. Some have argued that metaphor is the mainstay of original thinking. Donald Schon elaborated such a perspective in an engaging, thoughtful, and somewhat neglected book called *Displacement of Concepts.* William Gordon in *Synectics: The Development of Creative Capacity* urged that deliberate metaphorical thinking helps more than anything else in solving stubborn problems.

These testimonials don't quite settle the matter. Over the past few years, I've examined a number of sources where people have reported in detail their thoughts leading up to an insight. One aim was to determine what role *novel, remote* analogy played in reaching the insight. By "novel" I mean that the person devised the analogy at the time. By "remote" I mean that the analogy connected different domains, as with Kekulé and his snakes-as-molecules, rather than connecting similar domains, as with the analogy between a laboratory experiment and the natural circumstances it aims to capture. Excluded were insights from literary contexts, where the analogy might itself be the product. Examined instead were cases where analogy might serve as the means to achieve a nonanalogical resolution. The cases reviewed included the insight experiment mentioned earlier, accounts of personal insights gathered in the manner of one of the previous personal experiments, episodes from the history of science, and episodes from psychotherapy. The surprising result was that novel, remote analogy seldom – not never, but definitely seldom – contributed to these insights.

How can we make sense of such a counterintuitive result? First of all, perhaps the result applies only to small-scale insights, whereas the grand discoveries of science and art do depend on novel, remote analogies. Reasonable though this sounds, the fact is that some of the data concerned such grand discoveries. Second, if novel, remote analogies don't do the work of invention, what does? How can we understand the act of discovery? In fact, other mechanisms discussed earlier accounted for most of the cases reviewed – reasoning, noticing, realizing, and so on. Third, how can it be that novel, remote analogies, fresh and far-ranging as they are, would not be rich contributers to invention? I think a likely answer to this is that *powerful* novel, remote analogies are not only hard to find but are rarely there to be found. The lucky combination of superficial difference and profound but subtle commonality doesn't happen often.

But if novel, remote analogy doesn't do that much for discovery, why have so many thinkers thought it has? One reason, surely, is that many clear-cut cases of novel, remote analogy leading to discovery do exist. These distinctive and arresting cases attract attention and, unless systematic studies are done, the impression easily arises that such cases occur much more often than perhaps they do. Another reason is the very plausibility of the hypothesis. Here there seems to be a bit of "magical thinking" – the expectation that causes resemble effects. Because the result of invention transcends old frames of reference, it's tempting to think that the means of invention has to be intrinsically some sort of boundary breaker. Novel, remote analogies fit this prescription perfectly. However, the prescription itself is unwarranted. As we saw earlier, reasoning, remembering, and so on, although not always and intrinsically boundary-breaking operations, often break boundaries.

This is by no means an argument that analogy has little to do with invention. The proposal that novel, remote analogy seldom leads to invention is a rather restricted one. First of all, seldom is not never. Moreover, many fruitful analogies connect things or domains not so remote from one another, and many disciplines milk the same – and therefore not novel – remote analogy over and over again for insights. Analogies – novel and remote or not –

can figure in thinking in other important ways beside triggering discovery. For instance, in my own thinking, I have the impression that analogies often serve as a means of formulating for further exploration ideas that occur in a vague and evanescent way. For another instance, Vernon Howard has emphasized that analogical speech can be a powerful director of action in mastering complex intellectual and physical skills.

THE TROUBLE WITH BISOCIATION

I've argued that sudden insight can be explained in terms of recognizing, realizing, and reasoning, to a considerable extent. I've examined some more particular mechanisms of mind which contribute to insight and to creating generally – directed remembering, noticing, and contrary recognition. All these mental resources function routinely in everyday matters, but also on some occasions do the work of invention. Such resources are parts of a case against the need to posit special mental faculties to account for creating.

The still-waters theory, the blitzkrieg theory, and the better-mouse trap theory were all approaches to such a special account, approaches I criticized on various grounds. However, I dealt with them in their naive forms. Better-mousetrap theories especially have been developed at some length by various authors. A closer look at one of them is in order.

Koestler explains his bisociation theory of creating in his rich and detailed *The Act of Creation*. I can hardly do justice in a few paragraphs to that book's scope and to the many individual examples discussed with great insight. However, Koestler's general theory is my concern here. Koestler maintains that normal thought proceeds within what might be called a frame of reference or, alternatively, an associative context, a type of logic, a universe of discourse, or a particular code or matrix. Koestler mentions all these terms as roughly equally appropriate. He claims that in normal personal and professional life we function with many frames of reference, but usually only within one at a time. Creating involves a relating of normally independent matrices. Koestler's name for this is *bisociation*.

It's easy to see how bisociation describes some of the insights discussed earlier. For instance, clearly the synectics group comparing their problem of jack design to the Indian rope trick was relating matrices normally far apart. Archimedes connecting his bath to the problem of the king's crown and the poet comparing her babies with air raid sirens were doing no less. In other examples, the alternative frames of reference were not so far apart and the juxtaposition of unlikes seems less dramatic, but, with a little thought, one can make a case for bisociation. For example, the joke about sons converting to Christianity extends a possible problem of fathers beyond its usual human scope to include the concerns of the heavenly father. Even for the lowly four-dots problem, one could say that the difficulty comes from a too narrow frame of reference, the problem solver presuming that adjacent dots should be moved. Only by either reasoning out the logical requirements or by moving the dots around and discovering a partial square accidentally does the problem solver transcend this frame, and these activities could be said to involve frames of their own. If such pleading for bisociation seems a little weak in this case, as it does to me, the problem does not require that much invention anyway.

In a table at the end of his book, Koestler clarifies his concept of bisociation further by contrasting bisociative with merely associative thought. Koestler proposes the following oppositions:

Habit	*Originality*
Association with the confines of a given matrix	Bisociation of independent matrices
Guidance by pre-conscious or extra-conscious processes	Guidance by sub-conscious normally under restraint
Dynamic equilibrium	Activation of regenerative potentials
Rigid to flexible variations on a theme	Super-flexibility
Repetitiveness	Novelty
Conservative	Destructive-Constructive

All of this sounds plausible. What reservations could there be about such an account? One way to consider that question is to ask just what Koestler's concept of bisociation clarifies about the "act of creation." For instance, we might take Koestler to have named and characterized a distinctive psychological process called bisociation, similar across all acts of creation but distinct from other psychological processes. However, Koestler neither claims nor accomplishes exactly this. He does not specify the inner workings of a distinctive mental process. Bisociation seems instead to be defined largely in terms of its products. Bisociation is simply that process, whatever it might be and however it might vary, which yields a bisociative outcome. Indeed, most rows of Koestler's table suggest this interpretation. Bisociation of independent matrices, activation of regenerative potentials, super-flexibility, novelty, and destructive-constructive seem different ways of saying that the maker has accomplished something creative or bisociative. But just *how* the maker has done so remains unclear.

It's fair to ask, "So what?" What's wrong with taking Koestler's characterization of creative outcomes as a way of identifying a distinctive process? There is a ready answer. To do this is to beg the question of whether there *is* a distinctive process yielding such outcomes. In fact, everyday experience teaches that the same sort of outcome can result from very different processes. Consider fire, for instance. Someone might suggest a process of "firemaking" with the outcome fire, but we know of many very different firemaking processes – using a match, rubbing sticks, focusing the sun's rays with a magnifying glass, striking flint, and so on. Indeed, my own view of creative process is something like this firemaking – there are many different ways of getting the spark. Nor is it clear to me that Koestler thinks any differently. Certainly he acknowledges many varied routes to bisociation in the course of *The Act of Creation*.

Since Koestler's bisociation doesn't appear to name a single process, what else might his account do for our understanding of creativity? Perhaps Koestler characterizes in a broad way how bisociative processes operate. One of his principal points concerns the crucial role of unconscious thought in bisociation. For example:

The essence of discovery is that unlikely marriage of cabbages and kings – or previously unrelated frames of reference or universes of discourse – whose union will solve the previously unsoluble problem. The search for the improbable partner involves long and arduous striving – but the ultimate match maker is the unconscious. I have discussed several tricks which qualify it for that role: the greater fluency and freedom of unconscious ideation; its "intellectual libertinage" – as one might call the dream's indifference towards logical niceties and mental prejudices consecrated by tradition; its non-verbal, "visionary" powers.   (p. 201)

However, it seems to me that Koestler's notion of the unconscious as bisociator par excellence is wrong. First, people aren't all that unconscious during the process of creating, as the think aloud methods I've discussed show. Second, I've argued that there is no evidence at all for extended unconscious thinking. Third, clearly the work of the unconscious usually concerns routine, entirely uninventive matters – as when we get up in the morning and proceed through all the rituals with hardly a thought about what we're doing. Fourth, thinking that breaks the rules is easy to do quite consciously and deliberately. We can readily freewheel, talk nonsense, find silly puns, fracture logic, and so on. *Significant* rule breaking is rare, of course, but rare whether conscious or unconscious.

    Dreamtalk

Koestler mentions the unruliness of dreams. The idea seems to be that when, as in dreams, the unconscious is left alone, creative things happen. However, such fantasies can be quite wakeful and deliberate – we can easily make up dreams on purpose, for instance. Perhaps it's not clear what I mean, so I'll make up a dream right now. The following words report a sequence of thoughts and mental images that started because I asked myself that it happen and typed what came. Here I am. My chair disappears. I'm floating in space. The sun is to my lower left. I reach and pick a star, thinking of it as an apple. I eat it. It tingles like Pop Rocks, the carbonated candy. Suddenly I and a large green apple that abruptly appeared are falling side by side. The green apple hits Sir Isaac Newton on the head. I land on the ground and stare up at him, waiting for his eyes to widen with insight.

Certainly that was unruly, superficially interesting, unprofound and easy, as indeed dreams often are. Try it. However, do so without trying too hard. The aim is not to compose dreamtalk with calculation, but simply to direct yourself to loosen the usual constraints of literalism and range free of them.

But, someone might object, such exercises only demonstrate once again the whimsical inventiveness of unconscious processes. When you dreamtalk, you don't deliberately compose a dream. You turn over your activities to the unconscious and then simply report the dreamlike sequence unconsciously invented.

To which I say yes, of course, the unconscious does the work. Unconscious mental processing is involved in everything we do, inventive or not. However, usually more than this is meant. The intimation is that in dreaming or dreamtalk you delegate *unusual* control to unconscious processes and that *in consequence* something somewhat inventive occurs. Neither one of these is so. First of all, in dreamtalk we aren't abandoning deliberateness to an unusual degree at all. Much of our lives we function without directing our behavior with calculation. Second, the consequence usually isn't fantasy, but competent stereotyped behavior.

Rather than by nature creative, or by nature conventional, unconscious processes are by nature cooperative (up to a point). You get what you ask for. In dreamtalk, you implicitly request of yourself something dreamlike and so receive it. If you ask yourself for a plausible sequence of events, you'll get more or less that. For example:

I am walking down the street. I see a dime. I pick it up. I go into a drugstore and buy an Almond Joy candy bar. I haven't had one in years and it tastes as good as ever. I go out again. I walk along. I wonder whether I'll find another dime. I see only a gum wrapper.

Prosaic, certainly. One element of fantasy appears though: in 1981, a candy bar for a dime. Now would be a good time to try this kind of talk too, comparing the results with dreamtalk.

In sum, when we break the rules, unconscious processes do most of the work of breaking them, but when we keep the rules, unconscious processes do most of the work of keeping them. More spontaneous, less deliberate behavior can be dominated by convention as easily as invention, perhaps more easily. Degree of consciousness itself has little to do with whether you follow or flout the rules. Nor, indeed, is following rules necessarily uninventive. Flouting some rules often amounts simply to following others, sometimes rules that direct you to invent. Thus we can ask our waking thoughts to follow the pattern of dreams.

Still, Koestler's contribution doesn't stand or fall on whether he has adequately characterized creative process. Bisociation has some interest just as a description of outcome. To say that the outcomes we call creative are bisociative is to say that whatever creative process does, it somehow must bring about connections between frames of reference. Whether there is one or a hundred ways that can happen, it has to happen, so the story goes.

So is Koestler right in characterizing creative outcomes as bisociative? It's difficult to prove he isn't. Any very creative accomplishment has to innovate in some way and therefore transcends a frame of reference in some sense. The only question would be whether transcending one frame of reference necessarily involved relating it to another. To prove otherwise we would need to find clearly creative episodes where the maker clearly did not do so. This is difficult. On the one hand, vaguely plausible second frames of reference are easy to devise. On the other, Koestler, were he arguing particular cases with someone, might admit a case wasn't bisociative but simply suggest it wasn't very creative either. In other words, the boundaries between what is bisociative and not and what is creative and not are vague enough to make it difficult to demonstrate that the two are definitely misaligned. Such vagueness, of course, is a weakness and not a strength in the theory.

Nonetheless, Koestler has shown in a great number of significant cases that distinctly different frames of reference *were* joined. Regardless of borderline cases, these important observations pose a challenge to our understanding of creative process in general and to my proposals about it in particular. Processes are needed to connect frames of reference. This is a problem especially for me because I've suggested that the processes underlying creation are commonplace. One would think that such processes ought to function only within frames of reference. That is, Koestler's concept raises in an intensified form the problem with which I began the chapter: How can ordinary kinds of mental processes accomplish extraordinary acts of creation?

In fact, the ideas of this and the previous chapter provide a ready answer to that. Directed remembering, noticing, and contrary recognition, for example, are always bisociative in small ways. When we think of white, soft, and edible things, we retrieve items that would be unlikely to come to mind were we just groping for white things, or soft things, or edible things. Our command to memory yields items in the intersection of those three frames of reference. Likewise, noticing by definition always has an unexpected element and so always operates somewhat outside the dominant frame of reference. Likewise, even minor contrary recognitions always cross the boundaries of literal classifications.

Of course, most of the time such bisociations don't achieve much originality. Most of the time directed remembering and noticing and contrary recognition "invent" something either quite within the immediate purposes of the ongoing activity or simply irrelevant to it. However, sometimes the yield is richer: a truly creative synthesis of remote frames of reference to achieve a revealing insight. When this occurs, there's no reason to suggest that fundamentally different processes are at work. The contrast between dramatic and mundane rememberings, noticings, and contrary recognitions is of degree and good fortune, not of kind. The impressive instances shade continuously into routine or irrelevant ones and there is no natural breakpoint.

Besides such considerations, there is another way in which ordinary thinking contains bisociative potential. Thinking within a frame of reference requires sensitivity to the rules of the game, and events may occur that challenge the rules. Just by functioning within a frame, you are in a position to notice or more generally recognize the unexpected. Time and again in the history of science, investigators have accidentally encountered phenomena that should not have occurred, recognized them as anomalies, and gone on to revise or devise frames of reference to accommodate them. Of course, such a recognition does only half the work of bisociation, challenging the established frame of reference but not relating it to another one. Nonetheless, it's important to grasp that the work of bisociation – if bisociation is the ultimate outcome – has in a sense begun already when an anomaly in the prevailing frame of reference is observed.

Besides recognition, other processes also disclose anomalies. Reasoning within a frame of reference may reveal contradictory or otherwise unacceptable conclusions. In scientific inquiry, investigators reason out predictions, test them empirically, and, when the results diverge from expectation, strive to account for this. Rapid, reflexive understanding – I called it "realizing" – also has a talent for turning up anomalies: recall how people realize the oddity in the B.C. problem.

If reasoning and realizing can make a beginning on bisociation by disclosing anomalies, they can make an end of it by completing the process. For instance, in the B.C. problem, the problem solver would not only realize the anomaly in the date but proceed to realize how this resolves the other anomaly of the riddle itself, where for no apparent reason the museum director calls the police. Thus the modern tale of the museum director and coin seller and the ancient episode of dating coins are bisociated into the quirky pattern of the riddle as solved. As to reasoning, recall how the poet found her final metaphor by reasoning her way to a common property of sirens and wailing babies.

I could go on, but that should be enough. The point is simply that fruitfully challenging and crossing frames of reference aren't such difficult or exceptional matters as one might suppose. Events of this sort can occur in many quite straightforward ways. Processes like noticing which do most of their work within major frames of reference constantly cross smaller frames of reference inside them. Processes like reasoning and understanding, whose main business, it might be said, is maintaining coherent and consistent frames of reference can both detect anomalies and coordinate different frames. Extraordinary invention really does borrow the means of mundane thought.

THE ESSENCE OF INVENTION

What is the essence of invention? Somehow that question manages at one and the same time to sound both pompous and naive. Yet it's a serious question, which Koestler's account tries to answer. Bisociation is Koestler's proposal for what is fundamental about moments of creating. Other proposals I've only mentioned in passing include Arieti's "paleologic" and Rothenberg's "Janusian thinking" and "homospatial thinking". The trouble is that such concepts, as I've argued explicitly for bisociation, fail to respect the realities of invention. For example, they may emphasize a special role for unconscious thought, when unconscious thought appears to contribute to invention no more and no less than to mundane activities. They may propose rare, exotic processes 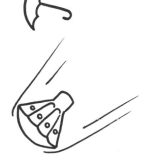 that distinguish the capacities of the creative person from those less gifted, whereas invention appears to rely mostly on the ordinary armament of recognition, noticing, understanding, and so on. They may stress blatantly creative processes, such as contrary recognition, although more conservative processes like reasoning and understanding often do the crucial work.

Another approach to the "essence of invention" would look to the formidable abilities great innovators have brought to their professions, the compositional facility and musical memory of Mozart, say. This is no place for a thoroughgoing appraisal of the relationship between abilities and inventiveness, a topic which will be taken up in Chapter 9. However, there's good reason not to count inventiveness as simply a matter of ability. Both history and everyday experience present us with people of immense competence who nonetheless do not seem to think very inventively. No doubt significant creating requires high ability in the processes that contribute to the sorts of creating involved, but this doesn't seem to be enough.

The accumulating reservations seem to discourage essence hunting. Creativity begins to look like a mulligan stew of this and that with nothing very distinctive about it except being creative. Yet just there is the paradox. If creative thinking is only "this and that," what makes it creative? Has some essence eluded us?

Yes it has, I think, because that essence isn't the kind being sought. The essence of invention isn't process but purpose. Purpose is what organizes the diverse means of the mind to creative ends. First and most simply, on many occasions people try to be inventive *as such*. Scientists seek new phenomena and theories, artists strive to develop fresh styles. It's odd that this has been so overlooked as an important explanation for creative accomplishment. If someone builds a birdhouse, surely a basic part of explaining the birdhouse is that the person didn't just happen to make one, but tried to. Similarly with inventing.

However, purpose operates in a somewhat different way, too. Invention often occurs not because a person tries to be original, but because the person attempts to do something difficult. Necessity, the saying goes, is the mother of invention. I would add: not only necessity, but the sort of commitment that leads some people to put "unreasonable" demands on themselves and their products. Of course, some unreasonable demands require stamina more than invention, and others lead only to frustration or to meticulous conventional resolutions. However, unreasonable demands often force invention, by excluding conventional solutions and requiring the maker to search beyond them.

Of course, because purpose is fundamental, this does not mean that all discoveries are purposeful. Any such conclusion would contradict the lesson of history, which records remarkably many occasions where discoveries were made by chance. But this is not so much of an objection to the importance of purpose as it might seem. As Pasteur said, "Chance favors the prepared mind." Discoveries made in, let us say, medical research, aren't made by bricklayers or businessmen or mathematicians. Nor are they made principally by family doctors or journeyman surgeons. They are the accomplishments of just those individuals who have committed their careers to exploring the complexities of medicine. Only such a focus leads the discoverer to explore the right phenomena with the appropriate frame of mind to make informative accidents both likely and meaningful. Although not "on purpose," such discoveries generally depend upon the discoverer's abiding purposes.

To say as much is to take what might be called a *teleological* view of creating. The term teleology implies that the ends govern the means. What makes creating special is not so much its component processes but their organization and direction, and that organization and direction derives from an end in view, however broadly characterized and vaguely grasped. Intents to create or to satisfy unreasonable demands, or both, pattern and bias those component processes toward creative accomplishment. There will be more creative thoughts and actions in response to such purposes, just as there will be more carpentering thoughts and actions if one is building a birdhouse than if one is assembling a stamp collection. Purpose shapes process.

The opening proposition for this chapter complained that there must be something special about the mental processes that lead to outcomes as special as discovery.

Revised proposition: Discovery depends not on special processes but on special purposes. Creating occurs when ordinary mental processes in an able person are marshaled by creative or appropriately "unreasonable" intentions.

4

CRITICAL MOMENTS

There is a famous anecdote about Albert Einstein that goes as follows. Once asked why he insisted on using handsoap for shaving instead of shaving cream and despite the discomfort, Einstein replied, "Two soaps? That is too complicated!"

The story is more than mere anecdote because, according to an article by Gerald Holton, it and the generally simple lifestyle of Einstein offer a clue to the nature of the man's genius. Einstein had a powerful drive toward simplicity, shown as much in his theoretical physics as in his soap. For example, in a fundamental 1905 paper on relativity theory, not yet known by that name, Einstein opened by mentioning not experimental evidence against classical physics but an asymmetry in the use of Maxwell's electrodynamics, the theory employed to relate electricity and magnetism. One sort of equation was used to calculate what current to expect when a conductor moved with respect to a stationary magnet, but another sort of equation was used when the conductor remained stationary and the magnet moved. Yet the same current resulted in both cases, and clearly in some sense there ought not to be any real difference between the mathematics for a moving conductor and a moving magnet. A pragmatist would say, "So what? The equations work. They tell us what we want to know." But not Einstein. Never mind adequate predictions; the aesthetics of the theory just would not do. In this and other ways throughout his career, Einstein strove for the simple and the symmetric and against the arbitrary in physics. This passionate purpose was an important part of what led him to remake our conception of the physical world.

The example of Einstein provides a good introduction to the theme of this chapter, the role of evaluation in creating. Usually we think of creative powers as a matter of productive powers: the creative person gets ideas that others would not. But of course, without some sense of values directing production and editing tentative products, the maker would make no significant progress at all. Einstein is a case in point. Though his ability to devise new ideas was crucial, equally crucial was his deep dissatisfaction with certain features of the established way and his persistence in striving for theories without those failings. A fortunate match between Einstein's values and the discoveries waiting to be made allowed Einstein to be the one to make them.

It is all the more apt to speak of a fortunate match because in other respects the match was not so fortunate. The same values that led Einstein to relativity left him a lifelong resister to the second major advance of twentieth-century physics, quantum mechanics, even though he had played an important part in its early development. Einstein found the statistical character of quantum mechanics, which allows only probabilistic prediction of many physical events at the atomic level, abhorrent. To quote another anecdote from the Einstein canon, Einstein was fond of saying,

"God does not play dice with the universe." To which Niels Bohr, fellow physicist and affable adversary, once replied, "Stop telling God what to do."

What to tell God to do or, more generally speaking, what the "right" values are for a particular creative effort is of course likely to vary a lot from case to case. So that problem I will carefully neglect. What I do want to examine is evaluative response in the ongoing process of making. Einstein's moments of disgustedly recognizing arbitrariness in a theory are the sorts of moments of concern here. As we looked at the nature and place of moments of invention, so now we want to consider the nature and place of evaluative responses – which of course are themselves insights of a sort, insights into the strengths and weaknesses of a product in the making or one already made.

ANALYSIS AND INTUITION

Proposition: Critical response is an intuitive process.
Proposition: Critical response is an analytical process.

I begin with two such contrary notions because they reflect common conceptions of critical response. The notions could apply to any discipline, but since both occur so often in the arts, I'll discuss them in that context. Our image of the artist supports the idea that critical response is intuitive. We think of the artist as intuitively making the many decisions that lead to a final work, sensing what has the desired effects and not standing back and cold-bloodedly applying criteria for unity, balance, or whatever.

Our image of the critic says that critical response is analytical. We easily can imagine the critic doing just those things the artist supposedly shuns: standing back, being objective, applying criteria. The pessimists among us fear that the critic therefore responds superficially and inflexibly. The optimists among us think that achieving something like objectivity and founding appraisals on standards of some sort are the specific and important missions of the critic.

The easy way to resolve these contrary notions is by compromise. First of all, the notions don't really contradict one another, since different people – artists and critics for example – might adopt different strategies. Second, the two strategies could occur mixed in behavior – the behavior of either an artist or a critic. In fact, this seems much more plausible than the extreme artist and critic types just described.

But I'm not satisfied with a some-of-this, some-of-that concept of critical response. I want to examine a deeper confusion. In brief, the most typical moment of critical response seems to be neither exactly analytical nor exactly intuitive, but something between. Both some logical points and some data from experiments are needed to make that case.

First, the meanings of "intuitive" and "analytical" have to be considered. Analytical seems clear enough. An analytical way of behaving involves deliberate analysis. One scrutinizes the object for various features and rates them against explicit standards, or something of that sort.

The meaning of intuitive is a little more subtle. Essentially, we say a judgment is intuitive when there are no conscious reasons for it. Suppose you are watching a mystery film. You might say, "Right away, I knew intuitively he was the villain. There was just something about him." That sounds like a proper use of the word "intuitive." On the other hand, suppose the remark was, "Right away, I knew intuitively he was the villain. He was wearing a black hat." That sounds wrong. Having a reason for identifying a person as the villain seems contrary to the meaning of intuitive.

But having a reason needn't mean reasoning out. It doesn't imply an analytical process. Imagine the scene again: The character with the black hat enters, and the viewer recognizes him as the villain. To do this, the viewer need not see the character enter, note his black hat, think "Now what do black hats mean?" and conclude "Oh yes, he's the villain." That might happen, but instead the viewer might simply recognize the character as the villain because of his black hat, much as one quite spontaneously might recognize a mailman or fireman or policeman by his hat, knowing it's the hat that tells you but not going through any conscious reasoning process. Lacking reasoning out but having a conscious reason, judgments of this sort are neither analytical nor intuitive. It is just there, I suggest, that much of critical response occurs.

Some evidence for this conclusion comes from my think-aloud

process tracing studies of poets and artists. The relevant analysis involved four different groups: twenty professional and amateur poets and several professional painters developing works of their own, eight amateur poets attempting to edit a poem given them, and eight students, some design majors, attempting to design trademarks for specified purposes. In all cases, the participants thought aloud as they proceeded with their tasks.

One question was whether people had particular evaluative categories in mind as they inspected their developing products. Would a poet examine an evolving poem for clichés, or a painter for problems of balance, for instance? The answer was no. Rarely did any of the participants judge their works with a specific standard already in mind, although they might examine their works with a general evaluative intent. Another question was whether long chains of reasoning appeared on the way to evaluative conclusions. This also rarely occurred. So evaluative response on the whole, in amateur and professional makers alike, involved little explicit analysis.

I also examined the judgments the participants made to determine whether reasons accompanied them. Did the participants come to evaluative conclusions without saying why? Here three different kinds of reasons were sought: "where" reasons – the evaluation attributed an asset or difficulty to a particular part of the work rather than to the work broadly; "what" reasons – the evaluation explicitly concerned some aspect of the relevant part of the work, such as meter, rhyme, meaning in poetry, rather than referring to the part in general; and "why" reasons – the evaluation explained the difficulty or advantage by explicit or implicit reference to a critical principle such as unity, variety, originality. Any of these where, what, or why remarks actually could serve as reasons in critical argument. For example, a drama critic faulting a play might say, "The ending is poor," a case of where, or "The plot is poor," a case of what, or "The work is full of clichés," a case of why. These examples sound somewhat artificial because each includes only one kind of reason; a more typical remark might include two or three. For instance, where, what, and why all occur in "The revelation in the last scene is all too guessable." For another example consider, "The final soliloquy was incomprehensible." Notice how the word "incomprehensible" makes a negative judgment and also indicates an aspect (meaning) and a principle (clarity). Very often critical remarks combine in a single term the pro or con judgment and reasons for it.

The scoring of the reports showed that nearly always evaluations involved considerable localization – the where component. Furthermore, from about 50 percent to 80 percent of the time, depending on the group, an evaluation referred either to an aspect (what) or principle (why). Aspects occurred from about 30 percent to 80 percent of the time, principles from about 40 percent to 60 percent. Furthermore, thinking aloud does not give the person time to say all that occurs consciously, since the procedure requires above all that the person continue with the task more or less normally. So these figures are underestimates of the fraction of time reasons accompanied judgments.

All the results support the suggestion that critical response involves judgments neither intuitive nor analytical in character. Rather than reasons not accompanying judgments at all, or judgments resulting from applications of explicit standards or other sorts of extended reasoning, or reasons for judgment deriving from an extended effort to reason out the causes of one's likings and dislikings, rather than any of these, for the most part reasons come spontaneously right along with one's pro and con reactions. Much as the movie viewer might experience a single recognition which amounts to "villain because black-hatted," so an artist would experience a single recognition like "Bad image because too balanced." I mentioned above that in fact many critical terms both report a judgment pro or con and give a reason for it. Such terms aren't merely conveniently compact; they mirror the fused nature of our evaluative reactions.

 Reasonable Reading

All the above concerns the critical response of the maker to a developing work. But I think much the same holds for the audience member responding to a work. In fact, a good way to get a sense of this is to try it for yourself. Below appears a playful poem by John Lyly, "Cards and Kisses." The work comes from an Elizabethan tradition of rhymed couplets to one's love. Try reading the poem as you normally would. Enjoy it or not. But note in passing how whatever pleases or displeases becomes conscious. Reread the poem several times. Each time, describe afterwards a couple of moments of delight or dismay. Consider whether at the time you knew just where the words were that affected you, what about them affected you, and why they affected you.

> Cupid and my Campaspe played
> At cards for kisses – Cupid paid:
> He stakes his quiver, bow, and arrows,
> His mother's doves, and team of sparrows;
> Loses them too; then down he throws
> The coral of his lips, the rose
> Growing on's cheek (but none knows how);
> With these, the crystal of his brow,
> And then the dimple of his chin:
> All this did my Campaspe win.
> At last he set her both his eyes –
> She won, and Cupid blind did rise.
>   O Love! hath she done this to thee?
>   What shall, alas! become of me?

If you let yourself read as you normally do, you probably did not read analytically. Even so, the experience was probably very specific and detailed. One might say the results proved analytical without the conscious process being so. Important effects and the reasons for them were noticed without being sought out deliberately. All this shows why critical response shouldn't be considered dominantly intuitive. "Intuitive" is misleading. It suggests a vague consciousness filled only with pro and con reactions, when in fact consciousness typically contains something much more specific.

Revised proposition: Critical response is predominantly nonanalytical but also nonintuitive – free of overt reasoning and intentional analysis but full of reasons.

Those reasons have an important function. The where, what, and why of a particular response are valuable information for the maker. They are guides to resolving difficulties. When – as certainly happens – the maker doesn't sense the where, what, or why of a negative response, the maker can't modify the work too readily. The maker can only take fairly simple actions like keeping or discarding, or attempt to discern those reasons that this time didn't occur spontaneously. In addition, such reasons provide for understanding of works and meaningful critical discourse. When we talk about works of art, spontaneous reasons make up a large part of what we say.

Beyond these particular concerns, there is a small object lesson here in the use of such words as "analytical" and "intuitive." These terms are easy to apply casually. We say that this or that is intuitive or analytical without care for two matters: What do the words mean, and what is the experience we want to describe really like? Being fussy about the first is an important way of understanding better the second. In the end, you can discard such terms as "intuitive" and "analytical" altogether if you want to. The crucial thing is to understand the nature of the experience they so often inadequately describe.

LOOKING HARDER

How worthwhile is an idea? People aren't always happy with spontaneous answers to such questions. On the contrary, they devise systems to help them make more careful evaluations. These systems usually amount to standards to apply or questions to ask. Here's one example, a list to be used in evaluating business ideas.

Is the idea simple? Does it seem obvious? Is it too clever, too ingenious? Too complicated?

Is it compatible with human nature? Could your brother

or the man next door, your cousin, or the service-station attendant all accept it?

Is it direct and unsophisticated?

Can you write out a simple, clear, and concise statement of it? Can you do this in two or three short sentences so that it makes sense?

Can it be understood and worked on by people of the average intelligence level found in the field.

Does your idea "explode" in people's minds? Does someone else react to it with "why didn't I think of that?" Can people accept it without lengthy explanation? If it does not explode, are you sure you have really simplified it?

Is it timely? Would it have been better six months or a year ago? If so, is there any point in pursuing it now? Will it be better six months from now? If so, can you afford to wait?

Such strategies occur in many contexts. The used-car shopper may review a list of tips before shopping. Diving and gymnastic competitions and other athletic events without simple first-over-the-line standards of victory require judging according to established criteria. Satellite launches depend on the countdown procedure, an exhaustive evaluation of whether "all systems are go." And so on.

Deliberate analytical evaluation, whether guided by a list or not, depends on a strategy that might be called "looking harder." Looking harder involves two important tactics: "looking at" particular parts of the thing to be assessed, and "looking for" particular features or kinds of features. The used-car shopper looks at the tire treads to look for excess wear. This is just the opposite of noticing. The strategy is completely unremarkable. By focusing attention on a particular

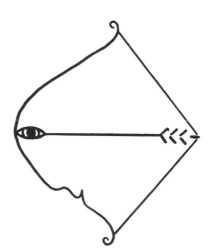

part and on particular sorts of properties, the person maximizes the likelihood of detecting certain advantages or disadvantages. The more focused the probe, the greater its sensitivity. Lists guide the evaluator through a systematic series of probes to ensure a thorough evaluation.

Proposition: In general and in creative activity, people maximize sensitivity and thoroughness in evaluation by "looking harder" – directing attention systematically to the various parts and aspects of something.

  Visit Your Head

The sensitivity resulting from focused attention can be truly impressive. This simple exercise demonstrates how attention can reveal sensations people are rarely aware of. Most of the "visits" conducted in this book have been to the inside of the head – the mind. This visit concerns the outside. Find a comfortable seat and follow each step below before reading ahead to the later ones.

First, attend to the feel of the outside of your head. Name whatever you notice. Spend about thirty seconds. This isn't an evaluative response to anything, of course, but it is "looking at" narrowed to a part. Probably you will find some sensations you haven't been conscious of before.

Second, narrow attention even further. Focus on your nose. Do you feel more sensation there than before? Focus on your ears – not the sound but the tactile and temperature sensations. One area may have stronger sensations than the other.

Third, ignore particular parts. "Look for" instead, by attending to a particular aspect. Let yourself become aware of the feel of the air wherever it occurs on your head. Then let yourself become aware of the pattern of loose and tense muscles. Now of the force of gravity – where it pulls and where it does not. Now of tiny muscular twitches. Where do they occur? You may find some places on the head where a pulse can be felt.

Fourth, combine "looking at" with "looking for." Concentrate on the area around your mouth. Feel the pulse in your gums. Feel the dryness or moistness of your lips. Sense the temperature of your tongue.

Fifth, put aside these literal guides and try to sense your head in a metaphorical way. A metaphor can direct perception just as attending to actual properties can. Imagine that your head is an enormous island with vertical cliffs. Your mouth is a grotto at sea level. The waves entering and receding are your breath. Consider what other sensations fit themselves in as you hold this image in mind.

Exercises like this one show why the best makers would look harder in evaluating. The same directing of attention that reveals so much about bodily sensations can reveal just as much about a creative product. The maker would discover the most about the assets and difficulties of the product by examining the poem or painting or article or mathematical proof part by part and aspect by aspect. Makers who did not do this simply would miss much of significance. The failure to monitor the developing product would lead to inferior results.

The trouble is that this logic bumps up against the facts. The poets and painters I studied with think-aloud techniques did not usually look harder. They simply noticed strengths and weaknesses. Did these makers, good as some of them were, proceed as they should for best results? Is looking harder, despite the gains in sensitivity, not what they ought to do after all? Any why not?

Certainly, competent performers might persist in an inferior strategy. History is full of such occurrences, for one reason because it is easy for people to mislead themselves about the effectiveness of a practice – animal and human sacrifices provide grim examples. Also, looking harder has some unattractive features, at least superficially. Looking harder makes more work out of an aspect of creative process that otherwise would proceed more simply. Because more flaws are found, even more work is made – the unwelcome work of correcting the flaws. This may discourage makers from looking harder routinely.

On the other hand, it's also possible that focused evaluation does not yield the gains it promises. It may be inefficient. True, looking harder results in much more sensitive detection of those features looked at and for. However, a narrow focus necessarily neglects features outside the focus. To evaluate the product thoroughly, you must review the many parts and aspects one by one. In contrast, the maker expecting to notice whatever needs attention stays open to everything at once. In the long term of months and years, the trade of more sensitive evaluation for more time spent may not be worthwhile: the maker could gain more by doing more projects faster and by becoming a better and better noticer.

A very different concern applies as well. Piecemeal evaluation may provide a seriously distorted picture of the whole. The problem is the classic one of making mountains from molehills. Difficulties may appear which in fact have little significance in broader perspective. Certainly this is so in art where, whatever the maker does, the audience wouldn't analyze a work piecemeal. By adopting a more global strategy, the artist simulates the audience; by adopting a focused strategy, the artist would simulate a sort of audience that didn't exist.

I've outlined reasons why a maker might not look harder despite the advantages and why those advantages might be spurious. Which account explains my own finding that artist and poets rely mostly on noticing difficulties rather than seeking them out? I can only offer a judgment here, since real data are lacking. I think there's more truth in the latter than the former account. Gains in efficiency and the distorting effects of piecemeal evaluation both lead the maker to adopt a noticing strategy.

However, there are some crucial qualifications. For one, circumstances make looking harder less important sometimes and more important other times. Typically the poet or painter or writer of a technical article or designer of a small-scale experiment enjoys flexibility: decisions involve minimal commitment because revisions are easily made. Indeed, the poets in my study behaved just this way, settling on phrases quickly for the time being and revising later. But if one is launching a missile or a new national product line, matters are quite different. In general, when a decision involves considerable commitment of resources and minimal opportunity for revision, focused evaluation becomes especially important. You simply must be right. You need a comprehensive and focused evaluation that also deals with the mountains out of molehills. This is a lot of work but, in the circumstances, worth it.

The second qualification concerns another special situation. Sometimes makers discover that they usually overlook particular kinds of difficulties in their works. Then they look harder for those difficulties and correct them.

The third qualification concerns looking harder as a way of learning. Focused evaluation can sensitize a person to considerations that will become simply noticed later. A good example concerns the judging of sports like diving. In fact, specific and elaborate standards govern the quality of a dive, standards described in the *Official Rules for Diving* booklet of the United States Amateur Athletic Union. But a dive only lasts for a few seconds. Clearly, the judges can't sit with books in hand, applying the rules one by one as the diver drops toward the water. They have to assimilate the rules and learn to detect reflexively whatever good and bad features appear.

Revised Proposition: Makers maximize long-term efficiency in evaluation by noticing difficulties rather than looking harder for them in systematic ways. But focus increases sensitivity greatly, so makers use focused evaluation in learning to notice, in making especially crucial decisions, and in monitoring aspects of their work they know present special difficulties.

FEELING AS KNOWING

Let me describe an odd experience I've had several times in writing. I would be vaguely dissatisfied with something I had drafted. I'd acknowledge a few problems to myself, but proceed to edit the piece without any basic revision. But the feeling of unease would intensify. I'd begin to procrastinate. Finally, I would get to the point where I simply could not continue. I would have to rethink the situation, discard considerable work, and proceed with a new plan.

What fascinates me about these episodes is that they don't offer me much choice. I don't feel free – at least not as free as I'd like to feel – to make a cost-benefit decision about whether to correct the problems. Rather, I'm powerfully compelled to correct them because – well, the product has become ugly as it is. As I write the word ugly, I realize it is just the right word. So when these episodes occur, I end up doing better than I might despite myself.

It's standard lore about creative process that feeling and knowing both contribute to the success of an enterprise. Einstein provides a loftier example. He felt, more than knew, that classical physics included intolerably arbitrary and excessively complicated features. He strove for what he felt a theory ought to be. In fact, one can easily list many ways that feelings about a creative effort guide the effort. Progress may disappoint or encourage, the work so far may feel tight or loose or thin or strong, the present problems may excite or bore. This is true as much for the scientist or businessman as the artist to whom we freely grant the emotional life of invention we may foolishly deny to the more supposedly hardheaded professions. But one might look at it this way: creating is too much work to be worth the bother, were it not a passionate enterprise.

People often express the contributions of knowing and feeling to creating and other activities in more technical language, speaking of cognition and affect. Such language contributes extra terms without much extra understanding. "Cognition" means nothing more than acts of knowing or psychological processes involved in attaining and processing knowledge. "Affect" means about the same as emotions or feelings. So whether you speak casually of feeling and knowing or more academically of affect and cognition, much the same results.

Proposition: Feeling and knowing enter distinctively and essentially into creating.

The best part of this notion is the "essentially." That word warns us not to forget the role of feelings in making. We should recognize their importance in explaining creative process and cherish their guidance in our own creative pursuits. The worst part of this notion is that "distinctively." The above way of emphasizing the importance of feelings adopts an unfortunate tactic. It says: "On the one hand there is knowing. But on the other hand there is feeling, and feeling is important too." This obscures just how feeling contributes because it divorces feeling from knowing. In fact, feeling contributes in large part as a *manner* of knowing. So considered, it becomes clear that feeling helps in the usual ways that other sorts of knowledge assist in achieving an end.

I want to examine the idea that emotions are sources of knowledge under three different headings: felt emotions, which both depend on and indicate how a situation is understood; cognitive emotions, which are felt emotions that particularly concern creative inquiry; and expressed emotions, which occur when we say a person or a work of art expresses a feeling.

Felt emotions. Contemporary analyses generally recognize that the emotions we feel imply particular understandings of the situations in which we feel them. Take anger, for example. Being angry at George requires perceiving that George has committed some offense against you or things you hold dear. Such understanding sustains the emotional reaction and, if the facts change, so does the feeling. For instance, our irritation at George's missing an appointment stops when we hear of a death in his family.

This leads to another respect in which emotions are like knowledge: emotions can be right or wrong. Of course, emotional reactions are not right or wrong in the way that statements are true or false. Emotions aren't propositions. But we do think of emotional reactions as appropriate or not. The old saw about elephants being scared of mice depends on this. The notion amuses not because any such fears an elephant might have wouldn't bother the elephant, but because they would bother him so inappropriately. To give a more serious example, in clinical contexts we distinguish between a person's rational, well-founded fears and irrational fears.

All this suggests that felt emotions and the physiological symptoms of them – red face and a surge of adrenalin, say – follow upon understanding a situation. But that account is too simple. There is evidence that sometimes the physiological symptoms come first and understanding second. In one classic experiment, some subjects were injected with a drug they didn't know accelerated the heartbeat, caused sweating, altered breathing, and in general produced the physiological symptoms of strong emotion.

Others were injected with a placebo. Each one waited for the experiment to continue in a room with a confederate of the investigator's, supposedly another participant. For some subjects, the confederate pretended to be angry over the study, muttering about this and that and finally throwing a questionnaire into a wastebasket and leaving. For others, the confederate pretended to be euphoric. In a while, the subjects were questioned about their moods. The drugged subjects reported feeling either angry or happy, depending on the confederate's actions. Cued by the confederate, they had spontaneously given very different interpretations to their physiological symptoms. The placebo subjects, however, reported feeling fairly unemotional. Finally, other subjects, who were warned about the physiological effects of the drug, reported no strong feelings. They had another explanation for their physiological reactions and so did not perceive themselves as feeling an emotion. Such experiments suggest that we identify an emotion by gauging our physiological states in circumstances appropriate to the emotion. So we can be fooled when for some special reason the physiological state has other unrecognized causes.

These general points about emotions have implications for the role of emotions in the creative process. Because feelings involve understandings, feelings toward a developing work of science or art may carry important insights about the work and its potentials. For example, boredom with or excitement about a work may indicate whether a work rehashes old themes or develops new ones. Because feelings may be inappropriate, the maker must learn when to trust them. As the experiment illustrated, the more physical manifestations of an emotion sometimes can come from other sources altogether. The maker may be misled if boredom with a work really derives from unrecognized fatigue.

Earlier I emphasized that a person's pro or con evaluative reactions included reasons. Now I want to add another point. Those pro and con reactions aren't cool assessments, but felt reactions. You object to a garish wallpaper when the garishness bothers you. Furthermore, to be bothered by the garish colors isn't just to be bothered and, on the side, to realize that the garish colors are doing the bothering. Rather, the sensation is distinctive: a being-bothered-by-garishness feeling. Affect and reasons typically occur not divided but fused. The affect would not be the affect it was, without the reasons.

Despite these ways that affect and cognition mingle, an important question remains: What does the affect really add to the cognition? Couldn't the maker get by just as well with the understandings and no emotions? Of course not. The emotions are not merely incidental additions to the understanding. They draw attention to it, a very important function. They also measure the degree of a problem, which amounts to further understanding. The potentially garish look that doesn't bother you much perhaps needs no attention. Furthermore, felt emotions themselves sustain the understanding of a situation. Were an emotion taken away artificially, the perception of the situation would fall into a new pattern; different features would stand out and those consonant with the emotion would recede.

Cognitive emotions. Besides emotions involving knowledge, certain emotions specifically concern the process of cognition – the process of coming to know. Israel Scheffler has developed this idea in an essay entitled "In Praise of the Cognitive Emotions." One point he makes is that certain emotions channel and motivate inquiry. Effective inquiry, for example, requires "rational passions": "A love of truth and a contempt of lying, a concern for accuracy in observation and inference, and a corresponding repugnance of error in logic or fact. It demands revulsion at distortion, disgust at evasion, admiration of theoretical achievement, respect for the considered arguments of others." But Scheffler warns that such commitments shouldn't make inquiry seem a grim grind. While some emotions constrain inquiry, others inspire it: a spirit of adventure, joy in discovery, a sense of intellectual daring.

Besides these roles for emotion, Scheffler identifies two specifically cognitive emotions. By specifically cognitive, he means that these emotions do not just guide, but occur specifically in response to coming to know. One of these Scheffler calls the "joy of verification." This is the delight we often experience in confirming a prediction. The other is simple everyday surprise. We feel surprise when circumstances contradict an expectation. Depending on the situation, the surprise may please or trouble the person, but in either case the surprise can only occur through thwarted expectation – a circumstance fundamentally cognitive. Neatly paired, joy of verification and surprise are emotional responses to success and failure at prediction. The two feelings relate to these two fundamental kinds of events in our cognitive lives.

Such examples illustrate once again that emotional reactions involve understanding situations in particular ways. Accordingly, they should remind us that the emotions Scheffler writes of, besides enriching, rewarding, and policing our efforts at inquiry, inform us about the course of those efforts, providing insights we can use rationally to guide inquiry.

Expression. Affect also influences everyday life and creating in particular through the perception of expression. For instance, a person might discern joy expressed in another's face or joy expressed in the abstract design of a painting. As before, the emotion identified depends on an understanding of the whole situation. In different circumstances, the same weak smile might express the anguish of a headache, fear of an agressor, or thinning tolerance for a bore. And if the perceiver understands the situations, the same weak smile will look different in the three cases – pained in the first, fearful in the second, and explosive in the third.

Despite this importance of context and understanding, expression differs fundamentally from the felt emotions discussed earlier. Expressed emotions are properties not of the perceiver but of the thing perceived. When you see an expression of joy, it is *that* person's joy, not your own.

Obviously true for people, this even holds for paintings. So argues Nelson Goodman as part of his philosophical analysis of symbols and their role in art. According to Goodman, what a work of art expresses is a property of the work. Of course the work cannot literally feel joyful as a person can. Goodman explains this by saying that the work shows the property of joyfulness metaphorically rather than literally. Just as when a person is said to be "hard" or "soft," it's the person who is hard or soft, even if metaphorically, so when a work of art is said to be joyful or sad, it's the work that is joyful or sad, even if metaphorically.

There's an alternative interpretation: when we say a work of art is joyful, we mean that we feel joy in response to it. The problem with this theory is that it's simply false. What you feel in response to a work *or* a person and what you see a work *or* a person as expressing aren't always the same. You might feel sad in response to a sad painting or person. But you might feel amazed – at the brilliance of the painting. Or pleased – because the person is a s.o.b. Or you might feel pity rather than sadness. Or indifference – you have troubles of your own. Whatever you feel, the painting and person are no less sad, and recognition of their sadness provides knowledge about them. This is why Goodman writes: "In aesthetic experience, the *emotions function cognitively.*"

So far I've emphasized that affect carries knowledge without suggesting that there might be difficulty in attaining that knowledge. Indeed, often there isn't. When we're angry, we usually know what we're angry about. But sometimes the reasons for an emotional response or an expressive appearance are not so obvious. A provocative experiment on face perception makes the point nicely. Imagine it this way: You, the subject, are shown photographs of identical twins Jane and Jeanne. You're told that these twins have developed contrasting personalities. From their looks, can you decide which is the warmer, more outgoing person?

Psychological research has shown that most people choose the same twin but without knowing just why. One simply looks warmer and more outgoing than the other. The trick of the experiment is that Jane and Jeanne are the same person, and the photographs are even the same photograph but for a single difference. One photograph has been retouched to enlarge the pupils, the other to narrow them. Viewers respond to this characteristic without realizing just what is affecting them. Furthermore, their reaction is a wise one. Research has also shown that pupil dilation really signals a person's attitude. Dilation is a symptom of attention and interest.

Here, then, is a simple case where affect leaves us ignorant of its causes. Cases like this occur constantly not only with emotional reactions and emotional attributions, but with perceptions of all sorts. A commonplace example concerns face recognition. We readily recognize our friends, but know little of the facial features that help us to do that. Without special training, we have slight success in drawing a recognizable portrait of a friend or describing to another the features important to our sure intuitive knowledge of our friends' identities. This is amazing ignorance, amazingly sensible. We know just what we need to know. We recognize our friends when we meet them, the warmth of warm people, the coolness of cool people. We do all this without our awareness being bothered by nose lengths, eyebrow slants, pupil dilation, and so on. For ordinary purposes, the arrangement is perfect.

But there are extraordinary purposes – the purposes of art, for example. Where the person on the street can ignore the causes of a perceptual response, the artist cannot. The artist needs to know how to render a recognizable face and an expressive one. The novice artist's emotional reactions and recognitions of expression provide information only very indirectly suggestive of the forms the artist has to manipulate. They are hints rather than clear declarations. Gradually, the artist learns to coordinate feelings with their causes in the work and to control those causes for artistic purposes.

The negative view of this would be: Too bad affect often tells us so little. But, remember, affect tells us what it's supposed to, for normal purposes. The positive view is that artists, and people in such other disciplines as psychology and philosophy, have found ways to extend human understanding and invention by seeking the covert causes of our more apparent reactions. In this long work of exploration, affective reactions have provided one very important set of starting points.

Revised proposition: Cognition and affect are not distinct aspects of creative experience. Emotions provide knowledge, point to knowledge, and constitute knowledge crucial to the maker. Emotions are a way of knowing.

BEING SURE AND BEING RIGHT

Proposition: When it's right you know it.

This notion, borrowed from a familiar beer commercial, testifies to the popular faith in spontaneous critical judgment. Supposedly when something is just the way it ought to be, your experience of it falls into place and feels right. Also, the opposite supposedly holds: when you have that feeling of rightness, then the something is just as it ought to be. In other words, we should be self-assured as my frogs are. It's right if and only if you sense the rightness.

Clearly that's a very strong claim. There are sure to be occasional exceptions, which wouldn't seriously challenge a proposition like this. But in fact the exceptions seem to appear more than occasionally. Symptoms of such a problem occur in ordinary discourse about scientific, artistic, moral, or political matters. Disagreement is commonplace or perhaps more than commonplace – the natural state of affairs. Furthermore, it's obvious that such disagreements can be heartfelt. Whoever is right, or whether either party is right, both parties are convinced of the justice of their cases. They're both right, and they know it.

More formal evidence about sureness and rightness comes from some research of my own, where I sometimes collected judgments of sureness incidental to the main purpose. In one study, some students performed a straightforward memory task. They were to remember as accurately as possible a sequence of steps describing a course of thought, a sequence like those quoted in Chapter 2. The students wrote down what they remembered and also rated how sure they were of each step. They remembered fairly well. However, the sureness they reported had little to do with being right; when they did err, they usually were still sure, and often when they were unsure, they were still correct.

Sureness doesn't always prove so unreliable. In another sort of memory task, the results agreed more with common sense. The participants in this study repeated back strings of digits presented in rhythmic patterns. The instructions asked some to remember whatever they could, and others to report only what they felt sure of. The latter had far fewer errors and as many correct answers as the first group.

However, a study in the touchy area of art criticism revealed further problems. The subjects, among other tasks, judged whether each of several differences between a pair of similar drawings favored the one drawing or the other. They indicated not only which choice, but how sure they felt about it. Now if people were sure just when they were right, those that said "sure" on a particular choice should turn out to agree with one another. But in fact the subjects were just as sure about judgments where they split 50-50 as about judgments where there was near consensus. (Testing this question in terms of agreement avoids having to decide who is "really right" in an aesthetic judgment while still examining the issue.)

The problems of agreeing with other people are not the end of the matter. There are problems aplenty simply of agreeing with oneself. It is a common audience experience to encounter a work of art again and react quite differently. The same may happen on rereading a paper in psychology or mathematics or history. Also, a maker returning to a work left earlier often judges it not to be so good as previously thought or, sometimes, better. If "when it's right you know it" isn't so right after all, makers should have adapted to this inconvenience. And indeed they have, in various ways. Creative activity includes a number of strategies for the further testing of judgments the maker was sure, or unsure, about. For example, the poets in my study reported distancing tactics such as setting a poem aside for a long while, typing a poem to objectify it, working on another poem, reading poetry, stepping away physically for a few minutes.

The poets also reported seeking criticism a great deal. This was a surprise, since the traditional romantic image of the poet presumes an individual stubbornly pursuing a personal vision. But the study revealed something quite different. Most of the poets claimed they valued criticism and took pains to find it. About half sought criticism for nearly all their work, and several others did so occasionally. And there were signs that this paid off. A panel of professionals rated a sample of work from each poet. A comparison of the poets in the top half with those in the bottom half revealed that the better-rated poets sought and valued criticism significantly more. Also, the better poets on the average had had three times as many classroom or tutorial experiences in poetry writing, experiences that typically emphasize criticism of the students' work.

These adaptations to the problem of sureness and correctness concern behavior other than the actual moment-to-moment creative process. But there, too, features appear that foster objectivity. By making an idea more concrete – for instance, a mathematician attempting to write out a proof from the idea for the proof – the creator not only approaches a final product but tests the idea. Flaws in an idea may show themselves only as the idea becomes realized. Often someone may make an idea concrete explicitly to test it and not to finish it. An architect may construct a model from the plan so that architect and client alike can know better how the actual structure would appear. I'll have a little more to say about this in the next chapter.

Another feature of the poets' reports is pertinent here. The poets spent little time assessing particular options. They accepted or rejected one relatively quickly and continued. However, the poets would revise poems again and again. I understand this pattern of behavior as in part an adaptation to the difficulties of sound judgment. Evaluations done in the midst of making are likely to be unsound, however protracted. So the poets did not waste time on them. They judged quickly, accepted tentatively, and reviewed later and repeatedly to gain perspective.

Makers have discovered another aid to objectivity: choice between alternatives. Contrast permits a more sensitive assessment of pros and cons, whether the assessment is intuitive or analytical. That paired choices foster better discrimination than options considered one at a time has been established for some basic perceptual judgments such as color discrimination. And, indeed, matching hues by placing two samples side by side is much safer than arriving at the paint store and trying to remember the exact color of the woodwork.

 Making Waves

The gains that result from paired comparison apply as much to supposedly more subjective judgments, such as what a shape expresses. This simple exercise demonstrates that, and also explores how sure our perception of expression is. First, look at the "wave" here. Describe an emotion it might reasonably represent. If more than one emotion seems appropriate, make a list.

This can be fairly confusing. One doesn't know what alternative words or phrases to choose from. That problem can be solved by providing a context of alternatives. Here is such a context for the wave: Choose an appropriate term from these five: peaceful, afraid, happy, angry, lonely.

Most people find that narrowing the field helps them to make a choice they feel much more confident about. Nevertheless, two or even three options on the list still may seem fairly plausible. At least, if a first choice appears obvious, close seconds may occur.

In part that's because there's only a context of alternative labels, but not a context of alternative waves. So I'll add the latter, giving the first wave again along with four more.

On turning to the picture, plan to cover it with your hand. Slide your hand down to examine the first wave, which you've already associated with one of the five emotions.

Then move your hand down to reveal another wave. Decide which emotion that might express. But it's a rule that no more than one wave can go with the same emotion. If two compete for the same emotion, one will have to be assigned to another emotion.

Then move your hand down to show the next wave, and repeat the process. Those are the instructions. Now turn ahead to find the waves. After finishing, return here and read on.

By the time the bottom is reached and all the waves are matched with all the emotions, you probably will have changed your mind about what words went with some of the waves. When choices were necessary between two waves for the same emotion, their features became significant in ways not evident before. By the end, some of the waves actually looked quite different than on first encounter. It's just this contrast effect that makes paired comparison a powerful resource in the creative process and decision making of various sorts.

Revised proposition: The maker's feelings of rightness or wrongness reveal only rather unreliably the actual state of affairs. Adapting to the reality of confusion, makers acquire many strategies to compensate for the unreliability of their judgments, however sure or unsure they feel.

THE IMPORTANCE OF JUDGMENT

For most of this chapter I've tried to describe how evaluations occur during the moment-to-moment process of creating. Makers typically evaluated spontaneously, but not exactly intuitively because reasons accompanied their pro and con reactions. Makers relied mostly on undirected scrutiny, detecting significant features simply by noticing them, but makers did "look harder" in various special circumstances. Makers used their emotional reactions and expressive attributes of the developing product as ways of knowing that product better. Although they had to trust their momentary judgments momentarily, makers adopted various strategies to compensate for unreliability. And so on. Taken together, these behaviors support the teleological view of creating advanced earlier. They provide an image of the maker in the midst of the task, adjusting the product toward a valid final form.

Whereas in the last two chapters I studied and celebrated idea getting, here I've studied and celebrated good judgment. It's natural to ask about the relative importance of the two, granting that both are necessary. Is creating more likely to falter and fail because of weaknesses in idea getting or weaknesses in judgment? The question needs asking because conventional wisdom may give too quick an answer. We usually think of idea getting as the characteristic problem of creating. After all, creating, by its very meaning, depends on acts of invention. But this is not a proof.

I want to argue that, very often, creating is clearly judgment-limited. When a poem is troubled by clichés, forced rhymes, excessive obscurity or clarity, when a painting suffers from lack of balance or too much balance, garish or dull colors, when a theory in physics exhibits inconsistencies or a mathematical proof *non sequiturs*, we can be reasonably sure the maker has failed to perceive the flaws. We can conclude this for the poet and artist because the flaws mentioned are not that hard to correct; had the maker apprehended them, something would have been done. We can conclude that the physicist or mathematician missed the anomalies mentioned because such anomalies are intolerable in proper physics and mathematics. Detecting the flaws, the maker would have solved the problem or not presented the product in the first place.

Failures of judgment deserve recognition all the more when we remember that judgment applies not only to close editing of the final product but to decisions made much earlier in the course of creating. Is such-and-such a problem worth pursuing? Is such-and-such a theory worth developing? What initial approaches seem most fruitful? Questions of these sorts are answered, at least implicitly, at the beginnings of a creative effort, and the answers send the maker down one or another path. Failures of judgment

peaceful   afraid   happy   angry   lonely

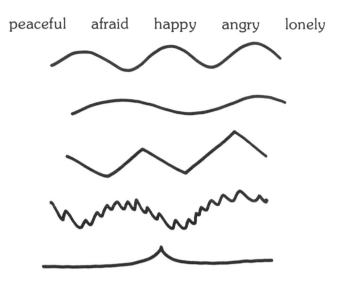

in those early decisions therefore constitute just as much of a limit on a maker's creating as failures of judgment later on. Furthermore, such early judgments may be more difficult simply because they often concern abstract, general, and tentative visions of how a work might develop.

This theme aside, makers' evaluative powers contribute to their creating in yet another way, improving abilities months and years later. This function of critical skill contributes to the creative products we learn from and enjoy as much as the function of refining the individual work does. After all, however well the maker's current work achieves the maker's current standards, if the maker did not grow, lost to us would be the more mature productions of five or twenty years later. In this learning process, critical judgment seems crucially involved.

A fundamental fact – maybe even *the* fundamental fact – about making is that critical abilities are more advanced than productive abilities. We can discriminate differences we can do little to produce. A maker can appreciate the insights of Einstein or the art of Picasso without at all being able to fashion anything of that quality. This difference between judgment and production describes mundane situations as much as creative ones. We can perceive the pitcher's curve ball without being able to throw one, discern good and bad carpentry without being able to build a house, know what square roots are and how to check them without knowing how to extract them. For many reasons, the test for a certain property requires much less of us than producing something with that property.

Now the editorial function of criticism has been my main concern. But besides the improvement of the product underway, something else important occurs as a result of constant correction, something that helps the maker achieve those difficult ideals. The properties the maker imparts to the product in after-the-fact, corrective ways gradually become imparted in original acts of production. The poet no longer checks and corrects to achieve interesting meter or forceful expression; the poet simply writes with interesting meter and forceful expression, just as second-language learners eventually stop criticizing and correcting their grammar and simply speak and write correctly.

One other feature of this process requires attention. It's not, of course, that makers necessarily improve until they can perform according to their highest aspirations, and that's that. As criteria come to constrain acts of production, the maker may also become able to perceive distinctions not previously apparent. Makers do not always – and maybe never – catch up with their critical sensitivities, which continue to develop. All this is rather like the carrot dangling from the stick tied to the donkey, which tempts the donkey forever forward. Makers' own critical sensitivities are the carrots they chase and never really catch. But, in the process, they do get somewhere.

5

SEARCHING FOR

Creative products, whether paintings, plans for aircraft, or Monty Python skits, are devised, revised, and redevised until slowly and sometimes painfully they take final shape. So far, this exploration of creating has given many pages to the momentary – those inventive and critical moments that lead to the final creative product. However, creating involves more than a swarm of insights. We also have to understand how such moments weave together to make organized progress.

Here everyday speach provides some unexpected help. Suppose someone were to look for something that had no shape; to pursue something that didn't move; to find something that wasn't in any real place; to dig for something that wasn't under anything; to look out for something that had no appearance.

That someone might be searching for ideas. In talk about problem solving and invention, as in talk about many other things, our language often borrows words describing everyday physical actions. We freely speak of looking for the best ideas as well as the biggest strawberries, pursuing problems as well as blown-away hats, finding the right approach as well as the right road, digging for meaning as well as potatoes, watching out for mistakes as well as for wasps.

All such phrases are ways of talking about invention as a process of search. Trying to invent something like a poem, a plot, or a theory resembles in important ways trying to search for something physical. In physical search, one often examines many items to find the right item, such as looking through coins for the coin with the rare date. Likewise in inventive thinking, one often finds and considers alternative ideas. In physical search, one often looks in different places – under the couch, on the table, in a coat pocket for the lost pen. Likewise in inventive thinking, one looks in different "conceptual places" – for instance, by taking different approaches to a problem that might lead to quite different solutions. Just as invention can be thought of as a process of search, so can effectiveness and efficiency in invention be understood as effectiveness and efficiency in search. In invention also, it makes sense to ask whether you've looked long enough, looked in the right places, dug deeply enough, ranged widely enough.

The search metaphor begs to be used, and I'll put it to work now, discussing some simple but crucial characteristics of creating in terms of search. As always, the aim is to explain how the originality and high quality get into the developing work.

SOMETHING FOR NOTHING

The labor of creating needs to be acknowledged. In emphasizing creative and critical moments I have neglected it, but the concept of search provides a good chance to set the record straight. A search, after all, can demand resources of time and effort suitable to Stanley's quest for Livingston or even Galahad's for the Holy Grail. Worse yet, a certain amount of search would seem to require that amount of labor.

Proposition: In creating as elsewhere, conducting a search requires the labor of taking the individual steps of the search. You get no more than you pay for.

This is sort of true. Yet it is not as true as it could be. Consider, for example, the classic tale of inference by Edgar Allan Poe, "The Purloined Letter." The Prefect of the Paris police approaches C. Auguste Dupin with a problem he can't solve for himself. It seems that a certain daring Minister has stolen a compromising letter from a lady "of most exalted station," in fact stolen the letter from the royal boudoir. The Minister has been using this letter for political leverage. If the Prefect can recover the letter discreetly, he'll get an immense reward.

The Prefect has – searched. There is good reason to believe the letter must be concealed on the Minister's premises, not elsewhere or on his person. Yet the Minister has been away frequently, and an exhaustive search has revealed nothing. Cushions have been probed with needles, the joints in furniture examined with a microscope only to be found undisturbed, and so on. Can Dupin, the keen analyst, help him, the Prefect wonders?

Dupin can. The details are well worth reading, but Dupin's fundamental tactic is to try to think as the wiley Minister would. The Minister, Dupin reasons, would anticipate all this very competent police work. In fact, no doubt the Minister designed his convenient absences from home to allow the police to satisfy themselves that the letter was not there. Ergo, the letter *was* there, but not in the way the Prefect expected it to be. It would not be concealed, but in plain sight. And so Dupin finds it – folded differently, sealed with a different seal, half ripped and tossed idly in a letter rack.

Poe's tale teaches some straightforward lessons. For one, extensive search accomplishes nothing unless the person looks in the right places. For another, searchers do the work of search best when they do not search at all, but rather deduce where the thing sought *must* be. Dupin is suspicious of that "you get no more than you pay for" notion. The Prefect certainly paid with his efforts, but didn't get. Dupin didn't pay so much, but did get.

So there are bargains to be had, not only in Dupin's search but in the searches associated with more conventional creative activities. Understanding what some of these bargains are is crucial to understanding how makers search productively and efficiently. I'll describe some of the bargains below. This can be done quickly because most of them have already been discussed in earlier chapters. They deserve another mention though, since before they were not seen as ways of doing the work of search. To understand them so now is to appreciate better their contribution to creating.

Search not done. Surely the best of all bargains is Dupin's — search not done. How is that possible in general? By not searching through possibilities where there are general reasons to think that nothing will be found. An example from an earlier chapter was the four-dots problem, where one could reason one's way to a solution by logically eliminating possibilities. There was no need to move various pairs of dots into different patterns. For any solution, two dots would have to be left behind, those two would have to be a diagonal pair, and so on. No need for trial and error at all. Another example recalls how people can ask their memories to provide ideas meeting multiple conditions. For instance, a person can try to remember not just cities or colors, but unusual cities or colors. Without this capacity, matters would be more difficult. The person would have to remember just colors or cities, and screen for unusual ones. In general, the mind often avoids screening by making multiple criteria part of a command to remember or to perform some other mental function.

Yet another example concerns how people reach the conclusion that they do *not* know something. It's natural to suppose that people do this by searching their memories completely. However, Paul Kolers and Sandra Palef have noted that people often judge that they do not know something more quickly than they judge that they know something. From this and other evidence, these authors concluded that people often make accurate "don't know" judgments without a full search of memory.

Search done on the side. Free search also occurs when someone pursues another activity while the search continues. This can happen with *noticing.* After some work on a problem, a person turns to another activity. In the midst of that activity, the person discovers something suggesting a solution to the original problem. There was no deliberate search. But the mind remained alert to patterns significant to the original problem. Functionally, a search for relevant cues continued during the unrelated activity.

Search in parallel. Savings also result when several different items are sought at the same time. Consider a customer browsing in a book store. The customer might stroll between the shelves alert to titles touching on any one of several topics of personal interest. For another example, a scholar might read a paper drafted earlier, ready to react to any problems of various kinds – punctuation, spelling, grammar, lapses of style, misstatements, and so on. This is an example of the role of noticing in critical response.

Search by scanning. Savings occur when each item tested is not inspected individually. For example, in scanning a list for certain names – or letters as in Chapter 3 – you can let your eyes run across the page without focusing on each item. The irrelevant items do not become conscious at all, but the desired ones stand out. As mentioned earlier, considerable laboratory research has been done on this "noticing" phenomenon. Investigators have found that with practice people can learn to scan for any one of many items about as quickly as they can scan for a single item.

      Looking for Bugs

Free and cheap search are important in creating. It's also worth remembering that they function routinely in everyday behavior, as this small demonstration shows.

Imagine you are quietly sitting, as perhaps you are. Suppose that someone behind you, having a view of the whole room, says: "Oh, look at that enormous spider."

So look for it. Allow your eyes to do what they want to do and notice what that is.

Now suppose that the person remarks, "Look at that enormous ant." Again, let your eyes look and consider how well they know where to look.

Suppose the person behind you says, "Mosquito." Let your eyes look once again.

What if the person says, "Hornet! "

Did you notice where you looked? In each case, it is as if your eyes knew how to look selectively. For the spider, people often look on the walls and ceiling, for the ant, down lower and on the floor, and for the mosquito, in the air nearby. Sometimes people find themselves spontaneously listening for the mosquito as well as looking. Sometimes they listen for the hornet, too. The thought of the hornet may lead your gaze to the windows because hornets so often cling there seeking a way out.

So, in part, this experience demonstrates *search not done*. You look only in certain areas, excluding others as a waste of time. Also, the concept of scanning applies. Probably you didn't examine every square foot of the wall for the spider. You let your eyes roam quickly about, trusting them to detect any spiders.

Another just as important feature of this experience is the spontaneous reflexive nature of the exclusion and scanning. Let me repeat: It is as though our eyes know what to do. Sometimes the resources for cheap search operate quite automatically. Other times – perhaps with the four-dot problem – they have to be more deliberately marshaled. Spontaneously selective search depends on learning. Research has shown that children scan a picture to pick up requested information much less selectively than adults do. That obviously applies to looking for bugs also: one has to have some experience with pests to know where to look.

Needless to say, the bugs one looks for might be flaws in some product instead of pests in the room. Suppose you were reviewing a prose passage. What would it be like to look for bugs in the punctuation? In the spelling? Suppose you were seeking fingerprint smudges instead. In each of these cases, your eyes would know where to look.

Revised proposition: By various means, searches often proceed with much less time and effort than in item-by-item searching. Creative activity and human behavior in general rely constantly on such economies.

SEARCHING LONGER

Here is a problem to solve. Working this problem now, before any propositions or explanations, will supply the example we need for the rest of the section. Try to devise a solution that seems entirely satisfactory. The problem is not misleading, and there is no one hard-to-find solution where everything falls into place.

     The Chickens Next Door

The Wendells enjoyed gardening while next door the Lees raised chickens. Unfortunately, the Lees were rather selfish people who did not care much what mischief their chickens did. The chickens were not penned. Again and again, they wandered over to the Wendells' garden and pecked away at whatever seemed tasty. The Wendells often had asked the Lees to deal with the problem, but the Lees did nothing. The Wendells considered a fence, but decided they couldn't afford one. The Wendells, peace-loving folk, also did not want to take any violent or strongly aggressive action. What might the Wendells do?

Ludwig van Beethoven was an amazingly fluent improviser, but, paradoxically, a painfully slow composer in the planning stages of his work. He would improvise on the piano readily and creatively. Such performances were much admired in Vienna high society. But when it came to producing a musical score, the fluency disappeared. Beethoven kept notebooks in which he outlined and revised themes and plans for his compositions. These notebooks reveal that he would rework such elements again and again before feeling ready to write out a composition in detail.

What to conclude? One interpretation sometimes suggested is that Beethoven "clutched" in front of a blank score. The ideas that would come so readily at the piano would not at his desk. Another interpretation, one I like better, is that Beethoven knew exactly what he was doing. Entertaining party goers was one thing, but composition was a serious endeavor. The easy ideas were not good enough. In the early stages of a composition, Beethoven meant to be sure that he produced the most compelling themes and structures he could. Therefore, he worked at it.

Beethoven's attitude – if this was his attitude – and anyway Beethoven's behavior were just contrary to a general difficulty in creative activities usually called *premature closure*. Premature closure is an explanatory notion in many writings on creative problem solving. Presumably, creative efforts often fail because not enough alternatives are considered. People accept the first adequate but probably mediocre solution they think of, when they could discover much better ones by persisting. Their failure could be described as a failure to search longer – to deliberately push beyond early ideas and find more options before selecting.

Proposition: Premature closure explains why many ideas and products are not nearly so original and effective as they could be. Superior creative efforts involve deliberately searching for many alternatives.

There is laboratory evidence that seems to support this conclusion. Some of the experiments involved genuinely creative tasks such as titling a cartoon or a short story. Some subjects were asked to write a single solution to the problem. Others were asked to write many. The solutions were rated for quality by two judges with good agreement. Although the average quality of the single solutions was higher than the average quality of the multiple solutions, in sheer numbers the multiple solutions group produced more high-rated solutions that the single solution group, simply because they devised so many solutions of all sorts. In other words, those in the multiple solutions group were more likely to devise one or more high-quality solutions. So searching longer seems to explain success, at least in part.

   The Chickens Again

You can test this conclusion against your own experience with the chickens-next-door problem. Your solution already could be excellent. On the other hand, perhaps there was a problem of premature closure. To decide, seek further solutions. Set a quota of four more candidate solutions. List four that at least seem worth a second thought.

How did it go? Was there a new solution you preferred to your original one? Experience with giving this exercise to others tells me that sometimes there is and sometimes there is not. Another common outcome: improvement of the original solution rather than a wholly new idea.

Superficially, premature closure seems to give a good account of some failures of invention, as well as advice on how to do better. However, such talk of searching longer neglects something important: in the last analysis, problem solvers' evaluations of candidate solutions are responsible for leaving them with mediocre ones. Consider the chickens-next-door problem. The first job was to devise an entirely satisfactory solution. If later, after inventing further solutions, someone feels that the first solution was not entirely satisfactory, that means he or she wasn't critical enough in the first place. The premature-closure concept leads us to think of premature closure as a matter of not searching long enough. But perhaps it's as much or more a matter of not requiring enough of the candidate solution we accept. Perhaps it's being sufficiently and insightfully critical that keeps the search moving forward rather than seeking many alternatives as such. Thus fussy old Beethoven searched longer.

Is any of this relevant to the chickens-next-door problem? Experience leads me to think that it is. I've asked a number of people for solutions they considered wholly satisfactory. Again and again, people have offered solutions that are clearly inadequate in one way or another. Surprisingly often, proposals do not meet the explicit demands of the problem. For instance, "The Wendells should get a tough dog" conflicted with their nonviolence. Often proposals violate plausible implications of the problem statement. For instance, someone suggested, "The Wendells should ask the Lees to share the cost of a fence." But it's clear from the problem statement that the Lees don't care about being a nuisance, so they probably wouldn't cooperate. Also, if the Wendells can't afford fence, can they afford half a fence?

Still other solutions were impractical in ways not relating directly to the problem statement. For instance, one idea was to "operate a tape recorder out in the yard to scare the chickens away." But even if the tape recorder would frighten the chickens, keeping it functioning would be a nuisance – rewinding the tape, protection from rain, and so on. For other proposals, carrying out the plan probably would not solve the problem. One person said, "Scatter corn soaked in tabasco sauce or something else hot about the yard. The chickens will eat it, not like it, and learn to stay away." But it's much more probable that the chickens would learn to ignore the corn, while eating whatever else they liked. Chickens aren't that stupid.

These examples suggest that problem solvers need to be more critical. But isn't this the very behavior that inhibits creativity? The answer seems to be yes and no. Experiments suggest that just how you are critical makes a big difference. In one investigation, some people were instructed to free-wheel, forget about quality, and devise as many solutions as possible. Others were to give only high-quality solutions. It was found that the first group produced more high-quality solutions, albeit with a lower average quality. So in this case the emphasis on quality impeded performance. However, in another study people were instructed not just to strive for quality but to try to meet specified standards. In a problem of inventing plot titles, they were asked to produce an "imaginative, creative, or unusual title for this plot." With even this slight clarification of standards, the results were quite different. Those given the standards produced a larger number of superior solutions, with a higher average quality of solution as well.

 ## The Chickens One More Time

Perhaps clarification of standards is important for the chickens-next-door puzzle too. Furthermore, the discussion above of difficulties in some proposed solutions ought to have done that. So step one: Review your own solutions. Compare them with the above examples and standards. How adequate do they seem? Very adequate, I hope.

But perhaps not. Step two: If the best solution so far doesn't seem good enough, try once again. Attempt to think of a solution without any of the failings described above.

Are there any "right" solutions to the chickens-next-door problem? Here, I think, are some reasonable possibilities. At least they satisfy the problem requirements better than those described earlier. One person recommended that the Wendells take a chicken into their house whenever one wandered over onto their land. Then the Wendells would call the Lees and ask them very politely to come get the chicken. The Lees would not want to let the Wendells have their chickens, and the nuisance would eventually cause the Lees to pen the birds. Another person suggested that the Wendells should share the produce of their garden with the Lees; although that sounds naive, this person claimed that such a tactic actually had worked for him in a similar situation. Maybe, given a chance, the Lees are nicer than they seem!

Finally, there is an "official" solution in the source from which the problem was drawn. When the Lees were out in their yard, one of the Wendells would go out, deliberately look about the yard, and find an egg that previously had been planted there. This would be repeated two or three times over several days. The selfish Lees, thinking that their chickens were supplying the Wendells with eggs, would find a way to keep the chickens home.

Revised proposition: Ideas and products are not so original and effective as they could be because of premature closure. Better performance occurs sometimes because a person seeks out and chooses from many options, but more typically because the person maintains clear and high standards that lead to looking longer for a suitable solution.

But I'm afraid that matters are just a little more complicated. The revised proposition assumes that *more* ideas are needed to do better. However, problem solvers who devised better ideas in the first place would not have to search longer. Furthermore, to hope for higher-quality ideas at the outset is not naive in principle. A higher initial quality means that a person has imposed further constraints on the process of generating ideas, constraints making the ideas more suitable. As discussed earlier, asking yourself to think of ideas meeting multiple constraints can be rather easy. Furthermore, such asking often occurs quite spontaneously and unconsciously. Certainly, then, a person might manage to think of better ideas at the outset.

In fact, there is evidence that this can happen. Some of it comes from my own studies of poets. One of the curious findings was that the better poets showed greater fluency on a test, but they did not appear to use this fluency to search longer when writing poetry. Let me describe this paradox in a little more detail.

Part of the study was an assessment of each poet's fluency. The poets took a simple test that asked them to list as many words or phrases as they could satisfying certain conditions. One task was to list properties of an apple – red, round, shiny, and so on. Also, samples of each poets' poetry were rated by expert judges. It turned out that the better-rated poets were considerably more productive on the fluency test.

This suggested that these poets would be using that fluency to search through more alternatives as they wrote, in order to produce better poems. But an examination of the think-aloud reports showed that this wasn't so. No poet, rated high or low, spent time searching through many alternatives. Usually, a poet devised only one or two options for a needed phrase, once in a while three or four, and rarely more. All the poets relatively quickly reached solutions satisfactory to themselves, at least for the time being. It is still possible that the better poets were using their fluency in another way. The better poets might have returned to the same place in the poem on other days, revising more often than the lower-rated poets did. There was no way of checking this in the study. But certainly the better-rated poets were not using their fluency in the straightforward way that usual notions of premature closure lead one to expect. They were not devising and choosing among many alternatives on one occasion.

What to make of this? My reading is that fluency as such is something of a red herring. To understand the situation, we have to consider the tradeoffs between fluency and quality that people can make. Research on problem solving has shown that people easily can switch strategies from generating many solutions of somewhat lower average quality to generating fewer solutions of somewhat higher average quality. But they have difficulty devising solutions both numerous and of high quality. In other words, a person's underlying capacity is best characterized as a tradeoff between quantity and quality. More of one means less of the other, and the person's capabilities are defined by just how much more of one means how much less of the other.

All this provides an explanation for the better poets' high fluency and short searches. The better and worse poets alike adopted different tradeoffs between quality and quantity for the fluency tests and for poetry writing. For the fluency test; the poets emphasized quantity because they were told to and also because poetic quality was not at issue. For writing poetry, they chose to emphasize quality. The better poets' high fluencies indicated that in general the better poets had a better quality-quantity tradeoff. They could get more quantity for the same quality, or more quality for the same quantity. They did the one for my fluency test, and the other in writing poetry.

Furthermore, the fact that better and worse poets alike wrote at the quality end of their quantity-quality tradeoffs suggests that this may be the most practical thing to do. Perhaps these poets had learned at least tacitly that trying for quantity at lower quality and then choosing required more time without yielding any real gains.

In fact, some results of other investigators support the same conclusion. When subjects attempted titling stories or cartoons, more difficult problems than sometimes are used in research of this sort, one researcher found zero correlation between number of solutions devised and number of high-rated solutions. In other words, those that searched longer did not devise more superior solutions for their pains. Other studies have shown that with undefined standards the better solutions often appear relatively late, but with defined standards nearly as many superior solutions occur among the first half devised as among the last half. Furthermore, I mentioned earlier that defining standards resulted both in a higher average quality and in a larger number of superior solutions. Not only that, but people reported fewer total solutions. They got more out of less.

Finally, all of the experiments discussed so far left the evaluation of solutions to judges, whereas normal problem solving situations require the problem solver to judge. What happens when people have to select as well as invent their solutions? Studies have shown that they will choose better-than-average solutions – but not much better-than-average. In fact, when people were even given criteria and some were instructed to devise a number of solutions and choose the best, the average quality of their final choices was no higher than the average quality of solutions from others asked to write a single solution.

A definite conclusion emerges from all this. When a problem solver has some idea of the pertinent criteria, deliberate long searches usually are a waste of time. The person does just as well if not better to try to think of one or two very good solutions in the first place. This is possible because the person can use the criteria in the very act of conceiving solutions, rather than screening for the best solutions after listing many.

Now "usually" does not mean always. For example, a deliberate long search becomes more desirable when it is very important to find the best possible solution. Also, if a person doesn't have a clear conception of the relevant standards, devising a number of alternatives may help to develop a sense of the significant differences. If the real problem is that the wrong standards are being used, haphazard exploration may help in recognizing the inadequacies. Finally and most simply, many problems are just plain hard. They require extended effort because the maker demands a good solution. Beethoven again.

But despite these qualifications, I do want to conclude that premature closure is not the kind of problem it seems to be.

Revised propositions: (1) The devising and quick acceptance of mediocre solutions is not a problem of short searches as such. This is only the superficial symptom. (2) It is a problem of not knowing or knowing and not maintaining standards, whether explicit standards enforced by analysis or implicit ones by impressionistic judgments. (3) In most circumstances, people deliberately searching longer do so by trading off quality for quantity and really gain nothing. (4) Ideally, standards control the very acts of idea production, so that outcomes are likely to be right in the first or second place and searches are short. (5) When this is difficult, next best is that high standards select among options produced from looser constraints; this keeps the search going as long as necessary.

GETTING GENERAL, SPECIFIC, CONCRETE, AND ABSTRACT

We've been considering what might be called a slot-machine model of search. You try to think of idea after idea, like dropping coin after coin in the slot and pulling the lever. Sometimes there is no payoff, sometimes a big one. Although results may differ, every try is much like every other. True, sometimes more or fewer tries are required, for many reasons. But basically, it's play until you've won enough, if ever.

Proposition: In trying to think of ideas, each trial is much the same except in its payoff.

Of course, this is a very naive view. No one asserts it as such. It is a convenient simplification when the purpose is to study matters of fluency, length of search, standards, selection of solutions, and how all this affects final quality. In reality, shifts often occur in the way people represent problem situations and possible solutions to themselves. Some of these shifts involve getting relatively more general or specific, more abstract or concrete.

Getting general. The brick problem mentioned earlier is a classic task in research on fluency. The problem solver is supposed to devise a long list of imaginative and practical uses of bricks, expected, in short, to play the slot machine. But imagine how someone might proceed: "Let's see, bricks – a paperweight, weight to hold down a tarpaulin, anchor, oh and build a bookcase, a border for a flower garden, a doll house, well, maybe use them for decoration – a planter, say, or a . . . well, maybe carve one to make a sculpture."

One argument against the slot-machine concept appears right away. Ideas often occur in related clusters, such as the first three ideas that use the brick as a weight or the second three that use the brick as construction material. In fact, changing from one kind of use to another is a strategy people adopt to continue to invent uses.

Now the slot-machine concept is just a convenient fiction. Research on creativity has long recognized this sort of shifting, devised a name for it, and used it as a measure supposedly relevant to creativity: *flexibility*. The measure scores not how many ideas a person produces, nor how original they are, but how many *sorts* of ideas there are. For instance, a person who listed many ideas, all of which used bricks as weights, would score very low on flexibility. Presumably, the ability and tendency to shift gears is important to inventiveness over and above whatever relevance the ability to devise many solutions has.

The flexibility in the above example is an example of spontaneously *getting general*. When ideas of one sort begin to occur less readily, the person may shift to ideas of another sort. This series of changes – first weight, then construction material, then decoration – amounts to a search at a more general level than the search for particular solutions. Tacitly, the problem solver produces a sequence of kinds of solutions.

Flexibility can be deliberate as well as spontaneous. Here are some more uses of bricks, beginning in the same way but continuing somewhat differently. "Let's see, bricks – a paperweight, weight to hold down a tarpaulin, anchor. But what about *kinds* of uses? Say weight, building material, decoration. But all that has the brick staying a brick. Say it was used as is, ground up, put in water, split into pieces – how about a puzzle made of a broken-up brick? Painted – how about a totem? But all that assumes *I* make something of the bricks. What if someone else does? Maybe I can 'use the bricks' by selling them. Trading them." So, by thinking of more and more general kinds of solutions, people can free themselves from unnecessary assumptions, assumptions that conceal opportunities for solving a problem.

Getting specific. Getting specific means defining more and more particular properties of a problem situation or a candidate solution. When you actually carry out a solution to a problem, you make everything entirely specific. The solution plan becomes physical fact.

Put that way, getting specific sounds like an uninteresting logical consequence of the need to get done. But getting specific has more to it than that. It can help the maker to deal with a task critically and inventively. For instance, getting specific often has a testing function. When people get specific, they tend to find difficulties in a candidate solution – difficulties that even may lead to another solution entirely. When people formulate ideas in general terms, they may not see the complications. Getting specific can even lead to dramatic insights. Remember, for instance, the poet who sought a better metaphor relating wailing babies to air raids. She got specific. In effect, she analyzed the concept of air raid sirens, asking "what do they tell me to do." She realized that they and her babies both told her to preserve herself.

Getting concrete. I've always especially enjoyed the tactics of one student of mine. A problem had been assigned to design a more effective coathanger. The details of the problem don't matter, but how the student approached it does. Not feeling that the problem was sufficiently vivid in her mind, the student went to stand in front of an open closet and think about it. That's getting concrete.

To speak more generally, getting concrete means confronting the physical circumstances of a problem, in reality or, slightly less concretely, through mental imagery, picturing, or role playing. It may mean looking at the open closet rather than just thinking about the problem at your desk; staring about the room to locate a lost object rather than just thinking where you might have put it; designing a bookcase with the materials rather than just a list of materials in front of you; trying a psychological experiment on yourself instead of only on others.

People get concrete because it helps. Like getting specific, getting concrete often reveals practical difficulties in an idea. Also, the physical stimulation of getting concrete leads people to notice opportunities they might not otherwise discover. Sometimes getting concrete helps because it discloses opportunities that shouldn't even be there – like tax loopholes.

Getting abstract. Paradoxically, getting abstract can contribute just as much as getting concrete. The four-dot problem provides a good example. The problem can be approached by manipulating the dots this way and that, but a more effective method was to reason from the problem requirements. Getting abstract in this way revealed the essential logic of the problem, something that shuffling the dots did not.

Here are some other examples of getting abstract: using plans, sketches, or outlines rather than working on the actual product; describing physical phenomena with mathematical equations; describing an experienced situation in words as a way of clarifying it for oneself. Such commonplace examples show that getting abstract, like getting concrete, is a natural strategy that people adopt all the time.

 The Prisoner's Nap

This design problem doesn't require much in the way of equipment, only yourself and a room.

You've been traveling in a foreign country. You are mistakenly arrested for revolutionary activities and locked in a completely bare cell for the night. In the morning, you'll see officials and you hope to be able to prove your identity and innocence, but for now you're stuck. You're worried, of course. But you're also very tired.

You'd like to sleep. Try to find the most comfortable possible position. In exploring alternative postures, notice the different levels of specificity at which you can search – from minor adjustments of an arm or leg to different positions of the whole body. Get general freely when you're not happy with a specific approach. Get specific freely when you want to know whether a given approach will really work. Remember also that you can get concrete and abstract. As to getting concrete, you may discover something important by trying various postures. As to getting abstract, you might discover something important by reasoning about what makes positions comfortable or uncomfortable. (It's humbling to consider what a luxury it is to do this sort of problem as an exercise, when so many have faced it in fact.)

Have you found a solution? So far as I know, there is no one perfect solution to find, but keep searching until you've devised something fairly satisfactory.

Experiences like this where one is examining one's own process reveal the complicated nature of search. Shifts from general to specific, specific to general, more abstract to concrete, and more concrete to abstract are important elements. Such shifts occur quite spontaneously. But also you can undertake them deliberately. Since shifts of opposite sorts often help, there can be no conclusion that creative thinking depends crucially on abstract or concrete or general or specific thinking. Rather, creative thinking has to be understood as effective navigating among the alternatives. Presumably the better creative thinker develops rules or intuitions about what to do when. Of course, the simplest rule is, when something isn't working, try something else.

Revised proposition: The slot-machine model does not describe what people do when they search for ideas and even less what people can do. It's natural and beneficial for successive ideas to differ in their specificity or generality, their concreteness or abstractness.

HILL CLIMBING

Imagine Sherlock Holmes trying to find the top of a hill in a thick fog. He can't see where the top is, because only the nearby terrain appears through the fog. But at least he can see which direction is uphill. So he does the logical thing. He walks in that direction. If he walks uphill long enough, he's sure to get to the top.

In a way, he is searching – searching for the top. But his search differs considerably from the sort of search discussed earlier. That was search in the sense of devising alternative after alternative, examining one thing after another. A person might search at different levels of specificity or concreteness, but at any level the next idea would not routinely be a revision and improvement of the previous idea. It's as though someone were seeking the hilltop in a helicopter, landing here and landing there, but never sure just where to land because of the fog. This could be called a *sampling search* because the searcher simply samples alternatives.

The climb up the hill could be called *progressive search*. Unlike sampling search, progressive search proceeds by a series of improvements. Step by step, the progressive search homes in on its objective.

Hill climbing is a good metaphor for many human activities, among them creative activities. The metaphor requires that the maker have a couple of characteristics. First, the maker has to be able to discern the uphill direction, to judge whether a step would improve the product. Second, there is the fog. The fog means that the maker can't see the whole way to the desired outcome. But because of hill climbing, the maker only needs limited vision.

Proposition: Progressive search explains how the maker can achieve a creative outcome – through a series of progressive steps unimpressive in comparison to the final attainment.

Does this simple idea really explain much creative accomplishment? I think it does. Eventually, I'll mention some important qualifications, but for a while let's consider the good sense the proposition makes.

For certain kinds of problem solving, the hill-climbing metaphor can be very precise. Suppose a manufacturer can set the price of the product and the volume the factories produce. Price and volume, two numbers that define the current operation, are like coordinate numbers on a map, numbers that define the whereabouts of the hill climber. In addition, there is an analogue of the height of the land at any point: the profit at any given price and volume. Now obviously the manufacturer will lose money on very low price and volume. But if prices are very high, no one will buy. If volume is very high, people won't consume it all, not even "at cost." So somewhere at an intermediate price and volume is the top of the profit hill, the point of maximum profits. The manufacturer's task is to climb the profit hill – to vary the choice of price and volume so as to move toward the combination where profits are maximum. The manufacturer might try to do this by actually experimenting, or more likely by using a mathematical model of the relations among price, volume, and profit.

The manufacturer's efforts do not seem very creative. For activities more obviously creative, the hill-climbing metaphor usually applies more loosely. But allowing some latitude, the hill-climbing metaphor fits nearly any sort of inventive or problem-solving activity. One only needs a situation where the language of hill climbing makes sense – that is, where there are analogies of being at a current location, of taking a small step, and of evaluating before or after taking a step whether it makes an improvement.

Consider writing a poem. Let's say the text of the poem as currently drafted defines the "current location." The quality of the poem so far measures the height at the current location. When the poet makes additions, deletions, and substitutions, these are steps designed to improve the poem. In this way, the poet climbs toward a high-quality poem by a series of small improvements. Of course, poets do not spend *all* their time on piecemeal improvements, but both my own studies and various autobiographical writings show that most poets commit most of their time to just that: hill climbing.

But a natural question arises: Do such examples necessarily have anything to do with creativity? Poets often write mundane poems. Perhaps progressive search accounts only for the competence in creation, not the creative part. Perhaps small short-sighted steps cannot lead to really big results in principle.

They certainly can, and the process of evolution provides a good example. Of course, evolution is not a deliberate search process. Evolution simply happens. But intention aside, evolution does proceed by a sort of progressive search, within which occurs a sampling search – another way the two can mix. In the sampling-search part, generation by generation, random variation within a species yields subtly different candidates for survival. The natural selection of survival allows those most fit to produce more offspring. Here the progressive search begins to operate. The characteristics that improved the parents' chances of survival tend to reappear in the offspring. The genes preserve the progress, the differences that helped the creature to survive.

Is the result really inventive? Well, it has invented ourselves, and indirectly everything we invent. It's produced the many marvels of adaptation, marvels that certainly would be called inventive if anything but a blind process had yielded them. There is, for instance, the orchid that mimics the sexual characteristics of a female bee. The orchid guarantees its pollination by male bees through this bit of seduction. If that isn't inventive, what is? And yet the stepwise process proceeds blindly in the most extreme sense. The standard for uphill versus down is simple as can be – mere survival, with no specific concern for intelligence, aesthetics, and so on. But here we are. Along with scorpions and bloodworms, of course.

In fact, Donald Campbell has argued that only blind variation and selective retention of progress according to some criterion can explain real innovation in the world of plants and animals or in the world of human invention. Whether this really holds true depends, I think, on what one means by "real innovation." The stricter one wants to be there, the fewer processes besides blind variation and selective retention would do. In human creative activity, trial and error with preservation of those trials that produce progress does seem important. And probably the more extremely creative the results, the less creators know exactly what they are doing.

In summary, the hill-climbing metaphor expresses vividly the idea that small shortsighted steps can lead to creative results. Progressive search offers an alternative to other accounts of creative activity, an explanation that sometimes applies more and sometimes less of course. Hill climbing contrasts with an insight account of creativity, where the essential idea of a creation comes abruptly through the operation of insight. Hill climbing also contrasts with a sampling account of creation where sheer persistence eventually produces a useful idea. Hill climbing is on the one hand a process more "on call" than insight and, on the other, a process more efficient than sampling.

So much for the case in favor. A very important reservation is long overdue. Despite the important and pervasive role of progressive search in creating, progressive search does not guarantee success, even when the maker can take the individual uphill steps. Although the maker certainly will get to the top of the hill by going uphill, that hill may not rise high enough. The higher summit the maker seeks may lie three miles away. In more technical terms, a local maximum is not necessarily a global maximum. Also, remember that fog. The climber on one hill can't tell whether there is a higher peak nearby.

What kinds of difficulties in creating amount to local maxima? Consider a situation where an only fair solution resists improvement. Suppose you have developed a design for a logo. The idea seems good. Some promising sketches are on the table. But try as you might, you can't achieve the simple appearance you want. Giving up the idea is difficult, though. You have worked hard to get this far. In fact, a local maximum has captured you. The real need is for a somewhat different approach. You need to find a new hill to climb.

This caveat certainly does not mean that hill climbing loses its pertinence. Granted, alone it will not explain creating. But the fact remains that makers commit most of their time to progressive search in one way or another. Almost any activity of scope depends primarily on preservation and extension of progress rather than a repeated starting afresh. If hill climbing will not do it all, it will do a lot.

          Perceptual Hill Climbing

I have said little about the rapid processes of perception and insight discussed earlier. Instead, various metaphors of search have explained something about how makers organize their activities over time to achieve a creative outcome. I've even contrasted a progressive-search explanation with one in terms of insight.

But in fact hill-climbing activities occur in perception and in insight, which often depends on perceptual and perceptionlike processes. This is worth knowing about because it means that the problems of local maxima might occur in insight. Let's consider how hill climbing appears in perception and what this suggests about insight.

It's not difficult to find hill-climbing processes in your own seeing. Here are some simple examples that have nothing to

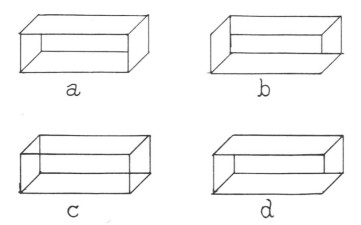

do with invention in the usual sense. Consider drawings *a* and *b*. Both show rectangular shapes, one open downward to the left, the other upward to the right. Drawing *c* is different, though; it is ambiguous. Sometimes it will appear like a transparent version of *a,* opening downward to the left, but often it will "reverse" to resemble a transparent version of *b*. After a while, it will reverse again, back to its original appearance.

These reversals by themselves hint at a hill-climbing process in perception. Perhaps for the transparent drawing *c* there are two local maxima – two ways of making complete sense of the drawing. Sometimes perception climbs to one of those maxima and sometimes to the other. But there's good reason to be cautious about this suggestion. Just because drawing *c* has two appearances, that need not imply a hill-climbing process. Perhaps you alternately recognize two distinct wholes, rather than coming to one and then the other in some stepwise way.

But drawing *d* shows that hill climbing does occur. Drawing *d* combines the left end of *a* and the right end of *b*. Examine it. You will probably experience something like this. As you glance at the left end, it appears much like the left end of *a*. As you move your eyes casually rightward, something goes wrong. The sense of shape shifts abruptly, and you find yourself seeing something like the right end of *b*. As your gaze moves leftward again, the same happens in reverse.

What does this imply? If your perceptual equipment was trying merely to recognize *d* wholistically, as *a* or as *b*, without any hill-climbing process, there would be simple failure. Instead, there is partial success, success that can't carry over as attention shifts to the other end of *d*. That implies hill climbing. Apparently, in this case the perceiver begins with a local interpretation and attempts to extend that interpretation to other parts of the figure. But when the interpretation isn't consistent with the other parts, a new local interpretation suggested by the other parts supersedes it.

Since hill climbing occurs in perceiving *d*, perhaps it does in perceiving *a* and *b* also. Let's take a more careful look. Gaze steadily at the upper right corner of *a* and you will see it start to reverse. But that seeing gets suppressed quickly because it won't extend to the other parts of *a*. A long look at the lower left corner of *b* will reveal the same effect.

It's very comforting that one sees both appearances of figure *c*. That shows that the hill-climbing process spontaneously starts over every now and then. It has a chance to locate a maximal solution other than the one it found in the first place. For unambiguous drawings like *a* and *b*, these further tries either produce the same result or simply fail. But for *c*, you discover the two appearances. This doesn't always happen, however. Recent research on just such figures shows that a person not already acquainted with the possibility of alternative seeings may very well never experience them. Such a viewer is like the person at the top of the hill in the fog, never suspecting there may be another peak nearby.

Even when one perception does not fit all that well, a shift to another may come slowly. An interesting experiment from the early 1950s demonstrated such an effect. The investigators projected slides of scenes at successively sharper degrees of focus. During each stage from the most blurred to the most focused presentation, the subjects guessed at the contents of the pictures. The investigators discovered that the subjects became trapped by their own earlier hypotheses. Comparison subjects who only viewed the pictures at a given degree of focus correctly identified the slides more frequently at that degree that did the subjects who had made earlier, mistaken guesses.

These examples of perception suggest something important about creative process. They warn that problems of local maxima probably will limit the reliability of insight. Insight, remember, depends on rapid reflexive processes of perception and understanding. These processes commonly involve a sequence of partly or wholly unconscious events as things fall into place. Falling into place is a kind of hill-climbing process; the various elements of the situation become assembled into a coherent meaning or pattern. The danger, of course, is that there may be more than one way for a situation to fall into place. Each amounts to a local maximum, one way of fairly comprehensively perceiving the situation. But some ways may be better than others.

I'm inclined to think that the problem of local maxima in insight is even more serious than in the more extended kind of thinking discussed earlier. Insight has a compelling quality that makes doubting an insight and considering alternatives especially difficult. "Seeing is believing." Just that sort of convincingness comes with insight as well as ordinary sight. But ordinary seeing shouldn't always be believing, as magicians demonstrate over and over. Neither should insight.

Whatever the degree of the problem, the way to avoid local maxima in insight is much the same as in more extended thinking: find a new hill to climb. In the case of insight, this means trying to discern new patterns and significances in a situation, trying to get the parts to fall into place in a new way.

Revised proposition: Progressive search explains much of the accomplishment of creative activity. But the hill climbing of progressive search may not get the maker as high as the maker needs to go, because of the problem of local maxima. Effective creative activity must cope with local maxima in both sudden insight and prolonged effort.

MAXIMIZING AND SATISFICING

How high is up? The answer depends on the activity. In thought, up is forever. In a manned rocket, up is the moon so far. In an airplane, the edge of the atmosphere; for a man on foot, the top of Everest. For a hill climber in a hill-climbing metaphor, up is the top of the highest hill.

But how high is up *enough?* We've taken it for granted that creation is an effort to maximize. The maker seeks the best possible outcome. How high is up enough? – as high as possible.

Proposition: Whatever the problems of local maxima, creators typically try to maximize.

But in creative or any other activities, do people really behave that way? Indeed, *can* people really behave that way?

Herbert Simon, a psychologist interested in computer models of human thought, for a number of years has defended quite a different theory. Simon argues that in general people do not so much maximize as *satisfice*. (Simon uses the term "optimize" rather than "maximize." I'll say "maximize" to convey the same thing and keep the hill-climbing metaphor prominent.) By satisfice, Simon means that people strive until they achieve so much and then stop. They work to satisfy standards of adequacy. In hill climbing, this amounts to ascending until you attain a certain altitude, but not necessarily the summit. Simon's claim applies to sampling searches as well as to progressive searches. In a sampling search, satisficing is searching until an alternative appears that exceeds some threshold of acceptability.

Simon's claim makes good sense in many everyday problem-solving activities. The manager of a factory probably cannot find the most efficient way to run the operation. Too many variables confuse matters too much. But an adequate way can be found. The shopper probably does not canvass every store in town for the cheapest price on a new washer. But he or she looks to find an acceptable price. The designer of armchairs does not strive for perfect comfort. What would that be? But the designer aims for a very comfortable chair, knowing customers will be happy with that. And so on.

However, Simon's assertion does not seem to fit so well certain activities, activities that stress a quest for perfection. Athletic and artistic endeavors usually are thought of as perfection-seeking. Of course, perfection may prove elusive, even unattainable. Just what perfection would amount to might be unclear. But even so, in such activities people might act as if seeking the fastest time or the purest expression in a perfectionist way. Perhaps people's behavior in athletics and the arts would show that Simon's claim doesn't hold true universally.

Consider athletics. Perfection seems to be a constant demand. Championship performance requires continuous discipline and effort. The feats by their nature involve attaining extremes – the briefest times, the greatest weights, the highest heights, and so on. In athletics, if anywhere, serious seekers ought to be maximizers.

Or should they? Logically, victory in an athletic event does not require doing one's best. It simply requires doing better than anyone else in the event. Even breaking a record does not demand the best – only the best so far. The athlete need only exceed any prior performance. In other words, the rules of athletics require satisficing – achieving some threshold of performance. This does not imply that the athlete doesn't maximize, but does imply that an athlete doesn't have to.

A recent study of footracing suggests that indeed runners do not maximize. If runners trained and ran as hard as they could, record times should approximate the limit of human capacity. Runners at various distances should break the current records more and more rarely. On the contrary, an historical review revealed that records had been, and still were being, broken at about the same rate. Runners were steadily improving their performances and not approaching any obvious limit. For this and other reasons, the investigators concluded that runners strove not for human limits of performance but for the latest record. Records

fell periodically as the most competitive athletes worked just a little harder to surpass them. This, of course, is satisficing, albeit
with a very high threshold for success.

What about the arts? There again perfectionism is expected.
The poet presumably labors for the *mot juste* and works until
every word is right. The pianist polishes the performance until
every note sounds clearly, expressively, and correctly. And so
on.

Here we don't have a study analogous to the one for athletics.
But merely a little more thought reveals a little less perfectionism.
Consider the composer. Surely the composer always might make
this passage or that just a little more telling, or perhaps a lot more.
If all outright flaws have been eliminated, more expression, more
intensity, more unity might yet be introduced. And if the composer does not see how to, who is to say but that the composer
does not see far enough? However effective the passage may
seem, there is no way to know whether the passage is as effective
as possible. The circumstances allow satisficing but not maximizing.

This concerns effort on an individual work. In the course of a
career, quite likely factors similar to those governing the runners
influence the efforts of an artists. Artists who "make it" profes-
sionally probably feel considerably less motivated to refine or
renew a manner of work. A few exceptional individuals may
achieve more than one artistic breakthrough. But then a few exceptional runners achieve more than one record. Neither occurs
commonly.

But perfectionism seems so obvious in athletics and art. How
can Herbert Simon be right and this simple intuition wrong? The
answer is that we tend to measure things on relative rather than
absolute scales. Certainly, the excellent artist or athlete strives for
perfection compared to the Sunday painter or jogger. Such a person works much harder and examines outcomes more critically.
Such a person does anything that obviously needs doing. The
less committed person probably does not do many things that obviously need doing, lacking the heart for it. In all these senses, the
committed artist or athlete is a perfectionist. But these are relative
senses and "perfect" is not really a relative word. In the last
analysis, even the committed person has to satisfice.

In fact, perhaps the lay public and the less able artists believe more in the perfectability of art than the best artists do. Some information suggesting just this comes from the previously mentioned study of male art students conducted by Jacob Getzels and Mihaly Csikszentmihalyi. Each participant in the study first completed a still life for the investigators based on an arrangement he made from a collection of objects provided. Afterwards the artist answered several questions, among them, "Could any of the elements in your drawing be eliminated or altered without destroying its character?" The investigators wanted to know whether a student artist considered his work to be fixed or subject to change and possible improvement.

Getzels' and Csikszentmihalyi's results revealed a fascinating relationship between participants' answers to this question and artistic ability. A panel of judges rated each participant's work. The analysis showed that an artist who said his work might be changed achieved higher ratings on originality and overall. Also, Getzels and Csikszentmihalyi conducted a follow-up study, assessing the participants' success as artists seven years later. More success came to those replying that the work done for the investigators might be changed. In summary, Getzels and Csikszentmihalyi found that the artists rated best were not those who imagined they had produced fixed and finished works, but those who recognized the possibility of change.

 I'm Going to Catch You
Not Maximizing

That should *not* be difficult, considering all the above. Here is a simple example. Right now you're probably sitting down reading this. But most likely you're not sitting nearly as comfortably as you might. To test my claim, try to get more comfortable. Shift around here and there until you feel as comfortable as possible. You probably found that you were a long way from maximizing your comfort.

Now the conclusion is that you weren't maximizing, not that you ought to have been. Sitting comfortably isn't so easy, in fact.

One can't stay in the same position too long. One needs to shift to another, also comfortable, position to keep comfortable. To take care to do this well would require considerable effort. In other words, here is one of those summits not worth climbing. You'd be so busy keeping comfortable, you wouldn't have time to read my book.

Revised proposition: Search in creative and other activities typically satisfices rather than maximizes because typically one can't maximize, doesn't know how, or wouldn't gain overall.

SEARCH IN SUMMARY

Certainly I haven't told the whole story about search in these few pages. The metaphor of search provides many ways to discuss human invention. The reader interested in a somewhat more detailed, rather different, and still quite accessible account could look to Herbert Simon's little book *The Sciences of the Artificial*. The more aggressive reader could approach Allen Newell's and Herbert Simon's *Human Problem Solving*, where they discuss the mental processes involved in solving cryptarithmetic and logical problems and in playing chess, and present a general theory of problem solving. A pervasive metaphor in these books is problem solving as a search through a space whose structure is determined by the nature of the problem. The concepts of sampling search and progressive search used here are very general. Investigators such as Newell and Simon have described in much more detail the organization of search for some particular tasks.

But whatever the further story of search, I hope I've made clear how search helps to explain creative outcomes. Search does so by being intrinsically goal-oriented, in line with the teleological view of creating. Search does so by explaining how some of the quality (including originality) gets put into the outcome. In general, search occurs because the maker cannot devise a satisfactory outcome in a simple act of production. The maker has to produce alternatives and select among them, as in sampling search, or produce successive improvements, as in progressive search, or combine sampling and progressive search in various ways. So a creative outcome depends as much on the maker's critical abilities to choose the better options and distinguish genuine improvements as on the maker's actual productive abilities.

However, a kind of paradox appears in the several sorts of search discussed: search seems to be trying to get rid of itself. The first section of this chapter discussed various tactics of free search, where the results of searching were achieved without item-by-item search. The second section revealed that findings on fluency do not for the most part recommend searching long; being clear about objectives and trying to produce high-quality ideas at the outset yield results as good or better, and more efficiently. Also, hill climbing preserves progress and eliminates some of the wasted effort of sampling search. Satisficing rather than maximizing not only is necessary in many circumstances but is economical in many more. Maximizing doesn't pay for itself, and satisficing saves the extra search that maximizing would have required.

In a sense none of this should surprise us. Naturally human effort tends toward efficiency. But in another sense perhaps we should be surprised. The literature and popular ideas about creativity often emphasize fluency, flexibility, brainstorming, and other behaviors that amount to extra search. They do so in the belief that extra search now costs less in the end. But the themes I've discussed reveal few signs of extra search now costing less in the end. Instead, it seems that one should view tactics of extra search rather critically. Certainly a deliberate effort to brainstorm up some alternatives or to abandon a seemingly fruitful approach just to explore others sometimes can be crucial. However, on the whole, such actions aren't what gets the work of creating done.

The lesson of looking at search seems to be that creative behavior advances toward less search for a given accomplishment rather than extra search. This doesn't mean that skilled and committed makers work less, of course. They reinvest their gains. With the greater facility of less search for a given result, they try to accomplish more.

6

PLANS DOWN DEEP

The late mathematician Norbert Wiener was a remarkably gifted individual, a child prodigy and a fertile researcher who founded the field of cybernetics and made other important advances. A professor for most of his career at Massachusetts Institute of Technology, Wiener earned a reputation for his mental agility. Such reputations naturally nourish many dubious stories. Here is one. It seems that a student approached the savant, complaining of trouble with an integration problem. "Can you show me how to do it?" the student asked. Wiener wrote the problem on the blackboard, stared up at the ceiling a moment, and wrote $\pi/4$ next to it. "Well, all right," said the student. "But can you show me *how* to do it?" Wiener again stared at the ceiling, and then below his original answer he wrote the same thing once more. "There," he said. "You see, I did it another way."

Certainly not so, this story remains true to Wiener's talents. Another remarkable mind was that of the mathematician A. C. Aitken. As well as being a productive researcher, Aitken could perform arithmetic calculations in his head with startling efficiency. Here are two examples quoted from an article on Aitken's ability:

> He is asked to express as a decimal the fraction $4/47$. He is silent for four seconds, then begins to speak the answer at a nearly uniform rate of one digit every three-quarters of a second. "Point 0851063829787234042553191 4, that's about as far as I can carry it." The total time between the presentation of the problem and this moment is twenty-four seconds. He discusses the problem for one minute and then continues the answer at the same rate as before. "Yes, 191489, I can get that." He pauses for five seconds. "361702127659574458, now that is the repeating point. It starts again at 085. So if that is forty-six places, I am right." The second example concerns a more difficult problem. He is asked to give the square root of 851. After a short silence, he gives 29.17. Then, at irregular intervals, he supplies further digits of the answer. By the time fifteen seconds have elapsed, he has given 29.17190429.

Such feats need to be explained in any account of creativity. Of course, they are not by themselves significant creative achievements. But they reveal abilities that helped Wiener and Aitkin to pursue their serious research, and abilities somewhat at odds with the previous chapter. There, small steps over an extended period let the maker do piecemeal what the maker could not do at once. This remains true even for Wiener and Aitken, but with a qualification: they were able to take much larger steps in the first place. With those larger steps, they could cover the same distance with less effort, or a greater distance with the same effort.

In this chapter, we seek an understanding of such ability. Actually I want to put off the question of underlying mechanism for a while and first examine the relationship between mastery and fluency. The examples of Wiener, Aitken, and similarly fluent individuals in other fields promote an image of the very creative individual as very fluent. But does fluency always accompany mastery? Some evidence suggests that fluency depends on the maker's having a large repertoire of unconscious units and patterns. In a way, such units and patterns are stereotypes. So the paradox of creative activity based on a repertoire of stereotypes will need untangling. The idea of "plans down deep" also leads to a particular question about creative process: Is there any down-deep plan for creative behavior in general? Oddly enough, despite the variety of creative activities, and in a limited sense, perhaps such a plan does exist.

FLUENCY AND MASTERY

I mentioned that the feats of Wiener and Aitken were not in themselves especially creative. Here is one that seems unimpeachably so. This story is told about Mozart's composition of the overture to *Don Giovanni*:

> It is generally esteemed the best of his overtures; yet it was only composed the night previous to the first representation, after the general rehearsal had taken place. About eleven o'clock in the evening, when he retired to his apartment, he desired his wife to make him some punch, and to stay with him, in order to keep him awake. She accordingly began to tell him fairy tales, and odd stories, which made him laugh till the tears came. The punch, however, made him so drowsy that he could only go on while his wife was talking, and dropped asleep as soon as she ceased. The efforts

which he made to keep himself awake, the continual alternation of sleep and watching, so fatigued him, that his wife persuaded him to take some rest, promising to awake him in an hour's time. He slept so profoundly that she suffered him to repose for two hours. At five o'clock in the morning she awoke him. He had appointed the music copyists to come at seven, and by the time they arrived the overture was finished. They had scarcely time to write out the copies necessary for the orchestra, and the musicians were obliged to play it without a rehearsal. Some persons pretend that they can discover in this overture the passages where Mozart dropped asleep, and those where he suddenly awoke again.

Tales of such prodigious achievement are endlessly fascinating. They feed our popular concept of genius. I can't think of a better example than Mozart's composition of the overture to *Don Giovanni* to illustrate one of our favorite ideas about creativity:

Proposition: The master of a creative activity is fluent.

And yet tales such as this one provide very shaky evidence. To mention a couple of doubts, how well does this and a few similar anecdotes reflect Mozart's workaday compositional practices? Naturally, the most impressive episodes are those that get told. Then there is the old matter of Mozart's memory. Various anecdotes suggest that Mozart possessed a superb memory for music and used it to develop compositions in his head. So, on that urgent evening before the debut, was Mozart busy composing or remembering?

And consider Beethoven, whose sketchbooks show that he composed with painful deliberation. He seems to be a counterexample to the above notion, an acknowledged master who did not produce fluently. However, the case against Beethoven's fluency needs qualifying as much as the case for Mozart's. Remember, Beethoven improvised with ease. So he was fluent on occasion. Perhaps we ought to consider Beethoven an odd exception to, rather than a refutation of, the proposition.

I mention these complications not to try to decide the issue but to emphasize how little a couple of stories prove. Individual examples, even assuming they are reliable, only show what sometimes happens, not what generally happens. A sound conclusion demands some sort of survey.

A survey is just what I'll report shortly. But before that, another job has to be done. We have to get clear about what fluency means here. It will help to say what fluency does not mean. Fluency here does not mean fluency as discussed in the last chapter, where subjects in experiments tried to devise phrases meeting certain conditions. That could be called *test fluency*. Also, fluency here does not mean fluency at the expense of quality. Anyone can produce a rapid sequence of sounds at a piano, if no more than that needs to be done. Finally, fluency here does not mean just fluency during the ongoing creative process. We could call that sort of fluency *process fluency*. Process fluency occurs when, however many hours are expended or revisions undertaken, the making process is fluent; the maker never is baffled or blocked.

Perhaps most masters most of the time do work that way. Or perhaps not. But the present puzzle concerns something still a little different: *product fluency*. Product fluency occurs when a quality product emerges quickly, with little revision. The issue is: Are masters usually product fluent, as Mozart might have been that night?

Biographical information about many makers helps somewhat. The question to ask is whether product fluency varies widely among established creators. Presumably, if extreme mastery requires great fluency, then near mastery ought to require considerable fluency. One ought to find that most makers of reputation are rather product fluent. I've casually surveyed a number of biographical sources for information about fluency. The sources have included biographies and biographical episodes about artists and scientists. Poets received more methodical attention. In certain sources, poets have described how quickly they write and how much revising they usually do. Simple ratings of such remarks on a "little-medium-much" scale provided for a rough tally of how many poets worked how hard.

The results of all this were very clear. Most established makers labored for their achievements. Only a small percentage seemed especially product fluent. Apparently, quality demands much of the maker. It would be easy to react to this conclusion with, "Of course! What else would you expect?" Naturally, to those already convinced, such results will not sound like news. But, remember, some people have supposed that talented makers produce effortlessly. This argument is for them.

Having said that, let me be cautious again and stress that the information found in biographical sources certainly could be better. Usually the evidence is anecdotal. Rarely does the maker report any exact information about hours spent and quantity produced. In fact, conceptual problems interfere with even attempting such a report. In many fields, there is no good way of measuring the extent of a product. What, for instance, is a fluent scientist? One who writes papers quickly? But the papers make up only a part of the work of science. One who formulates theories quickly? But how "long" is one person's theory compared with another's? In areas like literature, the question becomes somewhat more sensible. We could compare number of revisions or production rates in words per minute. Even so, this risks comparing people who write in more and less demanding ways. Thirty words of *Finnegans Wake* and thirty words of *Little Women* are very different endeavors.

Subject to these reservations, data gathered during my studies of poets thinking aloud provided an opportunity to test the fluency-mastery link more directly. Did the poets judged to write better poetry write more fluently? The question makes sense despite the conclusion above that most poets work hard. It still might be true, as a matter of degree, that the better poets worked less hard per poem. Since the poets usually did not complete a poem during their thinking-aloud sessions, the test employed the poets' estimates about how long they typically worked on poems and how many drafts they wrote. The distinction between professionals and amateurs and the ratings of sample poems by a panel of judges supplied two standards of quality to be compared to reported fluency. As in the biographical work, fluency varied widely and most poets worked hard. But the main point was this. The relevant statistics revealed no relationship between degree of product fluency and either professionalism or judged quality.

I've stressed the problems of measuring fluency. Nevertheless,

I think that the consistency of the evidence overwhelms the reservations. At every turn, in every respect, no relationship between mastery and product fluency appears. Perhaps more data and more statistics would reveal a weak trend of some sort. But clearly no strong association exists between the two. Instead, there are all kinds of makers: product fluent and effective, not fluent but still very effective, fluent and ineffective, not fluent and ineffective. Everything that might happen does.

That should settle the matter, but in fact a puzzle remains. Yes, the results contradict the relationship between mastery and fluency we might have expected, but they also contradict another exactly opposite relationship we also might have expected. It's worth examining why that should happen.

Contrary proposition: The master of a creative activity is not very product fluent because the master works harder to achieve higher-quality products.

Now this is just common sense. The proposition states the natural everyday relationship between effort and results. In fact, that relationship opposes the original proposition, the proposition based on the popular image of mastery. Both are plausible in different ways. But if the first notion isn't correct, why doesn't this one prove out instead? Why don't the better makers have to exert that much more effort to achieve their better outcomes?

A concept from the previous chapter supplies something of an explanation – satisficing. People typically work to exceed some standard or other, not to maximize quality. This suggests that the better makers are not so much those who labor more as those who somehow maintain higher standards. Some do this by working harder, while others do it by greater critical and productive abilities. Different makers solve the problem of achieving quality in different ways, with the result that some spend more and some less time.

All this helps to explain the relationship, or rather the nonrelationship, between mastery and product fluency. But there is one further assumption I want to question. Throughout this discussion, I've taken it for granted that fluency comes with the person; it is the maker who is more or less product fluent.

Hidden proposition: Degree of product fluency is a characteristic of the person.

How brash! This notion implies that Mozart, given the experience, would fluently compose something like Beethoven's Ninth Symphony. It implies that Beethoven would labor through the composition of something like Mozart's overture. And, of course, maybe each would. But clearly, just what a maker is making could have much to do with the degree of fluency. Quite likely, different genres and styles make different demands, even on the genius. I suspect that true product fluency reflects a fortunate match between the nature of the person and the nature of the product.

 Going in Circles

Here is a simple experiment exploring how the nature of a product affects the opportunities for fluency. The goal is just to draw a neat circle with smooth lines. Make the circle about two inches wide. Find a pencil and several pieces of paper – you may need to try many times.

First of all, draw several circles moving your hand carefully. Try to make the circles as round and smooth as possible. In fact, probably they won't look very satisfactory. Trembling of the hand makes the lines rough.

Now try to draw several circles moving your hand as quickly as possible.

The quality of line will improve. The ballistic motion of the hand produces a smooth trace. However, you probably had difficulty making the circles close.

Now try an intermediate pace – fast enough to achieve that smooth line but slow enough to have a better chance of closing the circle. Try to draw circles in single, moderately paced circular motions. Do several. With a little luck, or a page or two of circles, you will probably get quite a nice one.

There's nothing especially profound about this. In general, one can expect any task to have an ideal pace. A very rapid effort will introduce errors. One either has to try again or, if possible, to edit the original result extensively. A very slow pace at best will waste time. Also, a slow pace actually may cause errors that wouldn't otherwise appear, like shaky lines in drawing the circles slowly.

Somewhere between the extremes comes the perfect pace. With significant activities, as with the trivial one explored here, that ideal pace depends on many factors specific to the situation. Of course, the ideal pace may or may not be product fluent. Sometimes it is better to produce considerable error, since some kinds of errors are more readily fixed later than avoided earlier.

Revised proposition: Most makers are not product fluent. Even so, degrees of fluency exist, and more or less fluency does not seem to relate either way to more or less quality in products. Also, product fluency has less to do with the giftedness of the person and more with the genre and style of the product than is usually thought.

HOW FLUENCY HAPPENS

In exploring the link between product fluency and mastery, the nature of product fluency itself was left unexamined. I merely allowed that some masters worked in a product fluent way, although some did not. Now even though mastery does not require product fluency, product fluency remains a remarkable phenomenon, one that needs an explanation. Taken at face value, product fluency seems to mean that a maker creates a high-quality product from scratch with little revision and about as quickly as would be physically comfortable. The rate at which a maker can realize a product comfortably puts a natural upper limit on product fluency. For example, poets only could write poetry as fast as they could put the words on paper.

Proposition: The most fluent creators routinely produce about as fast as they can comfortably realize the product physically.

Is this so? First, take the question of production rate. Do the most fluent poets routinely write poetry as fast as they write? The evidence says otherwise. One among the twenty professional and amateur poets that helped in my study reported writing poetry routinely at a rate of about a half a pentameter line per minute. The figure does not imply that the poet steadily produced a line every two minutes but means that the finished poem required an average of two minutes per line. The other nineteen poets in my sample all wrote more slowly, many of them much more slowly.

The late poet L. E. Sissman, in print and in an interview I had with him some years ago, reported writing at the same rate: a pentameter line every two minutes. He also explained that he revised what he wrote very little, adjusting something every five lines or so. Most of what he produced was published. However, one qualification had to be made. Usually, when he sat down to write, he already had thought out how the poem might begin and end, not line by line but in a general way. So Sissman did not do all the work of writing at the writing table.

Sometimes, although not usually, enough information occurs in biographical sources to allow estimating a production rate. Reputedly one of the most fluent poets was Lord Byron. Some historical details allow estimating a plausible rate for one of Byron's most quickly written tales in verse, *The Corsair*. Again, the result is about a half a line per minute. Allen Ginsberg, a champion of writing as fluently and as much out of one's consciousness as possible, wrote his well-known long poem *Kaddish* in one intense period. The average rate – half a line per minute.

In summary, the most fluent poets do not write poetry as fast as they can readily write. Far from it. About a half line per minute seems to be the usual limit for consistent production on poem after poem or for an extended work. (Naturally, brief episodes of faster production might occur.) Note also that a half line per minute allows the poet time to think of alternatives, work longer on the stubborn lines, and so on. Certainly poems written at this rate need not have been written without revision or without sorting out alternatives, at least mentally. They need not have been written off the top of the head. Indeed, the still extant first manuscript of Byron's *The Corsair* shows considerable editing.

Such evidence might mean that extreme product fluency does not occur at all. But of course it does, and in works of unquestionable quality. Extreme product fluency can be found in traditions of oral epic, poetry sung by a bard. The *Odyssey* and the *Iliad* are two poems that were sung and were transcribed at some time to becomed part of written literature. Beginning in the 1930s, Albert Lord researched such a tradition in Yugoslavia and ultimately recorded its character in his *The Singer of Tales*. Lord's findings vouch for the fluency of poetry sung in an oral tradition, revealing a routine production rate far faster than that for written poetry. The poets Lord studied performed at rates from five to ten pentameter lines per minute, rates ten to twenty times faster than that of the fastest poets mentioned above.

Lord also testifies that, in some sense, the singer of tales sings from scratch. The oral poet does not repeat a memorized performance. He genuinely improvises. The poet will not sing the same tale exactly the same on any two occasions. For example, he may present a longer, more elaborated, and ornamented version to one group and a shortened version to another. All this sounds very much like an ideal example of the notion we began with. If only we could understand how the oral poet accomplishes his feat, we could understand how true product fluency can occur.

We can understand; Lord has laid the matter out. When we read his account, we discover that the oral poet, although he does not repeat memorized works, also does not produce quite as much from scratch as one might think. The oral poet relies on prefabricated units and patterns in several ways. First, he uses a vocabulary of standard phrases, lines, and half lines that fit into different tales equally well. For example, the poet will have a stock of lines to describe the maiden's loveliness or the hero's armor. The poet will sing about these themes out of that stock, whoever the maiden or hero. Often, for the sake of flexibility, these units have a variable element – a place where the singer can fill in the name of the current hero, for instance. Also, the same scenes similarly organized appear in different sagas – scenes like the wedding feast, the mustering of the army, and so on. In addition, various rhythmic and other patterns provide further structure guiding the singer's performance.

Contemporary psychology calls such repeated units and patterns *schemata*. A schema is a mental structure that allows a person to perceive or act effectively by anticipating the organization of what the person apprehends or does, so the person needn't function as much from scratch. One can think of schemata more informally as plans – plans for perceiving and producing. Indeed, plans not unlike those Lord identifies can figure very deliberately in creating. Rhyme schemes and refrain lines for poems are obvious examples. But the plans the oral poet relies upon operate mostly unconsciously. Lord emphasizes that the oral poet appears to know little about the means of his performance. For instance, he lacks the concepts of word and line, unless he has learned them from exposure to writing, and his closest analogous concept, meaning something like "utterance," can refer to anything from a word to a line to a whole song. If such naïveté about a very sophisticated performance is hard to accept, we can look to ourselves for a partial parallel. Suppose we'd had no English classes. Then what would we know about the rules of grammar? Yet our spontaneous speech follows those rules. The experienced oral poet sings proper songs as innocently as we speak proper sentences.

In fact, we ought to remember that the oral poet's accomplishment is not as remarkable as it might at first seem, because all of us are improvisers much of the time, in ways we take for granted. We all create appropriate behavior spontaneously in conversations and other everyday situations. This can only happen with the help of schemata analogous to those used by the oral poet. For example, in spontaneous conversation we depend not only on grammar but on many stock phrases and, more generally, stock responses to typical situations, as in saying hello, talking about the weather, asking "How have you been?" and following through on the standard "Fine! How about you?" conversation. Of course, conversations needn't be as schematized as oral epics, since there's less pressure. The speakers need not speak elegantly or aptly each time they open their mouths. Nonetheless, casual observation as well as research in a contemporary discipline called discourse analysis reveals that conversation is highly structured. Language performance aside, we get about our familiar environment with the help of mental maps. We cook and dine according to formula, from the rules and strategies of games like bridge and chess to the informal but just as regular rituals of having a picnic or attending a football game. Everywhere one looks there is pattern, pattern, pattern. Paradoxically, only this makes behavior reasonably spontaneous. Otherwise, our familiar activities would always be as tentative and labored as our novel ones.

As to behavior usually considered creative, an improvised performance like that of the oral poet requires the most in the way of supporting schemata. But more considered productions depend on schemata too. Both the ordinary rules of grammar and the plans for structuring narrative guide the work of the story writer. Indeed, nowadays the "grammar" of stories and how people acquire it are lively topics of psychological inquiry. E. H. Gombrich has argued in his *The Arts and Illusion* that the historical development of Western realistic art can be understood as an evolution of various schemata for picturing. Gombrich notes such evidence as the guidebooks instructing artists how to render various types of noses and ears, the styles characteristic of different schools and eras, and the way expectations produce inaccuracies, as when in an early drawing of a whale the flippers were drawn as ears.

So the concept of schemata provides an explanation for product fluency, not only the extreme product fluency found in oral poetry and other improvisational arts, but the lesser product fluency exhibited by the most facile of writers of poetry and the most facile practitioners in other artistic and scientific disciplines. The last section proposed that product fluency depends as much on the style as on the maker. In terms of schemata, that suggestion translates into something like this: product fluency requires a relatively schematized style where schemata can help a lot and, of course, requires a maker with the schemata.

To say as much is to challenge again the idea of unconscious creativity. Notions like the still-waters theory or the blitzkrieg theory proposed that powerful unconscious mechanisms fabricate creations and deliver them to consciousness. But here it seems that products which usually emerge relatively complete do so not because of a remarkably creative unconscious, but because of an unconscious repertoire of – well, one might even say stereotypes.

In the next section I will discuss the paradoxical relationship of stereotypes to creating. For now, it's worth noticing that there is a more positive way to think of these stereotypes. Lord's explanation for fluency exposes a very real and rich mental resource. The potential of product fluency exists whenever experience has provided a person with a repertoire of plans. The oral poet requires years of listening and practice to get started. But for some activities, this is not as much so. Drama makes a good example. Where in many art forms you begin naively, in drama you start with a repertoire of behaviors from everyday living.

In saying this, I'm certainly not suggesting that acting in general and dramatic improvisation in particular require no special skill or experience. Certainly the actor has to learn much particular to acting. Also, using old schemata in a new context can pose many problems. But I do want to stress the distinction between acquiring new schemata for a new purpose and applying old ones to the new purpose. Somewhat different sorts of learning are involved. Since, in practice, any activity involves a mix of new and old plans, this means that we need to try in different ways to get the best of both.

 Returning the Widget

Here is a simple personal experiment in trying to use old schemata. You can demonstrate your own dramatic resources by returning the widget. If you have a tape recorder, record your speech during the experiment.

Prepare the recorder, turn it on to record, and continue.

Suppose you purchased a widget at the local hardware store. You took it home, tried it out, and found it defective. So you returned it and they sent it out for repairs. Back the widget came two weeks later, you picked it up, you tried it out again and still it didn't work. Now you've gone back to the store. You're about to speak to a clerk you haven't seen before concerning the widget.

One more thing: you're a timid person.

Now say aloud what you would say. Don't stop to plan. Never mind if you don't have a recorder. You already know how to do this. You already have the unconscious plan. Do it.

Now try it again when you are: angry; flustered and busy; important and authoritarian; easy-going.

If you have a recorder, play back your speech and observe how it sounds. Don't expect Laurence Olivier. However, you probably can hear easily the different personalities and moods you tried to project.

Some people enjoy this exercise but others have difficulty with it. They feel silly and self-conscious. They can't seem to persuade those covert plans to work. Theatrical training ought to, and does, include some concern with the problem of getting covert plans to operate. For instance, in a contemporary text on acting, Robert Benedetti advises that going through the motions of expressing a feeling helps one to experience the feeling more authentically. The aim, of course, is not for the actor to savor emotions but to express the emotions better. Benedetti writes: "Our aim in 'doing the act' and letting the 'feeling follow' is to allow the internalization of our action to become *self-generating*. Our basic actions lead us in turn to fuller actions, which become the true extensions of the actions provided by the play." There is delicious paradox in this advice. By going through the superficial motions, you help yourself to achieve effective expression. As in the story of Pygmalion, the false turns real – or at least realer.

If you had trouble with returning the widget try again, following Benedetti's advice. Go through the motions and attempt to surrender to them so that you begin to function more spontaneously.

I've spoken so far about borrowing schemata from one context for a closely related one. But sometimes schemata can be carried to a radically different context. Metaphorical instructions show beautifully how this can happen. For instance, *Time* magazine recently published a list of metaphors the Russian cellist and conductor Mstislav Rostropovich had used to help performers toward the right expression. Here are some examples: "Whisper like a lady moving in a silk dress." "Like a cowboy riding a horse." "You must make it like two bugs fighting." In these instructions, Rostropovich took advantage of our schematic knowledge about locomotion and action in ladies, cowboys, and bugs to convey how a musical passage should sound. Notice that the metaphors are not just fancy ways of saying play softly or jouncily. They offer specific information. To play with a whisper like a lady moving in a silk dress is to play softly in a particular way. To play like a cowboy riding a horse is to play with a certain kind of jounce.

Revised proposition: (1) Extreme product fluency occurs only in improvisatory activities that demand it and depends on a large repertoire of schemata, prefabricated patterns and units which for the most part are unconscious. (2) Any activity requires some repertoire of schemata. (3) New skills are learned through a mix of acquiring new schemata and adapting old ones; the adapting can be a problem in itself. (4) Sometimes an activity can usefully adapt schemata from a radically different activity.

INVENTION AND STEREOTYPE

Even though schemata make possible some remarkable performances, they also raise a problem. Reliance on a repertoire of stereotypes seems very uncreative. Real innovation should require transcending schemata rather than depending on them. Schemata might go more with extreme competence than extreme creativity. Schemata might inhibit more than enable creation. Is any of this so?

The historian of science Thomas Kuhn has argued that established patterns of thinking in science do limit innovation. Kuhn begins his *The Structure of Scientific Revolutions* with the concept of a paradigm. By that term he wants "to suggest that some accepted examples of actual scientific practice – examples which include law, theory, application, and instrumentation together – provide models from which spring particular coherent traditions of scientific research." Examples of these traditions include Newtonian mechanics, Copernican astronomy, and the newer paradigm of relativity theory. Kuhn's idea of paradigm seems to fit the general notion of schema. A paradigm in his sense amounts to a collection of schemata that defines a unified way of scientific theorizing and experimentation.

Kuhn sees the normal process of scientific research as work within a paradigm. He calls such work puzzle solving. Kuhn asserts that puzzle solving hardly ever aims at producing major novelties. Rather, it stresses determining the facts important to the paradigm, explaining phenomena with the paradigm's theories, manipulating the paradigm to make and test predictions, and so on.

That doesn't imply that such puzzle solving requires no genuine creative effort. However, the more dramatic discoveries of science call for invention of another order. Scientific breakthroughs bring paradigm change. A new paradigm evolves and finally displaces an old one. This process begins with the recognition of anomalies – for instance, observations counter to the predictions of the current paradigm or inconsistencies discovered in the paradigm. If severe enough, the anomalies inspire a search for new approaches.

In many ways, the established paradigm is the enemy of discovery. An anomaly may not be perceived for what it is, precisely because it is not expected. A simple example concerns the discovery of the planet Uranus. The planets out to Saturn had been known since the dawn of history, and no one imagined that there might be others. The concept of planets included just that many and no more. Kuhn notes that on a number of occasions before 1781, astronomers had seen a star in the position of Uranus. One had seen the star on four successive nights, without noticing the motion against the background stars that would indicate a planet. Even when William Herschel, in 1791, observed that this celestial object had a visible disk, he interpreted it as a comet. Only months later did the scientific community conclude it must be a planet.

Furthermore, a seeming anomaly most often does not trigger paradigm change. Rather, it is resolved somehow within the dominant paradigm. Indeed, some have maintained that nearly always the dominant paradigm can give a better explanation of the phenomena than any new one. Novel paradigms arise not so much because they offer better explanations at the outset, but because some individuals have the luck, faith, and vision to pursue them. For instance, Paul Feyerabend has argued that a static earth fit the evidence at hand and general concepts of motion much better than Copernicus' thesis of an earth in motion. The latter could not compete on rational grounds until Galileo had argued for it in ways Feyerabend views more as progressive propaganda than proper logic and until time had allowed its development. Thus the maturity and authority of the established paradigm discourage new ones.

Sometimes one hears quite extreme versions of the limits imposed by scientific paradigms or, more generally, schemata for perceiving, understanding, and acting. People with different schemata understand the world in fundamentally different ways, so the story goes. They cannot communicate effectively. The reasons offered by one person mean nothing to the other person, not just for lack of shared assumptions but for lack of shared concepts. Change from one system of belief to another, which of course does occur, depends not so much on the weighing of evidence and judicious decision, but on something more like religious conversion, or like the sudden perceptual changes we've discussed earlier where new patterns fall into place.

Let me put all these worries into a couple of sentences:

Proposition: Schemata, while enabling skilled performance

within their scope, severely inhibit creativity beyond their scope. So far as real innovation is concerned, schemata do much more harm than good.

The discussion so far shows that this proposition contains much truth. But perhaps the proposition is not as sound as it seems. In fact, for some important qualifications I can't do any better than to borrow a few ideas from the noted philosopher of science Israel Scheffler. In his *Science and Subjectivity,* Scheffler describes more fully the "subjectivist" notion sketched above and reveals its limits. Scheffler writes mostly about scientific discovery. Here I can only mention a couple of his arguments and suggest that they apply to discovery in general also.

One logical point Scheffler makes is that extreme subjectivists rely on a self-refuting argument. They try to convince people of subjectivism through rational discourse – everyday and historical examples, psychological experiments, philosophical analysis of the nature of knowledge and knowing, and so on. But suppose the subjectivists were correct. This would mean that such arguments should convince no one, since the impotence of rational argument is part of what extreme subjectivism asserts. In short, the unqualified subjectivist argument declares its own irrelevance.

Besides exposing this oddity, Scheffler looks to the details of the subjectivist argument. A subjectivist maintains that the "facts" are wholly relative to the paradigm. Scheffler emphasizes that although categories may guide observation, those categories need not in themselves determine truth and falsity. Category systems are neither true or false, but simply ways of sorting the world. Having a category system with such categories as elephants and eggs neither affirms nor denies that elephants lay eggs. Whatever your belief about that, you can test the matter by investigating the behavior of elephants.

Of course, schemata produce expectations that may cause one to overlook anomalies and "read in" the way things are supposed to be. Such effects certainly do occur. But it would be silly to say that they entirely dominate perception and understanding. Scheffler puts it this way: "Our expectations strongly structure what we see, but do not wholly eliminate unexpected sights. To suppose that they do would be, absurdly, to deny the common phenomena of surprise, shock and astonishment, as well as the reorientation of belief consequent upon them." In fact, Kuhn can't really be considered a hard-line subjectivist. If he were, he would have to deny the perception of anomalies altogether and maintain that scientists inevitably become trapped by their own paradigms. On the contrary, Kuhn acknowledges the detection of anomalies and considers them spurs of scientific innovation.

Kuhn sees in the conservatism of science an important positive function. It guarantees that scientists will not be distracted lightly and that the most will be made of a fertile paradigm. Kuhn observes that throughout the eighteenth century scientists failed to derive the motion of the moon adequately from Newton's laws. Some investigators examined the possibility that gravity did not vary precisely with the inverse of the square of the distance. For the most part, however, science stayed with Newton and eventually discovered how Newton's laws ought to be applied to the case. The moral is telling: there's no point in inventing new paradigms left and right without taking the paradigms seriously enough to pursue them.

Second, and strangely, the more narrow and elaborated a paradigm becomes, the more it sets the stage for scientific breakthrough. Its very specificity makes obvious the occurrence of novelties. As Kuhn puts it: "Novelty emerges only for the man who, knowing *with precision* what he should expect, is able to recognize that something has gone wrong.

Revised proposition: Schemata play a paradoxical role in discovery, making possible discovery and fluency within their scope, inhibiting discovery beyond their scope, but at the same time preparing the way for such discovery by establishing a context against which anomalies and, in general, alternatives become meaningful.

 Food for Thought

We don't have to look far for examples of that revised proposition. Because all our activities depend on schemata, nearly any everyday activity will show the paradoxical contribution schemata make to innovation. Dining, for example, is highly schematized. We eat certain sorts of foods in a certain order, but not other foods in other orders. Certain foods will do only for certain meals. And so on. The conventions of dining provide the paradigm within which the better cook routinely invents, designing interesting combinations of foods and preparing them in the most scrumptious ways. Such a cook corresponds to the puzzle solver in Kuhn's account of scientific discovery.

However, such puzzle solving by definition doesn't challenge the rules. Consider food additives, for example. Do I mean chemicals? No, I mean the substances we routinely add to foods to heighten their flavor – salt, pepper, sugar, butter. We add something to almost everything we eat at the table. Meats and vegetables get salt and perhaps pepper, cereals and coffee get sugar, bread and vegetables butter. Whatever fine meal that better cook prepares, those additives aren't likely to be subtracted.

Let me suggest that you try subtracting them. Eat for an entire day without adding anything at the table. If you do this, you'll discover some interesting flavors. You never knew, or had forgotten, that steak or ham or carrots or broccoli could taste just like that. Some of the flavors may please and some not, but you're likely to discover a lot more flavor "there" in the food itself than you imagined.

But let's not fool ourselves. Such an experiment doesn't really set aside the old schemata, any more than the scientist noting an anomaly has set aside the paradigm. By leaving off the additives, you create an anomaly relative to expectations, and the food seems the way it does partly because of the anomaly. Just as only a newly developed scientific theory will accomodate the scientific anomaly, only a new consistently developed cuisine would reveal whatever potentials there might be in subtracting additives.

A PLAN FOR INVENTION

A while ago a student approached me and wanted to know what nature's secret plan for creativity was. He wondered what he would have to do to use his deepest resources. How would he have to think, what motions would he have to go through? He was hoping for so much that I hardly knew what to say. In fact, the chances of there being a "secret plan" for invention do not seem good. I've discussed the limits imposed on innovation by plans, at the same time stressing that those very plans make innovation possible. The give-and-take relationship between plans and invention makes a schema specifically *for* invention seem nonsensical. Also, the variety of situations where invention occurs has to be remembered. Schemata seem mostly specialized to particular contexts, as with the stock phrases of the oral poet or the assumptions of a scientist working within a paradigm. To ask for a natural plan for invention in general is to ask for a plan that cuts across these contexts, a plan of greater scope than any considered up to now. That much generality makes a positive answer all the more unlikely.

Proposition: No general plan guides invention because innovation is contrary to plan and is of so many varied sorts.

But such doubts haven't discouraged thinkers from seeking a universal pattern to inventive thought. And perhaps the quest is not entirely hopeless after all. Let me review one classic but not so sound idea, and then take up one contemporary idea that does better.

In a 1926 book called *The Art of Thought,* Graham Wallas proposed a simple four-phase organization for inventive thinking, *preparation, incubation, illumination,* and *verification.* During preparation, the person investigated a problem actively. During incubation, no conscious effort occurred. Illumination happened when an idea suggested itself out of the blue, perhaps as a result of a rapid sequence of associations. Then the person attempted verification, a deliberate effort to elaborate and confirm the insight. Wallas argued for this pattern with autobiographical accounts from notable thinkers.

In the 1930s, Catherine Patrick systematically tried to find evidence for the four stages Wallas proposed. Patrick conducted process tracing studies in which poets and artists thought aloud as they worked. She also studied the thought processes of scientists, using a somewhat different method. The poets wrote a poem in response to a picture given to them by Patrick. The artists drew in response to a poem. Patrick recorded their speech in shorthand. She also took great care to check whether her method might have distorted the processes under study. For example, she questioned her participants closely on their own subjective impressions about this, compared their productions during the experiment to samples of their usual work for any differences in style, and later determined the fate of the poems her poets had written (some were eventually published). Patrick concluded that from all signs her method had not interfered with the process of invention.

Patrick deserves praise for her pioneering effort, but there is a problem with her conclusions. She perpetrated something like a force-fit of theory to data. Consider, for instance, the evidence Patrick gave for incubation. She found that most often a subject, after conceiving the idea that in fact would turn out to guide the poem or drawing, went on to consider other approaches. After a while, the idea would reappear. Should that count as a sign of incubation? Incubation normally means that an idea appears out of the blue for the first time while attention is elsewhere, not that an idea reappears. Also, if a person simply explored alternative approaches and then selected one, as a matter of course the person most of the time would end up taking an approach other than the very last one discovered. This would happen even if the person were thinking fully consciously all the time. Finding that people often return to an earlier approach gives no evidence at all of the unconscious progress usually implied by incubation.

In general, the four-stage theory does not respect the variety of creative experiences. Other biographical accounts and other research reveal too many different dramas of invention for Wallas' script to be very meaningful. Sometimes a maker discovers an approach at once, with hardly any preparation or incubation. Sometimes no moment of illumination occurs, but only steady progress, and so on. It's been suggested that Wallas' four stages are better thought of as aspects of creative process that may occur many times in different mixes and orders during the course of creating.

If Wallas' account won't do as the natural plan for invention, maybe someone else's will. Worth considering here is Getzels' and Csikszentmihalyi's research on student artists. Remember that the students each selected a set of objects from a number provided and arranged them in preparation for drawing a still life. Then the students executed the drawings. Getzels and Csikszentmihalyi found a relationship between the procedures of the student artists and both the judged quality of their products and professional success seven years later. Roughly speaking, the artists who proved most effective worked as follows. In arranging their still lifes, they manipulated more objects, explored the objects they handled more thoroughly (looking closely, touching, working mechanical parts), and chose more unusual objects. They tended not to have a definite idea of the sort of principle they wanted to capture in their arrangements, but discovered arrangements through handling the objects. As they proceeded with their drawings, they more often rearranged or substituted objects, changed paper or switched medium, and transformed the scene in the drawing, for instance by changing or adding objects. The final structure of the drawing tended to become obvious later rather than earlier. These artists more often reported trying to develop the drawing beyond the physical arrangement. Also, in response to an interview after finishing, the more creative subjects said that elements of their drawings still might be changed without destroying its character.

Getzels and Csikszentmihalyi call this pattern of behavior *problem finding*. In their experiment, they thought of the arrangement that the artists made to draw from as the problem formulation. Their data showed that the more creative students gave much more attention to finding this formulation that did the less creative students. Also, the more creative students, as they proceeded with the drawing – solving the problem, so to speak – remained open to further changes in matters like the arrangement of objects seemingly settled during problem formulation. That is, they often found new problem formulations even while working from the original one.

The term problem finding is a little confusing because an inventive process does not split naturally into problem finding and then problem solving, any more than it divides neatly into Wallas' four phases. But think of it this way. Any creative activity involves narrowing down. You start with nothing, or nothing but a very general idea, and finish with a very particular product. As you proceed, more and more constraints emerge. The work so far, unless revised or abandoned, limits the possibilities of the work to come. Getzels' and Csikszentmihalyi's findings say that the more creative person spends more effort during the early part of the process, rather than quickly narrowing down. Also, the more creative person remains ready to revise decisions made earlier, not accepting as much the limits that the work so far tends to impose on the the work to come.

  Problem Finding

Most of the personal experiments have stressed problem solving more than problem finding. So, in this exercise, finding the problem will be the problem.

Here are a few constraints. Don't seek a world or national problem; they are too easy to think of. Also, don't seek a difficult personal problem. Instead, try to discover the most important problem you have that you might actually solve with a little thought. And don't start to work on a problem right away. Spend most of your time exploring thoroughly what problem to pick. Then try to solve it.

You may well find it very refreshing (or dismaying?) to make problems themselves the center of your thinking, discover what problems are there, and begin to map their shapes and relationships. Here is a whole world of entities we don't usually see as such.

All this began with wanting a schema for invention. Let's for a moment pretend that we have one:

Revised proposition: Problem finding is the schema that organizes inventive behavior.

However, this statement will not do. Important as problem finding may be, it doesn't really guide invention in the way the schemata discussed earlier did. They virtually guaranteed performance. Given the schemata for speaking grammatically, you can speak grammatically. Given the schemata defining a scientific paradigm, you can do science in the paradigm. But problem finding doesn't guarantee anything. In fact, a person could go through the motions of problem finding in a very uncreative way, considering alternative problems and revising earlier decisions obtusely. Certainly problem finding as such might enhance creativity, since the choice of a problem gets explicit attention it otherwise would not. But just as certainly *how* you problem find is more important than *that* you problem find.

Also, we can't be sure that problem finding guides creative behavior. Perhaps it's the other way around. A person's behavior includes problem finding simply because the person is creative. A creative person naturally would explore alternatives during the early as well as late phases of an activity and remain open to major alternatives during the later phases. That's what it would mean to perform the activity in a creative way. My own belief is that both are so. Problem finding occurs partly as a result of a generally creative disposition and partly from a habit specifically *of* problem finding. The two, of course, reinforce one another.

Rerevised proposition: A pattern of exploration in the early stages of narrowing down and readiness to revise earlier decisions in the later stages is characteristic of creating. The pattern seems to be part symptom and part cause of inventiveness.

HOW DOWN DEEP?

The title of this chapter pointed to the work of largely unconscious schemata in fluency. Despite their hidden nature, such plans are fully in keeping with the teleological view of creating. After all, conscious or not, plans are plans for something. Purpose is part and parcel of the very concept of a schema.

Yet the schemata underlying great skill may not always be as "down deep" as all that. For one example, and so far as problem finding ought to be called a plan, some of the artists Getzels and Czikszent-mihalyi studied appeared to problem find quite deliberately. Moreover, one of the first performances I mentioned in fact involved considerable consciousness: the lightning calculations of A. C. Aitken.

Earlier I quoted some examples of Aitken's feats without explanation. Now here is Aitken's own account of another computation, expressing the fraction 1/851 as a decimal:

> The instant observation was that 851 is 23 times 37. I use this fact as follows. 1/37 is 9.927927927, and so on repeated. This I divide mentally by 23, 23 into 0.027 is 0.001 with remainder 4. In a flash I can get that 23 into 4027 is 175 with remainder 2, and into 2027 is 88 with remainder 3, and into 3027 is 131 with remainder 14, and even into 14,027 is 609 with remainder 20. And so on like that. Also, before I ever start this, I know how' far it is necessary to go before reaching the end of the recurring period: for 1/37 recurs at three places and 1/23 recurs at twenty-two places, and the lowest common multiple of 3 and 22 is 66, whence I know that there is a recurring period of 66 places.

As I. M. L. Hunter, who studied Aitken, reports, this and other examples reveal two features of the mathematician's skill. First of all, Aitken relied upon a large repertoire of number facts, and second he also took advantage of a large repertoire of computational plans. Neither the facts nor the plans would be part of a person's usual arithmetic skills. But Aitken knew them, thought of them as needed, and applied them.

However, Aitken certainly did not produce his answer without awareness of his method, as the oral poets apparently sing their songs or you and I produce sentences. He went through an explicit process of planning and executing. Although the wholes he worked with were larger and more sophisticated, he performed as deliberately as you or I might in carrying out a much simpler arithmetic calculation. So the case of Aitken is a good bridge to the next chapter, where we'll consider "plans up front" – plans deliberately used for creative and other performances.

7

PLANS UP FRONT

It has often been pointed out that the state of the world, for better or worse, owes much more to cultural than biological evolution in recent years – the last 20,000, say. The trick that provides cinema, flush toilets, and nuclear devices is the preservation and transmission of knowledge. Historical studies of any era reveal the lively inventiveness of humankind. The Greeks, the Babylonians, the Incas were just as clever as we. But all this invention would amount to little if the advances of each generation, always modest on an historical scale, were lost and left to the next generation to reinvent.

It's easy today to think of this cycle of invention, preservation, and more invention as mostly a matter of snowballing science and technology. Less blatant but obvious enough is progress in the humanities, as philosophers, writers, and composers extend, reshape, or constructively turn upside down the works of their predecessors. But amidst all this emphasis on outcomes like theories, poems, and color TVs, something else is easily ignored: behavior. Behavior evolves too. One need only list a few behavioral patterns fundamental to modern life, but not to loping across grassy savannahs, to see how much this has to be so. There is, for example, language, writing, numbers, government of various sorts, and money – all technologies fundamentally of behavior rather than things. Such inventions often are themselves means of invention and problem solving in one way or another. Government defines a process for making decisions about courses of action for the group. Language is the tool of much individual thinking as well as communication.

Language and government are very old in human history. Are there less venerable invented behaviors that help with invention and problem solving? Certainly. There is mathematics. The fundamental trick of much scientific thinking is to mathematize the situation under study, representing it as equations, matrices, tensors, or other expressions that allow powerful formal manipulations. Another tactic old in essence but lately grown more varied and powerful is modeling. We use models or analogues as stand-ins for the real things, sorting out problems with the models instead. There are, for example, blueprints, mockups for aircraft, architect's models for buildings to be, casts of organs for student physicians, simulation games. Besides modeling and mathematizing, another important idea is automation applied to thinking. Of course, automation itself need not serve invention or problem solving at all, but only the manufacturing of shoes or soup. But it can. From the abacus to the slide rule to today's pocket calculators, computation devices have more and more freed the minds of mathematicians, accountants, engineers, and now practically all of us from arithmetic. Contemporary computers not only have done away with familiar drudgery, but taken up kinds of unfamiliar drudgery that provide entire new approaches to problems. Computer models of traffic flow can help to design thruways and street layouts. For another example, one sure to be a classic, in 1976 a famous intractable mathematical problem called the four-color-map conjecture was proved by computer. While mathematicians had long sought conventional proofs, Kenneth Appel and Wolfgang Haken wrote a sophisticated program to search through logical alternatives too numerous to manage by paper and pencil, and demonstrated the theorem that way. Although such tactics depend on technology, the tactics themselves fundamentally are behavioral inventions, ways people have found to use the new hardware at hand and very often ways never thought of when that hardware was designed.

I muster these examples to make a simple point. There is nothing odd or novel about the idea of inventing behavior to help with thinking, problem solving, and invention. On the contrary, modern life is full of such devices, old and new. We take them for granted. Given the precedents, we should be open to the idea of new inventions of the same kind, novel patterns of behavior that would help our thinking in unexpected ways.

There exists today a young "thinking technology" of just this sort – proposed procedures for making creative and problem-solving activities more effective. It emphasizes such tactics as deliberately thinking metaphorically, exploring a large number of alternatives, analyzing the problem requirements systematically, and so on. Unlike the examples mentioned so far, these tactics cut deep into the course of thought, providing not so much languages like mathematics to work in, or aids such as calculators, but a redirection in the pattern of thinking itself. Nonetheless, the fundamental continuity with earlier invented behaviors should not be overlooked.

To have a term for this technology let me use "heuristics," a name much used already. A heuristic is a rule of thumb that often helps in solving a certain class of problems, but makes no guarantees. Heuristics contrast with algorithms. An algorithm is an exact procedure that guarantees solutions to a given class of problems – the procedure for doing long division, for example. Heuristics, on the other hand, are hit or miss, hopefully helping but promising nothing. Although often the heuristics aren't conscious, most of thinking is heuristic in nature simply because true algorithms aren't possible. As a technology, though, "heuristics" aims to discover and impart the *best* heuristics, which may be much better than those people routinely use.

In the spirit of optimism, I've spoken of a young technology of thinking. But perhaps that's overoptimism. It's far from clear whether good advice about how to think is any good at all. Indeed, we shouldn't be too surprised to find that much of it isn't. By the measure of history, how many inventions of any sort for any purpose have been *that* good? Cultural evolution, like biological evolution, is viciously selective, discarding a hundred notions to preserve the few potent ones. Uncertainties are all the more in order because of another fact: general heuristics of thinking in the sense outlined above are a very new concept. Perhaps the beginning of extensive attention to the matter could be pegged down to Graham Wallas' 1926 book, *The Art of Thought*. But it is in the last twenty years, and even the last ten, that such ideas have multiplied most. There has not been much time for test and selection of any sort.

In this chapter I want to do what I can toward estimating the worth of heuristics, despite the youth of the ideas and the lack of much beyond hearsay evidence and common sense. Crucial to this is holding reasonable expectations for heuristics. "You can't manufacture Beethovens or Einsteins with a bit of advice," is a familiar commonsensical response to the idea of teaching heuristics for invention. But education never anticipates such gains in any field – tennis, for example. You certainly think lessons will improve your game but hardly expect to be made a winner of Wimbledon. Too many factors intervene for hopes to be so high: natural talent, time, drive, luck. We should demand no more of education for creativity than of education for any other activity: moderate improvement. This is nothing to neglect, but can heuristics do even so much?

BIG PLANS

The oral poet turned up with a full complement of plans down deep, all the way from small to big. There were the little plans – the innumerable half lines that equipped the poet to express particular ideas. Then there were the big plans – the trajectory of an epic from donning the armor to wedding feast. And indeed there were middle-sized plans inbetween. It's tempting to suppose that the biggest plans are the least important to epic performance. Given those small and medium plans, the overall organization would seem almost to take care of itself. A little experience and you could tell a tale easily enough, once you could sing the requisite scenes.

This view is no less sensible for more everyday activities. Big plans don't seem so crucial. Once one knows how to fix the parts of a car, one should be able to get on with fixing the whole. Once one knows the moves of tennis, one should be able to get on with playing the game. In fact, just such a principle pervades most of education. A repertoire of particular skills or pieces of knowledge is taught, and it's presumed that "getting it all together" just happens. Now of course no one makes that assumption out loud, but the way people behave says it clearly enough.

Proposition: The broad organization of behavior almost takes care of itself, once the person masters the contributing performances.

Now this proposition does not fit in with the hopes of a heuristic technology. The premise of heuristics is that people do not put together the pieces as well as all that. A little good advice about better management of your mind could go a long way. Consider an example: the writings of the mathematician George Polya on heuristics for mathematical problem solving. In one popular book, and other more technical ones, Polya set forth what he took to be the strategies professional mathematicians use to guide their thinking, and argued that students should do the same. Some typical advice? Ask yourself: Have you ever done a related problem and might you approach this one in the same way? Can you make a diagram to represent the problem? Can you think of a special case and understand how that case works? Can you divide the problem into parts and solve one part at a time? Clearly plans such as these are fairly "big plans" for problem solving, ones quite above subject-specific detail. Indeed, much of Polya's advice to the novice mathematician could apply just as well to mechanics or football coaching. That's how general it is.

However, the proposition we began with implies that Polya's sensible-sounding advice does not make much sense after all. If people assemble the parts of a performance without particular trouble, novice mathematicians should not need Polya. Education ought to get on with providing more of the separate skills they really require. There are other ways to doubt Polya as well. Perhaps professional mathematicians don't really behave the way he maintains. Or then again, perhaps they do and novices do not, but novices just can't take the advice so hopefully offered. Too general, it might become concrete and practical only in the expert who somehow has acquired it anyway. All in all, heuristic advice seems damned both ways, for being either too obvious to bother with or too vague to actually follow.

If these are the possibilities, then, what are the facts? One is that Polya appears dead right about mathematical minds, not only his own but others'. Professional mathematicians do use Polya's heuristics, not so much deliberately as with spontaneous craft and savvy. This has been generally acknowledged, and I'm personally satisfied about it too. My own university work was in mathematics, and though I never learned about Polya until I'd become skilled, I've since tried some introspecting in search of the promised heuristics. Sure enough, there they were helping, even though I'd given no deliberate thought to such things.

Another fact favoring Polya is that novices don't use such strategies nearly as much as they might. Studies of novices solving problems have disclosed epidemic disorganization when the going gets rough. A problem that matches a familiar procedure may be well enough treated, but otherwise the typical student gets stuck, little knowing how to search his experience for a trick to turn the trick.

This leaves one more reservation: that the novice can't readily take heuristic advice, but when one has the extensive background knowledge to take it, it takes care of itself. What are the facts here? The best data come from attempts to teach students heuristics and test for gains. Such efforts usually have recognized the dangers of overgeneral advice. They have not just set forth rules of thumb, but laid out illustrations and required practice in fitting heuristics to problems. They've made sure that the students possess basic knowledge to work from – one could hardly put heuristics to work on algebra without knowing the rules of the algebra game. Such preparations give the student the best chance to gain from heuristics.

And does the student gain? "Sometimes" is the vexing answer.

There have been no more than a few small and middle-sized studies. Some have reported gains on tests after heuristic training, by comparison with control groups who received normal instruction. Others found no benefits. No one, so far as I know, has reported a large scale demonstration of really dramatic improvements. We have every right to be unimpressed.

Perhaps that proposition was all too true. The broad organization takes care of itself given the various skills, and meantime there's nothing much to be done. But perhaps heuristic training falters for not going far enough. This at least is the thought of Alan Schoenfeld, a mathematician and educator who has spent much labor investigating when heuristics do and don't help and why. Schoenfeld maintains that the usual recipe for heuristic training lacks an ingredient. It is not sufficient to have the background knowledge and to understand how to apply the heuristics. You must know when to do what. Students who can plug in a heuristic when asked may not think to do so on their own.

Schoenfeld's attack on the problem has been to provide organizational strategies. Such strategies give the students a way to remind themselves of the heuristics they know and to match method to problem. To say as little as that reveals that the heuristic big plans mentioned earlier weren't so mammoth after all. What was lacking was yet a bigger plan to organize the lot, general though they already were.

In one demonstration, Schoenfeld provided nothing but managerial tactics. The particular heuristics were already in place, thanks to the normal curriculum. The mathematics of concern was integration problems in calculus, and the heuristics to be organized were the usual tricks taught in any first-year calculus course. Students learned these tricks of the trade well enough, Schoenfeld knew. But there might be something else they didn't learn: which trick provided the best bet when. So Schoenfeld prepared written guidelines for the students to help them with their final calculus examination. Half the students in a calculus class, not Schoenfeld's own, received these guidelines, and the other half did not. All the students were informed of this experiment, and all were frankly told that no one knew whether or not the guidelines would help. There was reassurance, too, on the question of fairness: grades would be adjusted statistically if either group showed an advantage. And the actual outcome? Schoenfeld proved quite right in his conjectures. The students who studied the guidelines outperformed those who reviewed in their usual ways. Moreover, the students returned estimates of the time they spent preparing for the exam, and those with the guidelines in fact used less time than the others did.

In another experiment, this one very small-scale, Schoenfeld sought even more direct evidence for help from heuristics. Four students were introduced to five heuristics and were shown how these could unlock several sample problems. Another three students learned how the same problems might be worked, seeing the same solutions laid out with one difference: nothing at all was said about those heuristics. The methods were not identified as examples of general strategies, ones that might assist with other problems too. In a following test, the heuristics students were reminded periodically to try to use the five methods. This bull-by-the-horns approach was calculated to force the issue – the worth of heuristics ought to show up clearly where students trained in heuristics had little chance to neglect them.

The results again favored Schoenfeld's viewpoint. The heuristics students improved considerably when their post-test scores were compared to a test administered before training; the others showed no gains at all. The heuristics students solved about twice as many problems on the final test as the others did. Despite the small number of participating students, the differences were large enough to achieve statistical significance. Moreover, Schoenfeld was able to make another and crucial point. He collected think-aloud reports of the students solving their post-test problems. Not only did those with heuristic training work more examples, but they did so by using the heuristics they were taught. Furthermore, it was clear that some students trained in heuristics had failed to solve certain problems just exactly through missing the right heuristic; some not trained in heuristics solved problems by applying the right heuristic anyway.

Now heuristic instruction might seem quite artificial. We do not think of master mathematicians as deploying managerial strategies. Yet, in fact research shows that skilled problem solvers in mathematics and physics do something rather like that. They do not dive into problems, but size them up first, considering general approaches in a qualitative way. In contrast, novices tend to start manipulating the givens without an overarching vision of a problem. So experts do just the sort of thing Schoenfeld instructs his students to do. No doubt they do it more spontaneously, noticing opportunities the students may have to search out. Still, with practice, the students' behavior would become more fluent too.

Mathematics is not the only area where payoffs from instruction in strategies have been demonstrated. Another such activity is reading. Most people comfortably persist in a word-by-word-begin-at-the-beginning-and-read-to-the-end strategy when reading for information. There's neither great need for nor much advantage to this. They have amply fluency for more artful ways of reading.

SQ3R

Here to try is a big plan for reading. It, and others more or less like it, have been widely recommended and taught in many high school and college classes. Plans like this yield better learning, so educational experiments have shown, at least when one is reading for information that has to be remembered. The plan itself includes five steps: survey, question, read, recite, and, finally, review.

Survey: Scan the material very quickly to understand the general topic and organization. Look at the title, introduction, section headings, illustrations and captions, and any summary at the end.

Question: Skim once more, asking but not answering questions concerning the topics.

Read: Read through the material thoroughly. Read to answer the questions framed earlier.

Recite: Skim over the material once again; at each section or other major division, ask questions, then answer them and, in general, recite as much as possible about the division. When something isn't remembered that should be, look.

Review: Go over quickly one more time.

Do try it. But don't just try it – do so critically.

Then, after the process is complete, list how you reacted to the SQ3R plan. Was it satisfactory in all respects, and if not where did it falter? Did the plan take longer than you hoped, or less time than you'd feared? Was it tedious or interesting? Would you use the plan again, and for what kind of reading? How would you revise the plan? Was one trial enough to test the SQ3R plan, or are several sessions needed to get used to it and evaluate fairly?

I ask those questions to emphasize a point. Merely to have a shiny new plan isn't so worthwhile – unless the plan does its job. Whether it really does, and does so better than competing plans, are matters that require much attention, some optimism, some pessimism, and perhaps quite a bit of art to judge. This labor of criticism should be undertaken for SQ3R and any other plans designed to help with memorizing, problem solving, and so on. *Caveat emptor* is a motto to keep in mind; in my experience, many of these nifty formulas are not so helpful as they sound, especially given the different needs and characters of different individuals.

Take SQ3R as a case in point. Personally, for the technical reading I usually have to do and the quantity and kinds of things I need to remember, I find the plan too thorough. A streamlined variant makes much more sense for me. I like to survey and question, but not read through – only read selectively to answer the questions. Then I sometimes recite or sometimes write notes without references to the text at all, and look up any really necessary points. This suits my current needs, but wouldn't do at all if I were studying for a fussy exam in Early American History.

Different people to whom I've presented the SQ3R plan as a sample big plan have reacted in varied ways. A few found it valuable. Many modified it considerably. Most, my impression is, felt their current reading really didn't require the extensive recall the plan doggedly aims to achieve. But one reaction was a bit dismaying. This student simply remarked, "Well, I tried it. It didn't help. It took much too long. So I think I'll just stick with my usual way of reading." This remark depressed me for no very subtle reason. At least such plans, however well they work, should raise questions in people's minds about how they organize their behavior, and how they might do so better. *If it doesn't work, forget it* seems a far less inventive and aspiring policy than *If it doesn't work, well then – what does?* In general, a critical posture toward new heuristics sometimes seems not so much productive as defensive, a tactic to maintain the individual's comfortable if less than effective habits. Here, as in many contexts, the distinction has to be drawn between defensive and constructive criticism of innovations.

Revised proposition: The broad organization of behavior does not necessarily take care of itself once contributing performances are mastered. Both particular heuristic advice and the more general heuristics of managerial strategies may be helpful. Most of all, one's big plans for conducting various activities deserve critical scrutiny and creative revision.

WHAT PEOPLE LEARN FROM HEURISTICS

Proposition: People taught heuristics become better problem solvers and creative thinkers by using the heuristics they are taught.

This is an odd proposition. What else would people learn from heuristics but the habit of using them? That's a long story, best forgotten for several pages. Eventually, though, I'll get back to it.

Besides the work on problem solving in mathematics, another tradition of heuristics for invention calls for attention here. It contrasts in several ways with the work of Polya and Schoenfeld. Although this tradition sometimes uses some simple mathematical problems, puzzle problems with a practical accent are more common, such as how to get a cat out from under a house, or how to achieve a fair settlement in a wage dispute, or how to wash the windows of skyscrapers more conveniently. The everyday world of pots and pans, salaries and spouses, corporations and products is much more its concern than the scholarly world of tensors and matrices, algebras and integrals. For another contrast, the two traditions emphasize somewhat different heuristics, heuristics that could be applied to both. The present one – let's call it "creative thinking" just to give it a name – especially urges avoiding premature closure. Recommended are the generation of many approaches and the deferral of quick and perhaps mediocre solutions in favor of longer searches for higher-quality solutions. Of course, such advice might make good sense in mathematical problem solving too. But it is not much stressed, just as the creative-thinking approach does not much stress such tactics as thinking of similar problems already solved.

While in mathematical heuristics the importance of managerial strategies seems to have been missed until recently, in the creative-thinking literature the biggest of big plans – broad outlines of the entire problem-solving process – have been around for a long time. I want to describe just one of these plans, one presented in a recent text by Noller, Parnes, and Biondi and developed to accompany courses in a creative-thinking program at the University of Buffalo in New York. It divides problem solving into five steps. The book labels the process, without a great deal of creative thinking it seems, the five-step plan.

Step 1. *Fact finding.* List what further information you'd like to have about the problem. List ways to find the information and the results of doing so when it seems worth doing.

Step 2. *Problem finding.* List questions that formulate the problem. After writing a few, ask, "What is the essential problem, the real objective?" and try to phrase that in different ways. Pick the version or versions that seem most suggestive to guide the further effort.

Step 3. *Idea finding.* Devise a number of candidate solution ideas without evaluating them. Some might be quite explicit, others quite vague – hardly more than approaches that might yield something if pursued.

Step 4. *Solution finding.* Evaluate the candidate solutions comparatively. List important criteria and gauge how well each solution meets each requirement. Classify the solutions as "use now" or "hold" or "reject."

Step 5. *Acceptance finding.* Consider what problems might arise in implementing the best idea and how to meet those problems. For example, could there be trouble in persuading those who would develop or use the idea to accept it?

I noted earlier that premature closure was the main villain of the creative-thinking school. This concern shows up in the five-step plan, which, through and through, puts off getting a solution and getting on with applying it. First, data must be gathered. But no solutions then, please – the problem must be formulated. You may think of candidate solutions, but not evaluate or select. And so on. Not only solutions proper, but other elements such as evaluative standards and one's concept of the problem are protected from premature closure by the methodical procedure and the emphasis on explicitly listing alternatives at each phase.

   Stepping Out

The personal experiment here is simply to apply the five-step plan, doing just as it says. The fact finding will have to be undertaken by plausible conjecture, of course. The following problem I've paraphrased from the same source proposing the five-step plan. It is the example they use to illustrate the plan with all its phases, after introducing each phase one by one.

An eight-year-old schoolboy fell into the habit of making trouble on the schoolbus, yelling, hitting other children, and so on. Distracted and upset, the driver came close to having an accident several times. Persuasion and staying after school did not help; the boy persisted in his wild behavior. The bus driver was warned that physically punishing the child might lead to a lawsuit. What should the driver do?

This problem certainly could have many solutions. So far

as I know, none is a completely compelling Eureka! sort of answer, but some do seem much better than others. What would your best suggestion be?

After applying the method, evaluate the experience. Was following the five-step plan comfortable? Did it seem fruitful? Was it difficult to "hold back" inventing solutions or evaluating them before coming to those steps? Did the plan lead to solutions that otherwise would have been missed? To come to a better personal answer about those questions, you may want to try the plan on additional problems.

Of course, it's difficult to say how any one person will react to a procedure like the five-step plan. But I've invited enough people to try it to have gathered an impression. Some like it, but many find the plan tediously complete. They come to an apt solution early on, perhaps even before intending to generate an answer. Good ideas simply suggest themselves. Then they find themselves undertaking the hollow ritual of all five steps, only to conclude that no or little gain resulted. Now admittedly the point of the five-step plan is to help people past those early solutions, on the premise that they aren't as satisfactory as they seem. But very often, they *are* as satisfactory as they seem. Furthermore, when they are not, is the best way to remedy this really a gradual approach to the problem and extensive searching at all points along the way?

The problem of premature closure was discussed at length in Chapter 5. I noted that premature closure tended to be diagnosed as a disease of not searching long enough. But various lines of evidence suggested that the difficulty had more to do with not having a clear concept of the problem and not maintaining high enough standards. When problems were clear and standards high, long searches would occur as necessary. But advised to search long as a matter of course, people would list ideas by trading quality for quantity, select not all that wisely, and finish with no better result than if they had tried to think of one or two "best" solutions in the first place.

None of this is to say that the five-step plan is silly. It has its moments. As mentioned in Chapter 5, problems with solutions that commit substantial resources need the help of cautious, thorough strategies. Also a faulty sense of problem demands can cause premature closure, and the five-step plan includes a step for pinning down just what the problem is. The difficulty with the five-step plan is not that it's too silly but too specialized, far more so than it seems at first. Like SQ3R, it does its best work in particular circumstances.

To generalize that point, I'd say the same about many of the recipes recommended for routine use by the creative-thinking school of thought. Such advice ought more to have a break-in-case-of-fire status. Persistence with these recipes is less to the point than having them around when the kinds of problems that most need them appear. But your average problem on the street can be approached in the most forthright way – by simply trying to think of a good solution at the outset. If that fails, or if circumstances are such that one can't take chances on a seemingly sound solution, time enough then for strategies and tactics. The steps of the five-step plan and similar ploys are best backed into as required, rather than run through as a matter of course.

We have here a problem of narrow advice. I've proposed that the creative-thinking school of thought has been up to some unfortunate schooling, with advice overgeneralized from special situations. Does research on classroom work corroborate or contradict so glum a circumstance? At first, the research seems to contradict it. In contrast with the research on mathematical heuristics, surprisingly many studies have sought gains resulting from training of this general sort. In a 1972 article, E. Paul Torrance tabulated findings from no fewer than 142 investigations, most of which adopted the creative-thinking perspective in one way or another. Torrance indicated that in most cases gains had indeed been found.

Can we be assured then that my doubts are needless and such instruction works after all? Not quite. The flaw in these attractive findings lies in the instruments used to measure gains. Most employed performance on the Torrance Tests of Creative Thinking. These tests ask people to devise many solutions for various sorts of problems. The tests are scored on number, variety, and originality of solutions. The person does not generally have to choose a best solution (although the instructions discourage routine solutions and request original ones, so this should lead to some selectivity). Other tests sometimes used in such studies proceed quite similarly.

It is no great surprise that such tests reveal gains in training of the creative-thinking sort: These tests merely measure what is taught. Students are drilled in generating many ideas, and unremarkably, when the post-test is administered, the students exhibit this very behavior more than do students in control groups. But have they learned to be more creative thinkers? I've argued already that the contribution of long searches to creative performance is problematic. Furthermore, efforts to show that the Torrance test and others like it measure what we really mean by creativity have yielded unimpressive results. One would like to know that people notable for creative achievement score higher on such tests. In an article wryly entitled "Creativity Tests: A Boon or Boondoggle for Education?," Susan Crockenberg reviewed several efforts to demonstrate just this and concluded that nothing compelling had been found. In a 1976 article, Michael Wallach, himself the codeveloper of the Wallach and Kogan Creativity Battery, reported that his own and similar tests as well as IQ tests had been shown again and again to be mediocre predictors of actual professional achievement.

The worst conclusion would be that creative-thinking programs using creative-thinking tests have wasted much time and money for no real gains. But we need not be that pessimistic, I think. Now is the time to call back the long neglected notion that began this chapter: people make their gains by learning what is taught. This isn't always so.

Consider the five-step plan again. What do people do when it seems to be a waste of time? Some proceed to do the exercise as given. But frequently people simply don't take the advice. If a seemingly good solution appears early, they omit the further steps. Even with no solution forthcoming, people often find the five-step plan too roundabout, and prune it to suit themselves. I've seen this happen again and again, not only with the five-step plan but also with various heuristics. It seems actually rare for a person to follow such advice straightforwardly, especially for more than one or two trials.

All this suggests a happier interpretation of what might be happening in those creative-thinking courses. People modify advice, rather than ignoring it or taking it, and modify it in the direction of streamlining – just what's needed at least in these cases. Also, practice with the five-step method and similar heuristics alerts the learner to methods that otherwise might be missed. The methods can be used when called for – their proper role. Furthermore, by being led to do long searches even when they may not be required, students do learn something: that ideas are "there" waiting to be found. Whether a person conceives of good ideas as rarely or frequently there might influence considerably the person's willingness to set high standards and search until they are met. Finally, more important than any particular advice in such courses may be the general message: you are here to do creative things. Change your behavior to make it more creative. Given the occasion and the motivation, many people can do much of that reshaping for themselves, never mind the advice good or bad.

I have no way to prove that all this happens in conventional creative-thinking courses, but I believe it does at least a little. I think I have seen people gain in such ways from heuristics in my own teaching, even though I don't particularly stress heuristics but introduce them in passing. For another example, E. Paul Torrance, in the article I mentioned earlier reviewing those 142 programs, begins by confessing his prejudices. He states: "I know that it is possible to teach children to think creatively and that it can be done in a variety of ways. I have done it. I have seen my wife do it; I have seen other excellent teachers do it. I have seen children who had seemed previously to be 'nonthinkers' learn to think creatively, and I have seen them continuing for years thereafter to think creatively." Torrance's testimony, I think, is worth more than his test.

Revised proposition: People often modify considerably the heuristics they are taught. But they may gain anyway, by improving poor heuristics, learning to think about how they think, and in many other roundabout ways.

Still, it would be much better when teaching heuristics to teach really good heuristics.

NO SUBSTITUTE FOR KNOWLEDGE

Heuristics do work, sort of, I've argued. They work when they're good heuristics with a managerial component and followed, or not so good and appropriately modified. Heuristics can add to the ability of a person well enough versed in a field for the heuristics to be meaningful. But "what do you gain when you add heuristics?" is just one way of asking how much heuristics help. Quite a different way is this: What sort of tradeoffs occur between general heuristic principles and knowledge in a field? That is, how much will having good heuristics make up for a lack of field-specific knowledge and knowhow? Profound implications would follow from a very positive answer to this question. If general heuristics could make up for particular experience, education could concentrate entirely on generalities and their application, never mind the niceties of sheep breeding or statistical methodology. Armed with a few reference books, the graduates of this educational utopia could sort out for themselves whatever was needed through effective reading, problem solving, and invention.

Proposition: Powerful general heuristics make up for considerable field-specific knowledge and know-how.

If any of these propositions deserves the name of "straw man," it is this one. Such fulsome optimism is, of course, plain silly. Yet the issue raised is not. Just what sense can we develop of the tradeoff between general heuristics and field-specific knowledge? An ideal answer involving systematic measures can't be managed right now. But we can get a feel for the situation.

What could it mean for heuristics to substitute for field-specific knowledge? Obviously, very general heuristics couldn't provide the "facts," the data of history or anthropology or the definitions of mathematics. Rather, it is upon just such facts that heuristics do much of their work — sorting, organizing, drawing implications. However, heuristics might make up for field-specific experience in handling the facts by providing in a much more general form the very arts the practitioner otherwise would develop only within a subject area. Mix heuristics with the facts and you get an expert. This, in somewhat caricatured form, would be the hope.

This hope quickly flounders on one particular fact: the existence of heuristics of intermediate generality, principles special to a subject area but not as piecemeal as are dates in history or recipes in cooking. Such principles are an important part of expert lore and understanding and a part often not well known to the novice. Very general heuristics plus the facts simply do not generate these middle-level heuristics. Their existence provides a way of understanding just what the limits of general heuristics are. All this needs examples to make it clear, and three follow.

The classical detective story is a perfect case in point. Some of the rules of the whodunit game might be put as follows. (1) The culprit is always a character throughout, rather than appearing newly at the end; (2) the evidence is sufficient to identify him or her; (3) the solution doesn't depend on exotic, specialized knowledge; (4) the villain is never the obvious suspect, and  usually an unobvious one – the person, for instance, who seems to have had no opportunity; (5) the villain is rarely a very sympathetic character, someone you would feel bad about being guilty. A novice at reading such tales certainly can understand them and sometimes even figure out who the culprit is. No doubt, general problem-solving heuristics could help in this process. But clearly one is also helped by knowing the genre, because this narrows the choices so much. It's sometimes even possible to guess the villain without sifting the evidence at all, because only one character is just right for the role of the unexpected villain.

You might think that genres and their tacit rules of the game arise only in such playful contexts as stories and riddles. But of course artifice is the business of being human, and rules of the game show up in nearly any pursuit. Consider psychological research. Anyone with some common sense can understand the gist of many psychological theories and the evidence supporting them. But in order to play the game at the professional level, you need to use the proper genre for establishing psychological results. For example, often results come from comparing performances on some task in different groups – children versus adults, male versus female, trained versus untrained, those exposed to one stimulus versus another. Claims are established by demonstrating a "statistically significant difference" between the groups. This means that, according to certain mathematical principles, the difference is large enough so that it would not be likely to result from chance alone.

In many ways, this style of inquiry helps the investigator, who can proceed with a clear sense of the form the results must take and what constitutes adequate evidence. On the other hand, in certain ways the genre is limiting. For example, investigators often settle for a statistically significant difference not very significant at all in another sense. The difference isn't big enough to matter much. Moreover, Herbert Simon has criticized the significant-difference form of typical psychological findings for its low information yield. Physics, Simon argues, has made great progress by devising equations that relate variables to one another. Such equations provide much more powerful theories than do simple demonstrations of significant difference, and perhaps in some cases psychology could move in that direction with profit.

Now why do I outline this little critique of the genre of psychological inquiry? Not for its own sake, but simply to emphasize that there *is* a genre, involving various somewhat arbitrary but motivated choices – as in the whodunits. Neither a rough understanding of psychological findings nor a host of general heuristics puts one in a position to play the psychology game or to perceive its limitations.

For a third example consider Zen koans, the riddles used to help the novice Zen Buddhist toward the proper frame of mind. The information comes from a fascinating book called *The Sound of the One Hand*, a translation with commentary by Yoel Hoffman. In the commentary and an introductory essay by Ben-Ami Scharfstein, the book tells a story of individual rebellion within the practice of Zen. In 1916, there was published in Japan an account of the Zen koans with their "official" answers. This caused some upset then, and its resurfacing in photocopied Japanese editions recently has created a further disturbance, because Zen tradition had kept it secret that there were official answers. But, the 1916 publication revealed, there were. The author made his motives plain. He considered the traditional answers and their transfer artificial and corrupt, and aimed to reform the conduct of Zen. Zen instruction would make little sense if the answers could be found in a book, he thought.

The motives of the koans' appearance in English, in *The Sound of the One Hand,* are quite different: a contribution to scholarship and recognition of a classic of Zen literature, for so the book is viewed by Zen master Hirano Sojo, who wrote a brief foreword and also advised Hoffman on the commentaries. My own motives follow upon this. Here is a remarkable chance to examine a tradition of riddling, to see whether the riddles and their answers can be understood as radical and patternless or as governed by regularities. Of course, the question would be a pointless one if Zen masters merely told their novices the answers. This apparently was not the practice. As Hoffman outlines, instead the Zen master would try to lead a novice to devise the answer for himself, hinting in various ways if the novice did not make enough progress. So the answers had constantly to be invented anew. How was this possible? Let's look at a few koans.

> A. *Master:*   In clapping both hands a sound is heard; what is the sound of the one hand?
>
>   *Answer:*   The pupil faces his master, takes a correct posture, and without a word, thrusts one hand forward.
>
> B. *Master:*   When someone asks you in a dream about the purpose of our founder coming from the west, how will you answer? If you can't

answer this, then the truth of Buddhism will have no effect on you.

Answer: The pupil snores, "Zzz . . . zzz," imitating one soundly asleep.

C. *Master:* There's a quarrel going on across the river – stop it.

Answer: "What the hell is that bastard muttering about?! You bloody fool! I'll kick your sides in and slam this damn bottle into your guts!" So saying, the pupil grabs his master by the neck and with his face raging with anger, he pretends to fling his fist at his master.

The inventiveness of such responses makes them especially intriguing here, where, of course, the deeper significance of Zen is not considered. The "answers" to koans stage a revolt against conventional rational explanation as well against anything magical or miraculous. We can appreciate their rebelliousness readily enough. In this limited way, we can appreciate the perverse sense they make. But it is hard to see how anyone could get from question to answer, other than by knowing the answer.

However, I want to argue that the responses are not as unruly as they seem. In fact, they are highly patterned, though not in the usual way for answering questions. Part of that order runs as follows. (1) The response always refuses to meet the question as asked and its tacit assumptions, ignoring the question's frequent absurdities, elements of the miraculous, metaphysical pretensions, and so on. (2) The response relates to the question by picking up some concrete element or part of it. Thus the pupil above thrusts forward the one hand, snores to imitate the sleep implicit in dreaming, or stages a mock fight. (3) The response often is an action rather than words. (4) The response often involves identifying yourself with what is not yourself, as when the pupil becomes part of the fight he was asked to stop. (5) Often the response is a "pretend" action, as when the pupil snores or fights. (6) Often the response is most disrespectful of "wisdom" and indeed of the master himself. Thus the pupil snores or attacks his master.

 Instant Zen

As koans B and C illustrate, a strong current in the practice of Zen is its refusal to take itself too seriously. To do so would be to defeat the endeavor. With that in mind, it's not so inappropriate to speak of "instant Zen." Below are five more koans. The principles have been outlined. Now try to propose answers in the same style as above. Suggest several for each koan.

D. *Master:* Now that you've heard the sound of the one hand, what are you going to do?

E. *Master:* If it's that convenient a thing (to hear the sound of the one hand), let me hear it too!

F. *Master:* Extinguish the light that lies a thousand miles away.

G. *Master:* Without using your hands, make me stand.

H. *Master:* How high is the sky?

Of course, whatever luck you have here (and luck as well as principle certainly helps), instant Zen is only ersatz Zen. The tricks above trade on structural regularities in the koans while hardly dealing at all with their significance. *The Sound of the One Hand* explores the meaning of the riddles and their answers in provocative ways I will have to pass by here, and only the Zen master would have a full sense of their meaning. But such reservations granted, this example, like the earlier ones, suggests that field-specific generalizations, known consciously or tacitly, powerfully inform invention. Think in what a poor position a person armed only with general heuristics of creative problem solving would be to solve Zen koans!

Revised proposition: Of course, one needs particular knowledge and experience to function at all in a field. But beyond that, knowing the informal rules of the game is more potent than knowing very general heuristics.

This might seem to say that general heuristics are useless. Indeed to a degree it says just that. There is no substitute for knowledge – experience, familiarity with a field, knowing the ins and outs, the rules of the game, whether explicit or tacit. Yet for all that, general heuristics have their place. When genre-specific principles are used, general strategies can add to their power. Moreover, we do not always operate in familiar problem domains. In fact, we encounter new kinds of problems constantly not only as we explore novel subject areas but as we go further in a familiar field. General strategies provide an initial approach that will give way to genre-specific understanding as experience accumulates. Finally, remember that the deliberate search for and use of genre-specific strategies can itself be a potent general strategy.

By the way, some traditional responses to the foregoing koans are:

D . "I'll pull weeds, scrub the floor, and if you're tired, give you a massage." [The notes to the koans observe that for the reader, an appropriate answer would be, "I'll keep on reading."]

E . Without a word, the pupil slaps his master's face.

F. With the tips of his fingers, the pupil makes the form of a rising flame. Then, saying "Whoosh," he blows it out.

G. The pupil stands up and walks two or three steps.

H.   Pointing toward the ceiling, the pupil says, "From here it's seven feet."

TEACHING INVENTION

This chapter began with the thought that people invent not only things and theories, but behavior. A novel kind of invented behavior was plans for invention, plans proposed by various writers mostly in the last half century. My main business has been both to review evidence favoring this idea and to worry over some serious difficulties. With all that in mind, what should be done about the promise and problems of teaching invention? Not much more here, I think. The main goal of this book is not to recommend but to explain, and I've tried not to burden these pages with too much advice to the maker. I'll limit myself to commenting on just two matters that seem central: advice giving as an approach to teaching invention and having the right advice to give.

For the first, advice giving seems much too narrow a concept. Indeed, such instruction by no means always proceeds by advising. In an imaginative program called the LOGO project, Seymour Papert and colleagues at Massachusetts Institute of Technology have sought to "teach kids to think" by teaching them a very simple computer-programing language. The students become involved in individual projects with the computer, projects that, it is hoped, help them to acquire general skills of thinking, such as how to organize extended problem-solving activities of the sort that occur in projects, how to abstract and formalize, and how to "de-bug" not only computer programs but any behaving system, including themselves. Though there are many advicelike principles important in the program, the program does not proceed mostly by presenting recipes. The main teaching strategy is to engage the student in the computer environment, which by nature and design promotes the desired behavior.

Matthew Lippman's "philosophy in the classroom" program provides another example. The program hopes to develop philosophical thinking, and other traits like creativity, in primary and secondary school children. Again, there are certainly particular patterns of thinking the program aims to impart. But the program relies hardly at all on advice giving. Instead, more than anything else it depends on modeling. Utilizing a novel, *Harry Stottlemeier's Discovery*, in which children of varying skills and personalities reason through various problems, and also classroom dialogue where the teacher serves both as a paragon and guide, the program shows students what philosophical thinking is like and gets them involved in it.

My own teaching experience in creativity makes a third example. Occasionally I've offered a course designed both to inform people about recent research on creativity and to help them to be a bit more inventive. Again, the emphasis is not on advice giving. Instead, people create their own advice. They investigate how they proceed with some activity like painting, consider their needs as they see them, and invent new ways to try to meet those needs. Of course, to encourage people to do this is to give advice of a sort, but not advice about how to carry out the particular activity.

None of these examples is offered as a perfect solution to the dilemmas of teaching invention. Both Papert's and Lippman's approaches invite various criticisms, and I'm all too aware of some uncertainties about my own. Indeed, from a purely practical standpoint, many approaches work more or less satisfactorily, and it's very difficult to find out how *much* more or less. But regardless of that, such approaches by their mere existence make a simple point: principles of effective thinking needn't be delivered to the student as advice.

My other target was the matter of "right" advice – or more generally, the "right" principles however delivered. Since I've grumbled about bad advice, it seems only fair to give a sample of what I think are good principles, the mainly explanatory aim of this book notwithstanding.

Try to be original. That is, if you want to be creative you should try to build into any outcomes the property of originality. This sounds almost too silly to mention, but I don't think so and have given some reasons for that in earlier chapters. Many supposedly intrinsically creative pursuits like painting can be pursued in very humdrum ways. Major figures in the arts and the sciences often were certainly trying to be original. As argued in Chapter 3, creativity is less an ability and more a way of organizing your abilities toward ends that demand invention.

Find the problem. This recalls Getzels' and Csikszentmihalyi's concept of problem finding. Early in an endeavor, explore alternatives freely, only gradually converging on a defined course of action and keeping even that flexibly revisable. The evidence is that creative people do this. The principle makes all the more sense because later on in the process is often too late – too late to build in originality or intensity or other qualities you might want.

Strive for objectivity. Chapter 4 on evaluation pointed out that problems of accurately and objectively monitoring progress pervaded creative activity. The judgment of the moment would prove different tomorrow, the revisions of today wrong in a week. As noted there, makers have adopted many strategies to cope with the caprice of their own impressions, such as setting a product aside for awhile. Also, learning to fashion products that have a potent meaning for others as well as for yourself is a complex process. Beginning with the child's first experiences of language and picturing, the problem of reaching others reappears throughout human growth in more subtle guises and plagues even the expert maker. Sometimes, it may be best to ignore such hazards and freewheel for a while. But if you always freewheel, you never really take advantage of your own best judgment.

Search as necessary and prudent. That is, explore alternatives when you have to, because the present option has failed, or when you had better, because taking the obvious course commits substantial resources that might be better spent. Of course, the conventional advice of many works on creativity is to explore many alternatives routinely. Chapter 5 presents experimental evidence to the contrary.

Try, but don't expect, to be right the first time. The research reviewed in Chapter 5 found that people trade quality for quantity. Aiming at fluency, they lower the standards governing their production of ideas, select imperfectly, and achieve no net gain.

This is advice against doing just that. Instead, ask your mind to deliver up the best possible results in the first place. Notice that this does not mean fussing over initial drafts, trying to make them perfect by editing in process. Neither does this say that the results *will* be right the first time. They likely will need revision, maybe extensive revision and maybe the wastebasket and a new start. This is why you have to adopt a paradoxical attitude: trying, while being perfectly comfortable about falling short. The point is to bias the quick unconscious mechanisms that assemble the words we say, the gestures we make, toward doing as much of the work as possible and leaving as little as possible for deliberate revision. To put it another way: ask yourself for what you really want – you may get it, or at least some of it.

Make use of noticing. The ability to notice patterns relevant to a problem is one of the most powerful gifts we have. This can be put to work deliberately by contemplating things connected to the quest. Suppose, for example, you are designing an innovative house and need ideas. Walk around a conventional house and see what transformations suggest themselves. Or examine a conventional house in the mind's eye with the same objective. The latter can be particularly powerful, and the mind's eye takes a willing traveler to places inconvenient for the body or billfold. Often books on creativity recommend exposure to seemingly unrelated things to stimulate ideas. This certainly sometimes works, as Darwin, Archimedes, and others have taught us. But, in my experience and judgment, sensitive scrutiny of things related to the task at hand usually yields a richer harvest of ideas.

When stuck, change the problem. Early on in the space race, NASA spent much time and effort seeking a metal robust enough to withstand the heat of reentry and protect the astronauts. The endeavor failed. At some point, a clever person changed the problem. The *real* problem was to protect the astronauts, and perhaps this could be done without a material that could withstand reentry. The solution, the ablative heat shield, had characteristics just opposite to those originally sought. Rather than withstanding the heat, it slowly burnt away and carried the heat away from the vehicle. Let me generalize this and similar examples into a heartening principle. Any problem can be solved –

if you change the problem into a related one that solves the same
real problem. So ask yourself what the real problem is, what constraints have to be met and which ones can be changed or sacri-
ficed. (There may be more than one way of formulating the real
problem.)

When confused, employ concrete representations. Darwin's
notebooks, Beethoven's sketchbooks, a poet's drafts, an
architect's plans all are ways of externalizing thought in process.
They pin down ideas to the reality of paper and prevent them
from shifting or fading in memory. All of us do this at one time or
another. However, despite such habits, we may not realize that
making thoughts concrete can help to cure confusion on nearly
any occasion. When paths lead this way and that, circle back, and
refuse to show the way, make notes, make drawings, make
models. Think aloud or form vivid mental images, for such internal concreteness helps some too.

Practice in a context. Most advice on how to be creative urges
the learner to apply it everywhere. However, sometimes "everywhere" is so indefinite and daunting a notion that it turns into
nowhere. When people want to improve their creativity, my suggestion is for them to choose some likely activity they often
undertake and try hard to be more creative in that. Focus breeds
progress. No need to hold back in other activities, but be sure of
one.

Invent your behavior. That is, people should think about,
criticize, revise, and devise the ways they do things important to
them. Too often, inventive thinking is limited to the customary
objects of invention – poems, theories, essays, advertising cam-
paigns, and what not. But part of the art of invention is to select
unusual objects of invention – objects like your own behavior.
This isn't just nice; it's needed. Performances do not necessarily
improve, even when you do them frequently. Indeed, it's common lore that people often end up practicing and entrenching
their mistakes.

There, then, are some possible plans up front, another contribution to that young and hopeful technology of thought. These
principles and others like them try to define and impart the limited
but very real "edge" which is about the best you can hope for from

very general principles. Perhaps the plans mentioned are hard to take, at least as advice. Their prescription is too broad, too much in the direction of telling the daydreamer to pay attention or the grind to daydream more. Just what they mean in particular cases and how one persuades oneself to behave accordingly are serious questions. But take them as general principles and take seriously the problem of translating them into practice, and then they make more sense. There's no reason why the right principles (whether these are they or not) have to be as easy as a recipe for boiling water.

8

LIVES OF INQUIRY

A familiar friend in many children's activity books is the connect-the-dots puzzle. There is a sprinkle of dots numbered from one to something, and the youngster must draw a line connecting them in order, to reveal the dinosaur or rocket ship or Raggedy Ann. An odd feature of such puzzles is that often they pose no puzzle at all. The supposedly hidden form shows through simply in the pattern of the dots, even as the sprawl of the stars across the sky allowed the eyes of ancient peoples to group them into constellations.

Here you will find something like connect-the-dots puzzles of that unpuzzling sort. This is a biographical chapter, putting into a broader perspective the processes of creating examined earlier. However, since a few pages hardly allow for real biography, I've tried instead to collect episodes that, like the dots on those non-puzzles, make meaningful constellations. Sampled here are periods from the lives of three scientists: Charles Darwin over fifteen months as he searched for an adequate theory of evolution; Marie Curie over more than a decade as she made herself a potent scientist, discovered two new elements, and struggled to demonstrate their reality; and a contemporary medical researcher, James Austin, over much of his life as he became a physician and then a research neurologist striving to understand degenerative diseases of the nervous system.

DARWIN: THE TRANSFORMATION OF A PROBLEM

Darwin's discovery of the principle of natural selection is one of the most celebrated moments of insight in the history of science. The circumstances are worth remembering. By July 1837, at the age of twenty-eight, the young Charles Darwin already was a confirmed evolutionist. Acquainted by his education and readings with the controversial evolutionary thinking of others, he had been impressed by symptoms of evolution observed during his five-year voyage of geological and biological inquiry on the *Beagle* – symptoms such as the variations in species on islands isolated from the mainland. In the months after his travels, Darwin pondered all this and finally reached a conclusion. Evolution was a reality. At least to some extent, species developed into others. Darwin set out quite deliberately to devise an explanation, a theory of evolution.

Darwin's mission proved a difficult one. The crucial insight came only fifteen months later, in September 1838, when he had been reading Thomas Malthus' writings on population, "for amusement," as he said. Malthus' book discussed population pressures and the struggle for survival that occurred when organisms outbred the available resources. Suddenly it struck Darwin that here was a principle to explain evolution. In the struggle for survival, the better adapted would have an edge over the less well adapted. These individuals would tend to survive and pass on their advantages to their progeny.

In Chapter 2 I discussed this discovery as an isolated insight, but now Darwin's moment of truth needs to be put into a larger context. Otherwise, it's tempting to embrace a "big bang" model of discovery, a model that has the conceptual work of invention occuring in one brief epiphany. Why did Darwin take fifteen months to put some simple facts together into so simple a pattern? Because, at first, his concept of evolution differed fundamentally from the theory of natural selection. Before Darwin was ripe for Malthus, he had to get free of some early ideas, find some new ones, and bring into focus the data that proved most telling. It is this story of conceptual change that I want to tell over the next pages. My source is a penetrating book by Howard Gruber, *Darwin on Man.*

In July 1837 Darwin opened the first of a series of notebooks that allow tracing the development of his ideas. There was a theory at the outset, the monad theory of evolution. To the hindsight of the twentieth century, the theory sounds naive, even magical. Darwin proposed that monads – individual primitive life forms – arose spontaneously all the time and tended, generation by generation, to develop into more complex forms. When geographical barriers separated some individuals of a monad from others, the groups would adapt to their slightly different environments. Different species would arise from the same monad over the course of millennia. However, radically different organisms, for instance fish versus birds, were the descendants of different monads. Finally, like an individual, a monad eventually would die, meaning that all the descended species would expire at once. Darwin believed that this mass death somehow had to occur because he had concluded that the number of species should be roughly constant over time; but, according to this theory, new monads were always arising. Odd as it sounds today, this theory seemed like a good start to Darwin. Notions like the spontaneous generation of life forms were common, and the idea that a whole group of species should have a natural life span and a timely death, much as an individual, seemed a fine analogy.

Numerous origins of life – a premise to reject. Darwin thought he had to assume numerous origins of life because some contrasts between species defied any effort to imagine a common ancestor. Also, the presence of living one-cell organisms seemed to require the premise, since Darwin at first thought that all life forms evolved to become more complex. So the only way to have primitive organisms today was to have them of recent origin. Darwin shortly became uneasy with all of this. He wanted a theory of evolution, and the more that could be ascribed to adaptive change and the less to independent origins of life, the better.

Darwin soon found reasons to reject numerous origins of life, along with the idea that life forms had to develop into more complex ones. Even at first, he had imagined the evolution of a monad as a kind of branching tree, the branches corresponding to adaptation of the monad to different environments. There was no need for a living "missing link" – an organism intermediate between two related species – because the division of the two had occurred long in the past, and intermediate forms were extinct. Darwin came to realize that this argument could explain even the radical differences between the plant and animal kingdoms. When the branch point was so far back down the complicated tree, one wouldn't expect a readily imagined common ancestor. Some new evidence also helped Darwin. Fossilized material was discovered containing preserved one-cell organisms essentially identical with living forms. This meant that all life forms did not become more complex over the millennia; some could remain simple.

The species as an individual – an analogy to challenge. Darwin's monad theory featured an analogy between the life cycle of an individual and the life of a monad, which would originate, develop, differentiate into more complex forms, and finally die. To make progress, Darwin had to think of a species not as a single organism but as a collection of individuals that could vary individually in their adaptations and chances for survival. One thing that helped Darwin to drop the analogy was the absurdity of supposing that the descendants of a single monad, scattered over the globe and diversified into many species, would all die out from monadic old age with no definite physical cause.

Direct adaptation – an idea to discard. Early on, Darwin supposed that plants and animals in a new environment somehow changed slightly in form to adapt to it. Darwin saw no necessity to explain how this happened – it simply did. The business of a theory of evolution was to account for the development of utterly different species by successions of such direct adaptations. But Darwin's ultimate theory did explain how plants and animals adapted to their environments. How did he perceive this need? For one thing, Darwin came to feel that assuming direct adaptation simply assumed too much. For another, over the months he observed that creatures could adapt to an environment in many ways. It was not that there was a unique template an environment stamped on a given species; clearly something more complicated was going on. Finally, Darwin noted that often species were imperfectly adapted, even though surviving. Apparently adaptation was not so quick and clean as he had thought. Eventually Darwin was ripe for a more roundabout account.

Change is continuous – a principle to sieze firmly. Natural selection provides a mechanism of gradual, continuous change. This was what Darwin wanted, since he identified continuity with scientific explanation and mysterious jumps with a mystical or religious explanation. But, at first, the seeming evidence forced Darwin to tolerate occasional jumps. Signs in the fossil record suggested sudden, massive extinctions of whole groups of species. The death of a monad was one way of expressing this. However, later on, Darwin became more aware of gaps in the fossil record which could create the illusion of extinction. Also he got the idea that species did not so much become extinct as evolve gradually into other species. Apart from extinction, Darwin initially thought that adaptation to a new environment would have to come in one generation, but later Darwin saw that some species weren't well adapted. One way and another, acceptance of discontinuities gave way to an insistence on continuities.

Favorable variation – a possibility to recognize. The theory of natural selection depends on favorable variations. Darwin had to work against a prevailing conception that spontaneous variations – not the adaptive variations Darwin had imagined might be caused directly – were always disadvantageous. Unfortunate mutations were a familiar phenomenon, and the idea of natural selection was already current in a negative form: "nature's broom" kept species neat by sweeping away mutants unfit to survive. What had not been recognized until Darwin's insight was that natural selection could be a progressive force.

The frequency of variation – an extreme to appreciate. Natural selection makes more sense if there is considerable variation to select from. Early on, Darwin did not recognize how much variation occurred within a single species. However, during the fifteen months following his first notes, Darwin became more and more aware of this. Indeed, the notebooks are filled with catalogues of variations. Five days before the Malthus insight, Darwin again was impressed by this, writing, "Saw in Loddiges garden 1279 varieties of roses!!! proof of capability of variation – Saw his collection of Hummingbirds, saw several greatly developed tails and one with beak turned up like avocette."

Superfecundity – another extreme to appreciate. The more reproduction of young, the greater the competition for limited resources. Over the months, Darwin became increasingly aware of such profligacy in nature. For one source, there was of course Malthus' book itself. Darwin certainly already knew Malthus' theories, and reading Malthus again at a ripe moment gave Darwin the last nudge he needed. Another influence was the report from a German biologist, C. G. Ehrenberg, of incredible rates of reproduction in microorganisms. At one point, Darwin wrote in his notebooks, "One invisible animalcule in four days could form 2 cubic stone."

Artificial selection – an analogy to make work. Darwin became intensely interested in artificial selection – the breeding of plants and animals – because he saw there a parallel to natural evolution. Creatures generation after generation "improved," albeit by the measure of humankind and not of nature. However, for a long time Darwin did not grasp that what was needed in the natural case was a mechanism of selection, to do the work done in stockbreeding by the judgment of the breeder. Initially, Darwin thought artificial selection and natural evolution to be quite different matters. The shifts of form introduced by human selection were impermanent. One could always make them disappear by breeding back into the parent population. The products of breeding programs were not the sorts of modifications wanted for adaptation; they were unnatural consequences of humankind's special needs and desires. Darwin saw no connection between geographical isolation, which prevents nascent species from merging back together, and the isolation imposed by breeders. He even pondered the odd notion that, for some reason, variations produced by slow causes stuck better than the quick work of humanity. Even after Darwin had reacted to Malthus with his theory of natural selection, for a while he did not make that much of the parallel between artificial and natural selection. But it was to become a dominant metaphor in Darwin's final statement of his theory. The concept of selection would be prominent in Darwin's mind and ready to participate with others in the pattern that finally fell into place on September 28, 1838.

I began with a paradox: respect for Darwin's great insight, but also puzzlement over his obtuseness – what took him fifteen months? I end with an appreciation of the real problems Darwin faced. When Darwin first set out to solve the problem of evolution, he simply was not ready for natural selection. The eight factors discussed above are a partial measure of his distance from his goal. Some notions were to be rejected – the idea of direct adaptation, for instance. Some were to be emphasized – the idea of continuity. Some were to be recognized – the frequency of variation and super-fecundity. What forces brought about these shifts in Darwin's thinking? There was Darwin the critic, surveying his own early positions – did they really explain what he meant them to? There was Darwin the inventor, devising new formulations. There was Darwin the learner, accumulating facts not present or not prominent before. There was Darwin the despairer, ready to postpone and finally give up trying to explain the mechanisms of variation.

In light of all this, Darwin's moment of insight no longer seems so focal. Clearly, much of the real work of invention was done before Darwin sat himself down to read Malthus. This isn't to deny the importance of getting it all together, as Darwin did, nor to forgo respect for the powers of the mind for rapid pattern making. But it is to insist that such moments have to be appreciated in the context of the work of the mind that prepares the way for them.

Darwin's notebook entry for the idea Malthus inspired was emphatic, but no more emphatic than many entries. Neither did Darwin drop his other lines of inquiry to pursue the new idea, indicated by an entry on the following day emphasizing the sexual curiosity of primates. Apparently, although the idea seemed good from the first, Darwin's appreciation of its potential grew slowly. Only six or eight weeks later did Darwin have his idea firmly enough in hand to write a succinct and forceful statement of its logic:

> Three principles will account for all
>
> (1) Grandchildren like grandfathers
> (2) Tendency to small change especially with physical
> (2) change
> (3) Great fertility in proportion to support of parents

Finally, twenty years later, twenty years of worry over that nagging problem of variation, nervousness about the response of a fundamentalist public, painstaking assembly of persuasive data, and only under the stimulus of Wallace's discovering the same theory, did Darwin go public (he had shared his ideas with a few associates). On July 1, 1858, a joint paper by Darwin and Wallace describing the theory was read at the Linnaean Society. Finally, six months after that, on November 24, 1858, Darwin published his thorough argument for the concept that would once again force humankind to reconceive its place in nature. The whole theory was in the title: *On the Origin of Species by Means of Natural Selection, or the Preservation of Favoured Races in the Struggle for Life.*

MARIE CURIE: DISCOVERY AS DEDICATION

In the last years of the nineteenth century, the first steps were taken that would result in the modern concept of matter, the quantum theory of the atom and nuclear energy. One of the key moments in the history of atomic physics occurred when the young Marie Curie, having taken degrees in physics and mathematics, having married Pierre Curie and borne a child, set out to select a topic for her doctoral dissertation. She chose to work on the recently discovered phenomenon of radioactivity, a name it did not yet have but which she and her husband later would give it.

Radioactivity had been detected in uranium. Marie Curie wanted to measure just how much radiation emanated from uranium, other elements, and compounds and ores of uranium under various conditions. She quickly found that thorium was radioactive, a result in which another investigator slightly anticipated her. She established that the amount of radiation emitted by uranium depended only on the quantity of the element present, regardless of compounds it had formed with other elements or other physical conditions. (This had profound implications, although Curie was not to recognize them yet. It suggested that radiation was an atomic property, a property of the atom itself, when atoms were then supposed to be indivisible and structureless.) But a third and yet a fourth discovery awaited her. The last of these would give her a life of intense labor, much grief, and considerable triumph.

The third discovery arrived when, measuring the radioactivity of pitchblende and chalcolite, uranium-containing minerals, she found they exhibited substantially more radioactivity than refined uranium. Marie Curie saw the likely significance of this: the samples contained an element more radioactive than uranium, a new element as yet unrecognized by science. In honor of her native country, Poland, Curie christened the element polonium and set out to demonstrate its reality by purifying a sample. In due course she was able to prove its existence. Meantime, though, the fourth discovery occurred. A residue left after refining polonium also turned out to be radioactive. Curie applied the same logic: yet another unrecognized element must be present. She would label this radium. In the course of the years, her labor and her honors would be most associated with this name.

Marie Curie's discoveries may well have come to her as moments of insight. However, such moments are not the concern here. Instead I want to look at what her ideas required in the way of commitment to study and research. It seems likely that another physicist in similar circumstances simply would not have had the will to undertake the program of investigation that Marie Curie pursued with her husband Pierre.

Maria Sklodowska came to Paris in the fall of 1891 at the age of twenty-four. She came to study science at the Sorbonne. She arrived with poor spoken French, a smattering of physics and chemistry picked up mostly from books, little in the way of formal education, and a small allowance from her father in Poland together with some slight savings. For the first months, she stayed at the home of her elder sister and her sister's husband, a Paris physician. It wasn't long, though, before she shifted her residence closer to the university, to live as many other students of meager fortune did. Her room was a sixth-floor garret and, in the winter, she had to carry her ration of coal up from the ground floor for whatever heat she needed. In the summer, the room was stifling.

Her poor preparation and equally poor spoken French did her no good. She had to work hard just to accomplish what others could with little trouble. But her commitment and interest did not flag. Indeed, as time advanced, she became more and more involved in the study of physics, a total recluse existing only for her work. "All my mind was centered on my studies," she later wrote. "All that I saw and learned that was new delighted me. It was like a new world opened to me, the world of science, which I was at last permitted to know in all liberty." "If sometimes I felt lonely, my usual state of mind was one of calm and great moral satisfaction."

In 1893, Maria Sklodowska faced her final examination in physics, the examination that would decide whether or not she would receive the degree for which she had undergone such deprivations. She was troubled by nervousness and despair for weeks beforehand, all for nothing. She took a first in physics, surpassing all the other examinees. The next year, she sought a degree in mathematics, and there took a second.

When Maria Sklodowska and Pierre Curie first met at the

home of a Polish physicist working in Paris, Pierre was thirty-five, a serious physicist himself with some recognized work. The year was 1894, and Maria Sklodowska had just completed her degree in mathematics. In due course, the two were drawn more and more together. It was a remarkable match between idealists. Both had dedicated their lives to scientific inquiry. Both felt that findings should be shared freely with the world, regardless of the advantage this might give other investigators working in the same area or the commercial rights that would be lost. Both expressed indifference to financial well-being. For the most part, they behaved accordingly, as the trials of the coming years were to testify.

There were some differences of temperament, however. Although both were shy, Pierre was vacillating even in professional contexts and, although imaginative and productive, made much less of himself than he might have. Marie Curie, for the most part quite as reticent, spoke firmly in professional discussions and tended to dominate a group in a quiet way. Though she didn't put herself forward, she would not shrink from seeking what she saw as her due. Later in life, she proved the irritant of many physicists and a puzzle to the public for her increasingly cold, authoritarian manner, the complex product of her own early bent, the hard work that had been necessary, her radiation-induced ills and weakness, and experiences with public media that sometimes had been painful.

Even early on and in connection with Pierre, she was meticulous about protecting her own preserve. It was her idea, hers alone, that the excess radioactivity in a uranium ore over that in uranium itself pointed to an unknown element. She took care in conversation and in publications to be perfectly clear about whatever was to be attributed solely to herself. She must have been conscious early on how easily the world could explain away her accomplishments as the work of her husband. Had the risks been reversed, Pierre Curie no doubt would not have had the forthrightness for this. But Marie Curie did.

In 1899, the Curies were ready to attempt the purification of radium. They were given a large shed to work in, of which Marie Curie later had to say: "Its glass roof did not afford complete shelter against rain; the heat was suffocating in summer, and the bitter cold of winter was only a little lessened by the iron stove, except in its immediate vicinity." A famous German chemist, Wilhelm Hostwald, who visited the Curies' laboratory out of respect for their work, said of the shed, "It was a cross between a stable and a potato-cellar, and, if I had not seen the worktable with the chemical apparatus, I would have thought it a practical joke."

Since the radium occurred only in minute quantities, massive amounts of pitchblende had to be processed. This job fell to Marie Curie. Working in and outside the shed, she spent all day handling iron pots of ore, the size chosen to be the maximum she could lift. All this was only the first stage of refinement, and other more finicky if less punishing phases came after. This cycle she would have to repeat again and again. One young physicist said later how privileged he felt to have observed "with my own eyes the birth of radium . . . I saw Madame Curie work like a man at the difficult treatments of great quantities of pitchblende." She herself confessed, "I would be broken with fatigue at the day's end," but characteristically counted this time as the "best and happiest years of our life . . . I shall never be able to express the joy of the untroubled quietness of this atmosphere of research and the excitement of actual progress with the confident hope of still better results." Marie Curie eventually was able to delegate her stevedore's work. However, there was much left to do. What with one mishap or another, it was not until March 28, 1902 that she had isolated a nearly pure sample of radium chloride. It weighed just more than one tenth of a gram.

As early as July 1898, when Marie Curie and her husband had discovered polonium but not yet recognized the existence of radium, they began to encounter health problems. Pierre Curie experienced pains in various joints, attributed to rheumatism, and Marie Curie had cracked and sore fingers. Both succumbed to minor ailments easily, and fatigue and lethargy were persistent difficulties. In the years to come, these symptoms intensified. In 1903, the Curies' second child, a girl, was born prematurely and died within hours. There were no obvious reasons. Contemporary medicine recognizes a likely cause, however. Particularly during the early months of pregnancy, the fetus is highly susceptible to damage by radiation. It can be estimated that Marie Curie would have been exposed to up to 1 rem per week. Recently .03 rem per week has been considered the maximum safe dosage for pregnant workers in radium plants, and with new awareness of possible long-term effects, such figures are under constant scrutiny. Also, Marie Curie would have constantly been breathing the radioactive radon gas emitted by radium. Her exposure would probably have been several hundred times that of today's safe dosages.

Through all their problems of health and weariness, even during Marie's pregnancies, the Curies worked on, ignoring their disabilities as best they could. Hindsight finds a sharp irony in one of their innocent pastimes. Sometimes at night, during the refinement of radium, they would return to the shed simply to wonder over what they had wrought. As their eyes became a little accustomed to the darkness, they would begin to see the radioactive glow emanating from the various containers on shelves about the room. Marie Curie, almost always the sober scientist, was to write later that such moments "stirred us with ever new emotion and enchantment."

Marie Curie was a compulsive taker of notes. In the laboratory, this habit stood her in good stead, providing the kind of definitive record invaluable to a scientist in making sense of a long program of work subject to mishaps and false leads. In the home, it would seem a meaningless waste of time. But not to the discoverer of radium. The dates when Irene, the Curies' first child, first tried various foods were dutifully recorded, along with the costs of two bicycle tires and a pair of woolen cycling stockings. Even up to the time of her death, Marie Curie persisted as an archivist.

Rarely did any personal flavor creep into these lists of dates, numbers, and items. Only once did Marie Curie break down to the point of fully expressing her feelings in writing. After Pierre was killed in a carriage accident, she began privately to scrawl a diary of love letters to the dead man, in a kind of expression she had never allowed herself before: "What a terrible shock your poor head has felt, your poor head that I have so often caressed in my two hands. I kissed your eyelids which you used to close so that I could kiss them, offering me your head with a familiar movement." But whatever passions Marie Curie harbored, her demeanor with others was almost always controlled. Within a month of her husband's death, she began her laboratory notebook again, and more and more she immersed herself in her work.

Marie Curie was the first woman to make a significant contribution to science. Although public acclaim and reasonable financial support for her work was slow in coming, her accomplishments, with those of Pierre, were recognized fairly early by major figures in the exciting atmosphere of end-of-the-century physics. In 1903, the Curies shared the Nobel Prize for physics with Henri Becquerel for their work on radioactivity. Public attention began to turn more and more to the shy and dedicated couple, who became reluctant and uneasy celebrities, ill equipped for and disinterested in the furor. In 1906, Marie Curie took over her dead husband's new professorship at the Sorbonne, one specifically created for him by the French parliament. Disconcertingly for her, her first lecture was a celebrity event, packed with journalists, sightseers, and socialites as well as students. She made no concessions, delivering a technical lecture in a nervous, barely audible voice. Nonetheless, great applause greeted her conclusion and hasty exit. One person characterized the day as "the celebration of a victory for feminism. If a woman is allowed to teach advanced studies to both sexes, where afterwards will be the pretended superiority of man? I tell you, the time is near when women will become human beings." But earlier, then and for the rest of her life, Marie Curie refused all association with feminist causes. She considered this "politics" and no proper concern of a scientist.

It was a point of honor with the Curies not to patent their procedures for extracting radium. Science should be a disinterested activity, and indeed "disinterested" became one of Marie Curie's terms of highest praise. Not only did the Curies take no patents, but they willingly provided information to whomever sought it. Even before Pierre Curie's death, radium had become a commercial commodity. Their investigations had gained some slight support from cooperative arrangements with manufacturing concerns, but for the most part, while the two were still laboring with inadequate resources, others were beginning to profit handsomely. In 1904, the price of radium salts in English pounds was 400 pounds per gram. By 1912, the price had risen to 15,000 pounds per gram. The couple never gained anything from the industry their inquiries had launched, a fact Marie Curie recounted with some pride for the rest of her life.

Madame Curie's commitment was crucial to what she accomplished. A person of the same gifts but less drive would have achieved nothing in the same circumstances. A person with more flair for theoretical innovation but less drive would probably have achieved something quite different. Of course, we have to avoid the trap of supposing that commitment plus ability guarantees greatness. People both very dedicated and very able are not nearly as rare as the likes of Marie Curie. But the importance of character cannot be gainsayed. Biographical studies of major figures in the sciences and the arts almost always reveal unusual commitment, whether or not of Curie's austere sort.

AUSTIN: TIME AND CHANCE

"Again I saw that under the sun the race is not to the swift, nor the battle to the strong, nor bread to the wise, nor riches to the intelligent, nor favor to the men of skill; but time and chance happen to them all." This sentence from Ecclesiastes, offered by James H. Austin as an epigraph to a chapter in a recent book, could not be more to the point, for the concern here is the vagaries of chance and how they shape the life of inquiry. Whereas Charles Darwin and Marie Curie are famous figures, James Austin may hardly be known to anyone outside his profession. Austin is a contemporary man, a research neurologist and chairman of the department of neurology at the University of Colorado Medical School. In his 1978 *Chase, Chance and Creativity*, Austin spoke out about his own career, and the twists and turns imparted to it by chance of one sort and another. Committing the first part of his book to biography, Austin went on to present a typology of chance and discuss other aspects of creativity.

Although the theme of chance is familiar in the history of science, episodes of actual discovery usually receive emphasis. There was Darwin's encounter with Malthus or Marie Curie's detection of a new element while testing the radioactivity of uranium-bearing minerals. Another classic case is that of Alexander Fleming, who in 1928 observed that a culture of staphylococcus in a laboratory culture dish would not grow near a bit of mold that had invaded the nutrient, and gave the world penicillin. Another concerns Wilhelm Roentgen, who in 1895 noticed that a completely shielded cathode ray tube he was experimenting with induced a glow in a card coated with a certain chemical that happened to be nearby, and named the penetrating radiation X-rays. In this tradition, Austin does give examples where chance immediately yielded a discovery. But Austin does much more with chance than that. He recounts its crucial role in events not seemingly pivotal at the time, events that put him in a position to discover something later or encouraged a new direction. He conveys a sense of the way chance infuses all aspects of the inquiring life. Austin sums the matter up in a few sentences:

> What factors shape a career? Are they readily definable? Are they the product of a free choice, decision, or logic alone? Not in my case. For thus far, the pivotal influences have been more subtle or unplanned things: the resonance of an uncle's voice, impromptu drama in a Saturday conference, the happenstance of military assignment and of job scheduling. And from now on, the turning points in the story will

hinge on other fragile events: the words of a friend, a mother's resolve against a fatal disease, and the vigor of a dog running wild and free on a chase in the field.

For a better sense of some of the influences Austin sees operating, let me review each one of these episodes, ones that only sample the many Austin describes.

James Austin spent many a summer in his youth on his uncle's farm in Ohio. The uncle was a physician and enjoyed discoursing on patients in his deep resonant voice before the youngster, who was generally intrigued by matters biological. Besides this exposure to thoughtful involvement, the young Austin found browsing opportunities in his uncle's medical library. The uncle's articulate concern was but one of many factors that led to Austin's later commitment to medicine. Another was his own risky encounter with pneumonia, where he experienced first hand the threat of disease and the remarkable work of a new sulfa drug in returning him to health.

In 1950 James Austin was twenty-five years of age. He had completed four years of undergraduate education, four years of medical school, and a year of internship. He was engaged in a first year of residency at Boston City Hospital, in neurology because he felt his knowledge of the area was inadequate. One Saturday morning, a patient was presented by another neurology resident; an incident occurred that ultimately was to change the direction of Austin's commitment to medicine. The patient, a women in her forties, had suffered for a number of years from a degenerative condition of the nervous system, one that affected the conduction of the impulses in the peripheral nerves and resulted in atrophy of the muscles in her hands and feet and in loss of feeling. The chief of service, Harvard professor Derek Denny-Brown, stepped forward to palpate the nerves at the elbows and knees. Austin had never seen this done before. Were the nerves enlarged? No, they were not. The neurologist in charge of the ward commented intelligently on several diagnostic possibilities and then asked Denny-Brown for his opinion.

His opinion was that the patient might have hypertrophic neuritis. But the patient's nerves were not in fact enlarged. Certainly this objection was more than reasonable, because the very name of the malady *meant* enlargement of nerves. Denny-Brown remained unshaken. He cooly remarked that sometimes in this disease the nerves were not enlarged. A lively exchange followed, with nothing resolved in the end. Years later, Austin was to find an obscure article confirming that hypertrophic neuritis did not always involve enlargement of the nerves. In any case, the drama of the occasion had fixed the odd disease and the test of palpating the nerves in Austin's mind.

About a year after that Saturday morning, James Austin found himself a naval medical officer, stationed in California and admitting to the hospital a young sailor, aged twenty-two, who for a number of years had experienced increasing weakness in his feet and hands. It did not take Austin long to confirm the basic condition of the patient, but which of many possible diseases did the sailor have? Now comes a crucial moment. Austin remembered to feel for the nerves, an unusual move relevant only to a few rare diseases. The nerves were decisively enlarged. He had encountered an unambiguous case of hypertrophic neuritis.

What to do about it? Austin in fact knew little of the disease and, hoping to help the young sailor, began to explore its causes and possible cures in the literature. The quest was not encouraging, since the medical profession did not understand the disease very well. Throughout the following months Austin continued to canvass the literature, assembling information and becoming more and more involved in his mission to comprehend the mysterious malady. By the end of the year, Austin's mind had been turned by his experiences. He no longer saw himself headed for a career in internal medicine. Instead, he meant to become a neurologist.

Austin took decisive steps in that direction. In 1953, out of the Navy, he planned in six months to start a two-year residency at the Neurological Institute of New York. A fortunate circumstance would fill the gap until then: Austin was granted a six-month fellowship at the Columbia-Presbyterian Medical Center in New York, an organization of which the Neurological Institute was a part. Austin would study neuropathology during this period. He continued his reading about hypertrophic neuritis and encountered an intriguing fact. In certain parts, the enlarged nerves when tested on autopsy proved "metachromatic" – this meant that a color change from blue to red appeared when the material was treated with a certain dye, much as litmus paper shifts from blue to red in an acid solution. Later, by chance, he came across a reference to another neurological disease involving metachromasia – one called metachromatic leukodystrophy, or MLD. This link immediately made MLD of special interest to Austin. On reading the article, Austin discovered that MLD involved massive metachromatic deposits not only in the nervous system but also in the kidneys. Austin experienced a heady moment of inspiration: Might one be able to diagnose the disease during life by a simple procedure, detecting metachromatic fragments excreted in urine?

Fascinated by this hypothesis, Austin finally found an opportunity to attempt his dye test on urine collected from two brothers with symptoms of MLD admitted to the hospital some ten months later. For a while there was confusion: the metachromatic effect appeared, but also appeared in control samples from healthy people's urine. However, Austin shortly discovered an unexpected color shift that occurred only in material from the brothers' urine, a shift to a golden brown. This seemed specific to MLD. But why golden brown and not the expected red, and, in any case, what was this metachromatic substance?

Austin's six-month fellowship came to an end and he moved to his residency. His inquiries continued. Chance had intervened several times, but here we come to the particular episode referred to by Austin as "the words of a friend." This friend had had some neurochemistry and, although not able to help Austin directly, pointed him toward some recent work in dissolving substances in the nervous system as a means of isolating them. Finishing his residency and moving to a new division of neurology at the University of Oregon Medical School, Austin applied the technique and succeeded in isolating the metachromatic material. But still "what was it?"

MLD is a rare disorder, thankfully. However, its very rarity posed a problem for Austin's efforts to investigate and understand the disease; post-mortem materials for analysis were hard to come by. A young patient at Oregon, suffering from MLD, eventually died from it. The child's mother insisted over the reservations of other family members that they should agree to a postmortem examination. This, along with other sources of materials and information, provided Austin with the wherewithal to push his inquiry further.

This final example, the oddest one of all, takes us ten years further along in Austin's career. By 1965, Austin's interests had diversified to include other diseases of the nervous system with metachromatic properties. One of these was called Lafora's disease. This could be recognized through use of the microscope, because small round bodies inside the nerve cells would stain red. But what were these Lafora bodies, as they were called, and what would the answer to that reveal about the disorder?

Austin and his colleagues tried several approaches to the puzzle, all of which failed. Then chance took a hand in a bizarre way. A sequence of events occurred which for some time had no apparent connection with the problem of Lafora bodies. Tom, Austin's spaniel, loved to wander far on country walks with his master. One day, Austin tied a small bell to the dog's collar to help him locate Tom. Apparently, Austin concluded much later, the bell irritated the dog's skin. In any case, a few days later Austin found an alarming lump developing on Tom's neck. Fortunately, surgery performed by a colleague revealed only some kind of mild inflammation. But what had caused it? Some sections of the tissues, stained, revealed a peculiarity under the microscope: round bodies, bodies that stained red. Could these be like Lafora bodies, Austin wondered? And could he find out what these bodies were made of? If so, that might be a clue to the nature of Lafora bodies.

Austin's first hypothesis was that the bodies in the tissue sections taken from the spaniel might be some sort of fungus. Not so. It was observed that the bodies occurred outside and not inside the tissues. Indeed, the bodies were soon found to be globules of starch from the surgeon's glove. Starch was routinely used to dust surgeons' gloves. The bodies had nothing at all to do with the revived Tom's unserious malady. Even so, the starch globules stained red. Could the Lafora bodies in that disease be some chemical similar to starch? Various techniques permitted Austin to confirm shortly that Lafora bodies, like starch, were a glucose polymer.

It may have struck you that, over these many episodes of good fortune in the investigations of James Austin, accident figured in different ways. Certainly this struck Austin, and in his book Austin attempts to characterize four kinds of chance. (1) *Blind luck.* This is the sort of chance that might happen to anyone, like finding a dollar bill on the street. (2) *Being in motion.* This kind of chance depends simply on the individual poking around within a circumscribed area, but without any focused purpose. The luck arises because one is on the move, exploring. (3) *The prepared mind.* This could involve a certain amount of blind luck and being in motion, but in any case something else is central: the person's mind has been prepared by experience to notice the significance of circumstances that might pass another by. (4) *The individualized action.* Chance of this sort depends on the unique contribution of actions arising directly out of highly individual traits and circumstances.

Austin does not categorize the incidents I reviewed, so I will try it for him. The resonance of an uncle's voice – this factor, which helped to move Austin toward medicine in the first place, seems to be blind luck. Impromptu drama at a Saturday conference – being in motion, I think; Austin was poking around, attending a presentation he probably need not have attended. The happenstance of a military assignment – the prepared mind certainly fits this well. Because of the Saturday conference a year before, Austin was prepared to examine the young sailor. The words of a friend – this seems to fit (2) best, being in motion. Again, Austin was poking around, describing his work, asking here, asking there. A mother's resolve to have an autopsy – blind luck; beyond a request, nothing to be done. The vigor of a dog – here we have the individualized action, in Austin's outings with Tom, which triggered the odd chain of events leading to the discovery of starch globules and their resemblance to Lafora bodies. That recognition, of course, is a case of the prepared mind.

It's interesting also to think how chance intervened in the investigations of Darwin and Curie. There was Darwin's encounter with Malthus, clearly a case of the prepared mind encountering the right stimulus. In discovering polonium, Marie Curie benefited from being in motion. She had systematically set out to test the radioactive properties of a number of minerals, just to see what could be found. Of course Curie's mind had to be prepared to appreciate the significance of what she found, and Darwin's reading of Malthus could be taken as part of his generally being in motion. Indeed, Austin writes that there is no particular need to take his four types of chance as exclusive of one another; two or more can apply to the same event.

Now all this could be dismaying if we came to see ourselves as constantly subject to accidents beyond our control, our lives as so many dice rolled by fate. What about that problem? In Austin's

story, not every accident changed wildly the direction this man set for himself. A steadiness of purpose developed over the years that would take advantage of what chance offered, but persist nonetheless. True, such an early episode as the presentation of the patient with hypertrophic neuritis may well have changed the rest of Austin's life. But contrast this with the last incident, where Austin's dog provided him with a clue about Lafora bodies. What would have happened had this luck not come Austin's way? A month or a year later, one way or another, Austin would have found the answer anyway. Even without Malthus, Darwin probably would have reached the same conclusion, since natural select fit his problem so well. As the concept of the prepared mind makes clear, the human response to circumstance can be active and selective, not just passive and accepting. When it is, the best of chance provides full advantage, while the worst of chance has its influences minimized. Right there is the concept that frees us from a fatalistic view of the forces Austin dramatizes.

REGULATING INQUIRY

How do we understand a creative career? The sketches of Darwin, Curie, and Austin emphasized the gradual transformation of a problem, the role of commitment, and the contribution of chance. All of these elements seem important to that complex compound that makes up the life of inquiry. But surely there must be more than this. Asking the right questions is crucial at such points, and one of those right questions was asked by Howard Gruber about Darwin: What internal factors regulate a career? How does the inquirer achieve and maintain coherence and direction?

One useful concept Gruber introduces is a person's "network of enterprises." The words are well chosen. One problem leads on to another in the context of a person's general missions and aspirations. Also, it's a network of enterprises, not a single enterprise or a disconnected set of them that needs to be considered, since typically several somewhat related enterprises will be pursued; one may spin off another; an enterprise may be dropped, now one and now another will receive emphasis; and in general you orchestrate your work in terms of them. Another provocative idea from Gruber is "images of wide scope," images that serve as a kind of conceptual and aesthetic focus for a person's developing inquiries. Gruber suggests Darwin's tree of nature, his image of evolution as a branching tree. This idea and sketches of it occurred early in Darwin's quest for a theory of evolution and survived to become the only figure in Darwin's *Origin*, thus informing the investigation throughout.

It strikes me that these notions of Gruber map readily into the lives of Marie Curie and James Austin as well. Polonium, radium, establishing a laboratory and raising funds to support it, organizing a fleet of mobile X-ray units during World War I, all these were part of Marie Curie's network of enterprises. For one image of wide scope, let me suggest the glow of radium itself. Remember how the Curies used to return to their laboratory at night to marvel over its luminance. Also, simply to hold up a vial containing a sample was a favorite demonstration of the Curies. Consider the choice of the label itself – "radium," for matter that emits rays, at first signifying the invisible rays of atomic radiation and ultimately appropriate for an element that emits light itself. There surely is both fascination for the eye and a puzzle for the mind.

Austin's case also can be read in such terms. From his first introduction to hypertrophic neuritis in 1950, Austin elaborated his network of enterprises to include studies of a number of degenerative disorders of the nervous system, particularly those exhibiting metachromasia. In that very word emerges one of Austin's images of wide scope, one predominantly aesthetic in character. I can make that case no better than by quoting from Austin:

> I made thin frozen sections of the MLD kidney material sent by Lowell Lapham and stained them with toluidine blue. This was to be my first real glimpse of the disease I had worked on for so long. I awaited the result with mounting excitement. Looking into the microscope, I finally saw the MLD kidney tubules – packed with vast amounts of the abnormal lipids. The deposits stained a sensational mixture of red, red-purple and golden-browned colors, and I immediately recalled the stained glass windows of the Saint-Chapelle in Paris, which until that moment had been my ultimate visual experience. I have never forgotten the way this slide looked; I can still see it vividly in my mind's eye – an aesthetic delight!
>
> If some symbolism is involved in this earlier work in MLD, surely it lies close to a profound appreciation of these colors. They are among my favorites, and working with them has always been deeply satisfying.

These examples deal with what Gruber has called the erotic side of science. In response to one of his articles, Michael Parsons urged that another more austere regulating force be kept in mind: the inquirer's sense of the discipline. In each of our three cases, Darwin, Curie, and Austin, there is something special to be said about that. Darwin, for instance, was not happy with his first monad theory of evolution. Gradually, over the months that followed, he discarded those features that amounted to no explanation at all and pushed toward a more meaningful account.

Clearly, most would have been satisfied with less. In the mind and personality of Marie Curie, the sense of the discipline concerned not just the proper form of theory and experimentation but extended into a kind of Puritan morality of science, with the key precept "disinterestedness." In the work of James Austin, a personal sense of discipline figured too. Austin wrote about the hard times he encountered early in his research career finding support for his neurological work. Metachromasia in the kidneys? In urine? What kind of neurological studies were these? But he saw the genuine relevance of this to the discipline, persisted, and eventually persuaded others.

So "sense of the discipline" often can mean more than following the rules of the paradigm. It can involve the kind of self-discipline that has a vision of the needs of the field and holds the self to the standard of meeting those needs. To people who feel this way, a discipline becomes more than good manners. It becomes a sort of ideology, and they are its idealists.

9

HAVING IT

When you have it – creativity, that is – what do you have? A good way to start on an answer is to think about *creativity* the word. It's a member of a little family of words including the verb *to create*, the adjective *creative* applied to things like *Guernica*, the theory of relativity, or Aunt Beth's cooking, and the adjective *creative* applied to people like Picasso, Einstein, or Aunt Beth. Which of these words is central?

I'd say it was creative as applied to things. The verb won't do because it is much more general than the adjective. For example, a person may create a problem, a hurricane create havoc, or a journalist create a stink without any of these outcomes being particularly creative. The kind of creating we are talking about is the kind of creating that leads to creative results. Creative people are people who often produce creative results. And creativity is whatever people who get creative results have. The idea of a creative outcome or product is the conceptual center; all the other words in the family get their meanings from it.

If creativity is whatever people have that leads to creative results, it might include many things. Creative abilities would be abilities that make a person's thinking creative. A creative style of thinking might be a style which gives novel ideas a chance by not rejecting them out of hand. Interest in and commitment to doing creative things would be important. Neither the enthusiast without ability nor the able but uninterested person would be called creative. So we ought to think of creativity as a mix of abilities and many other traits. But often we don't. Instead, we think of it as

creative abilities alone. Creativity becomes a kind of "stuff" which the creative person has and uses to do creative things, never mind other factors. If you have so much of it, that's what you have, and that's that. We think of intelligence in much the same way. Intelligence is the "stuff" people have that lets them think intelligently.

I don't know why people ever treat creativity as if it were only a stuff. Perhaps it's partly the influence of the concept of intelligence on the way we think about thinking. Perhaps it's the human tendency to make up entities standing behind processes, such as rain gods or wind gods. At any rate, sometimes I feel we ought to do away with the word *creativity*. What need is there for a word that removes us one step further from the key meaning of a creative result? To see what an odd and unnecessary idea creativity is, consider this. Just as we speak of creative people, we speak of athletic people. So suppose we coin a word to mean whatever athletic people have that makes them athletic – say *athleticity*. Now we can talk about how much athleticity people have, and maybe even try to measure athleticity in relation to IQ, sex, and race. All this sounds scientific because athleticity sounds like a single fixed stuff we could measure. But perhaps people are athletic for many different reasons and in many different ways, even reasons and ways which change with time. We could just as well

talk about how athletic a person is, instead of how much athleticity a person has, and the first way of talking doesn't make those
misleading suggestions.

Well, I'm not going to try to reform the English language and I'll
continue to talk about creativity. However, the "stuff" connotations of creativity beg questions that can't be begged here. We
mustn't forget that creativity may be as much a matter of style,
values and other factors as of abilities. In fact, I want to take seriously the possibility that specifically creative abilities may not even
exist. Maybe it is the creative orientation of a person that mar-
shalls the person's general abilities to creative ends.

TALENT AND CREATIVITY

The great creators tend to have talent. They reveal a natural
knack for thinking and doing in their specialties. Whether gifted in
mathematics, music, drawing, or whatever, they find that those
gifts support their creative endeavors. An apt example of such talent, again, is Mozart's musical memory. Mozart reportedly had a
phenomenal memory for music – both others' and his own – and
this memory served him well, making possible an in-the-head approach to composing which would not have worked for another.
So it's natural to urge a talent theory of creativity. If creativity is
whatever a person has that makes the person creative, then that
"whatever" might be talent.

Proposition: Creativity derives from a talent or set of talents.

This proposition does not state the issue too well. It would be
odd to say that Mozart's musical memory caused his creativity.
True, perhaps it made possible the sort of music Mozart composed. Certainly it made possible his approach to composing. But
just as certainly someone else might have had an equally potent
memory and used it quite uncreatively. As with Mozart's memory, so too in general a talent might relate to creating only in allowing a certain order of creative achievement, but without at all
making the person creative. Such talents, even if extraordinary,
aren't properly a part of a person's creativity, because a person
could have those talents without being creative. What would a

specifically creative talent be like? It might be an ability for idea getting or insight, for instance. Whatever its form, having such a talent should in itself make the person that much more creative.

I've stated this in terms of talent. However, it applies just as well to abilities in general. After all, what is a talent? Roughly speaking, a talent is an extraordinary and inborn ability for doing something – remembering music, say. A specifically creative ability, inborn or not, would be an ability that in itself made a person more creative. So we ought to refine the proposition to emphasize specifically creative talents. Let me also refine it to concern abilities in general. If there turns out to be any specifically creative abilities, time enough to consider then whether they ought properly to be called talents because they seem inborn.

Refined proposition: Creativity derives from specifically creative abilities.

I've urged caution about supposing that creativity derives from abilities. This view leaves no room for orientation, and orientation in general seems to have much to do with human endeavor. Nonetheless, what evidence is there for specifically creative abilities that account for all – or even part – of creativity? Basically, psychologists should propose an ability that withstands several tests.

(1) The ability in itself should make a person more creative.

(2) The ability should contribute to all or most sorts of creating, much as good coordination would contribute to nearly any athletic activity. We want this requirement because the aim is to explain creativity in general, not just in a particular domain like music or mathematics.

(3) The ability shouldn't turn out to be a more general ability sometimes applied with creative results. Likewise, in language learning we might casually speak of "good memory for vocabulary" as an ability. However, quite possibly, "good memory for vocabulary" is nothing but a good memory for anything, applied to vocabulary. When this happens, the "real" ability is the more general one.

(4) The ability should be measurable independently of a person's actual creative accomplishments. Likewise, to speak of

"good coordination" as a distinct athletic ability, we would have to be able to measure it independently of a record of success in athletic events.

I've tried to be specific about the needed evidence so that the implications of the available evidence will be clear. As the list shows, the conditions for a pure "stuff" concept of creativity are strict, certainly nothing to take for granted. Have creative abilities been proposed which pass muster?

Problem finding: Getzels and Csikszentmihalyi do not describe their concept of problem finding as an ability. However, since these investigators were able to demonstrate a strong relationship between problem finding and actual creative performance, whether problem finding might be creative ability seems worth considering. In my estimate, problem finding fails test number 3. Problem finding has the maker exploring multiple alternatives early in the course of creating, and considering seriously changes of direction that suggest themselves later. Now, anyone can explore multiple alternatives by trying. Anyone can take seriously, rather than hastily dismissing, ideas that suggest themselves later. But most people don't. In short, problem finding is a way of using your abilities, not an ability in itself.

Bisociation. Koestler does not advertise bisociation as a creative ability. Nonetheless, appraising it as such underscores the difficulties of meeting the standards. Bisociation involves bringing together areas of thought usually kept separate, so an ability to bisociate should indeed make a person more creative. However, bisociation fails all the other tests. As I argued in Chapter 3, it isn't clear that all invention involves bridging normally separate frames of reference. Even if it were, bisociation occurs as a result of remembering, pattern recognition, and other abilities rather than being a distinctive ability itself. Finally, there is no measure at hand for a person's bisociative ability, much less a measure independent of actual creative performance.

Ideational fluency. The most straightforwardly appealing and well-developed concept of a creative ability is ideational fluency along with its close relatives such as flexibility. The capacity to think of large numbers of ideas satisfying a given criterion, especially varied and original ideas, seems on the face of it to be fundamental to creating. Indeed, this sort of measure, suitably formalized, has become the core of a small testing industry and an associated body of research. Given such a good start for ideational fluency as a specifically creative ability, it is dismaying to think that this concept fails on almost all counts. As I mentioned in Chapter 5, poets did not use long searches very much in their moment-to-moment creating. Furthermore, the laboratory research reported by Donald Johnson suggested that long searches are often counterproductive. Not the "real" ability itself, fluency reflects an underlying capacity subject to a quantity-quality tradeoff, with people functioning at the quantity end of the tradeoff while taking fluency tests and the quality end while creating. True, underlying capacity might be called the "real" candidate ability. But in general, as emphasized in Chapter 7, scores on the standardized fluency tests do not relate strongly to actual creative accomplishment. In the end, about all that can be said for fluency as a measure of creativity is that fluency can be measured – surely the least of reasons.

Remote associates. In the early 1960s, Sarnoff Mednick developed a general analysis of creative ability based on the classical view that thinking, inventive or not, depends on chains of associations. Mednick argued that creative individuals relied on associations that reached further afield. Most people possessed "steep associative hierarchies," meaning that they associated one thing very quickly and efficiently with a few other familiar things – dog with cat, black with white, and so on. However, such people had trouble retrieving other less common associates. In contrast, creative people benefited from a "flat associative hierarchy." Unusual associations suggested themselves more frequently. This basic difference in the texture of people's associative responses endowed the creative individuals with their creativity.

How well does this concept of a flat associative hierarchy measure up against the standards for a creative ability described earlier? It's at least plausible that remote associations might contribute to all kinds of creating. However, there remains the matter of an adequate measure.

The RAT

Wanting to gauge the capacity to devise remote associations and hoping to relate this capacity to demonstrated creativity, Mednick developed a well-known instrument called the Remote Associates Test, or RAT. A person taking this test encounters trios of words and must try to think of a single word that fits all three. One trio might be rat, blue, and cottage. The remote associate of the three is cheese. Presumably, people with flat associative hierarchies can solve such problems more readily because contemplating each word excites in their minds associations other than common ones, other than trap for rat, sky for blue, or lake for cottage. Here are four further examples to try, taken from a paper of Mednick's but not on the published version of the test.

railroad	girl	class
surprise	line	birthday
wheel	electric	high
out	dog	cat

Does the Remote Associates Test distinguish individuals found more and less creative by the measure of actual accomplishment? Here a somewhat confusing picture emerges. In studies conducted in the early sixties, strong correlations were found between faculty ratings for the creativity of student architects as well as student psychologists and scores on the RAT. However, another investigator failed to find a significant relationship between RAT scores and creativity in a group of 21 engineers and in a group of 31 physical scientists. In another study, RAT scores did not relate to achievement ratings within several groups of scientists. In short, some findings encourage the idea that the

RAT might measure a kind of creative ability, but the inconsistencies remain to be reckoned with.

In any case, the RAT falters in another way, a way hinted at by the experience of working the above examples. People taking the RAT report forming and exploring hypotheses with some selectivity rather than the kind of associative blitz that the notion of a flat associative hierarchy suggests. Indeed, any one thing would have an enormous number of remote associates, just because the link to the answer need not be close; so a freewheeling exploration of them would seem to be a questionable way to score well on the RAT. In fact, several studies have measured people's capacity to produce remote associates fluently and compared this to scores on the RAT. These efforts have revealed no relationship. Whatever people do to perform well on the RAT, apparently they do not draw on a distinctive ability to generate remote associates, even though this was the rationale that inspired the RAT in the first place.

Such a finding puts into question what was not questioned before – whether whatever the RAT measures contributes to an activity in a specifically creative way. It was from the unconventionality of those remote associates that the relevance to creativity came, but ready access to remote associates is not the essence of good performance or, the RAT after all.

By the way, the standard answers to the four remote associates listed above are working, party, chair or wire, and house.

Intelligence. Just what intelligence is has proven to be an unsettled and unsettling issue over many decades, an issue with many tangles worth avoiding here. However, the kernal motivation for the concept of general intelligence can be sketched in a few words. When people perform a variety of formal tasks – tests of vocabulary, mathematical reasoning, and so on – they do not show entirely unrelated strengths and weaknesses on the various tasks. Rather, a person scoring high on one will tend to score high on the others too. This is a statistical and not an absolute trend, but it suggests the *existence* of some underlying factor enabling the individual to perform well across the board, a general factor whose influence is partly, but only partly, obscured by particular knacks for particular tasks. This factor need not be one ability; it could include several general intellectual abilities all tapped by seemingly disparate tasks.

How does intelligence rate as a creative ability? First of all, intelligence is not, on the face of it, specific to creativity, whereas bisociation or divergent thinking at least has the appearance of involving creativity. Instead, intelligence might be one – or all – of those general abilities referred to earlier, abilities that enable creative performance without being specific to it. So does intelligence contribute to invention? The intensive and protracted efforts to develop intelligence tests have established an ideal situation for answering this question.

Essentially, the reply is a qualified no. A number of investigators have sought relationships between achievement in a particular discipline, such as mathematics, physics, or writing, and IQ. In general, no or at best very weak relationships have emerged between creative achievements and IQ scores. Contrary to its popular image, IQ simply does not predict effectiveness within a professional field that well, although IQ relates somewhat more closely to academic success as a student. The needed qualification concerns what might be called entrance requirements for various professions. For example, one rarely finds physicists or mathematicians with IQs much lower than 120 or 130, as if a certain IQ were minimum equipment for mastering the fundamentals of such a field. However, the findings suggest that so long as that basic mastery can be attained, what a person accomplishes with the resulting expertise has little to do with general intelligence. Perhaps we should say so-called general intelligence, since such results of course challenge the meaningfulness of the concept.

Insight. In the preface to a 1968 book entitled *Toward a Contemporary Psychology of Intuition,* Malcolm Westcott mentions the genesis of the twelve years of inquiry behind his volume: "It began one evening at sunset on top of Rockefeller Center, where it suddenly occurred to me that some people 'get the point' more quickly than others do." Around this observation Westcott elaborated some questions: "Do they? How much more quickly? So what?" Although many have pondered this, Westcott would not let the matter rest with a little thought. He set out to try to operationalize what it meant to get the point more quickly. The consequence was a psychological measure and a series of studies of what Westcott calls intuition. To my way of thinking, insight is a more suggestive term than intuition. Intuition has to do with lack of reasons, not with discerning the point more readily. So I'll use the term insight here but depend on Westcott's views otherwise.

 Insight Operationalized

Westcott's concept is the best candidate in these pages for a creative ability, although Westcott did not call it that. His basic notion was that a person with more insight required less information to reach a sound conclusion. Westcott made this notion more concrete with a simple test. The items were designed so that a test taker could expose five clues one by one for each item. The five clues together made the solution obvious. However, the instructions asked the test taker to find the right answer by exposing as few clues as possible. Of the test items, the series problems asked the test taker to determine the final term in a sequence given as many as necessary of the first five terms. The analogy problems asked the test taker to understand the basis of an analogy from as few examples as possible and to complete another analogy in the same way.

On the next page there are some sample items from Westcott's test. Before looking at them, cover all but the leftmost column with your hand. In trying each problem, look at it with only one clue showing, then with two, and so on, revealing as as many as you need to figure out the logic and predict the sixth term or the completion of the analogy.

1. Verbal series

   BC   CD   DE   EF   FG

   Sixth term?

2. Verbal analogy

   over/under   in/out   short/long   up/down   black/white

   high/what?

3. Numerical series

   326-1957   732-6195   573-2619   957-3261   195-7326

   Sixth term?

4. Numerical analogy

   312-4   8-2   15-4   351-1   242-2

   216-what?

Westcott administered his tests to several groups of college students. He found that how many problems a student got right had little to do with how much information the student demanded before answering. Some students did poorly while requiring much information and some poorly requiring little; some students did well requiring much and some well requiring little. By the measure of Westcott's test, the latter were the most insightful. He also found that insightfulness did not relate strongly to academic achievement and conventional measures of academic ability, suggesting that he was on to something else.

Could that something else be creativity? Let's consider the four standards. Arguably, insightfulness would make a person more creative for all sorts of creating. An ability to detect patterns with little information would favor noticing, which has proved important in the creative process throughout these chapters. Insightfulness might turn out to be the application of some other more general ability to problems requiring insight, but I can't propose such an ability. Westcott also found some evidence relating insightfulness to creative activities and traits. From two of his samples, Westcott identified extreme groups of the four kinds mentioned above. In the high insight group, 86 percent participated in creative activities of some sort, mostly writing. The other groups fell closer to 50 percent. He also found that the high insight students tended to be unconventional and comfortable in their unconventionality. They did not base their identities on group affiliations, and became most emotionally involved in nonsocial pursuits and in abstract issues. As I'll discuss later, this is characteristic of people of demonstrated creative accomplishment.

Nonetheless, there are reasons to hesitate about identifying insightfulness with creativity. Westcott also found that interest and creative involvement in the visual arts was more typical of the students who were often right but required more information – not the high insight group. Furthermore, Westcott constructed a perceptual version of his test, where people tried to recognize a pictured object with as few lines showing as possible. High insight scores on this did not relate very well to high scores on his other tests, suggesting that his method did not measure some general ability which could be called insight, independent of task.

All in all, Westcott's concept comes closer than any other I know of to capturing a specifically creative ability. However, the anomalies in the pattern needed to be understood, and data from individuals of professional creative accomplishment need to be gathered to be sure a relationship to creativity holds up.

Revised proposition: There is no strong evidence that creativity derives principally from specifically creative abilities. Creativity probably depends considerably on traits other than abilities. This applies all the more to talents. If specifically creative abilities are hard to identify, specifically creative inborn abilities are all the more so. On the best evidence to date, creativity is in addition to talent, not made of talent.

LEFT BRAIN, RIGHT BRAIN

During the eighth decade of this century, it has become increasingly difficult to avoid knowing that the brain consists of two anatomically nearly identical hemispheres with different functions. Even the simplest distinction between the activities of the two hemispheres has an air of paradox, since the left hemisphere controls the physical actions of the right side of the body, while the right hemisphere directs the left side. However, the contrasts that have filled books and lectures and sparked public interest are more provocative. They concern the fundamental nature of human intellectual functioning.

Proposition: The right hemisphere of the brain is the intuitive, visual, artistic, divergent half. The left hemisphere is the rational, verbal, scientific, convergent half.

This proposition makes obvious why the functions of the left and right halves of the brain show up in this chapter. In effect, the proposition assigns creativity to the right half of the organ we think with, making the left half what might be called the "calculator." Of course, science as well as the arts involves creativity, but this would not bother those who like such binary maps of the mind. They might simply acknowledge that good science has much art in it, and good art a certain science. In effect, the proposition offers an alternative to the "abilities" approach to creativity of the previous section. Here we find creativity explained not by analyzing what makes it up but by emphasizing where that what can be found – left or right.

Although this proposition might seem overbold, it lists only eight of the many capacities that have been attributed to one or another hemisphere. In fact, powered both by legitimate scientific interests and public fascination, the area of investigation itself has developed an odd split. While careful scientific inquiry has burgeoned, so too more and more sweeping claims have emerged with all the unstoppable vigor of Jack's beanstalk. In the circumstances, two key questions about the supposed hemispherical functions need asking: Is it so? So what if it is?

I'll begin with the second question. One reason for the popularity of such concepts is clear. The notion that an entire half of the brain is specialized to deal with intuitive, visual, artistic, divergent matters has pleased those concerned with what they see as an overly rational, scientific, and language-oriented trend in our culture. Such a division of the brain could fuel their plea nicely, for who would deny that if 50 percent of the organ we think with is given over to a certain range of functions, those functions could be neglected only at the risk of missing much of what it is to be human? Besides this sort of significance, findings about what functions occur where in the brain offer insight about the way various skills and abilities relate. When brain injury impairs differently skills that seem much the same, this suggests that the skills do not relate so closely after all. Such findings are quite common. For example, some victims of stroke can read numbers but not words, despite the seemingly similar demands of the tasks.

The "so what" question has at least that much of an answer, but often even more of an answer seems needed. In fact, localizing a performance in one or another hemisphere reveals very little about it. People often seize on such information as though it were rich with meaning, but consider: What can we tell about how invention works, when it ought to work, and how to encourage it to work better, simply by learning that invention sets up shop in the right half of the brain? Although studies of hemispheric localization have some point, they also often do mischief by becoming ersatz substitutes for understanding.

Now let me take up the first question, the one that asked whether the proposition we began with was so. A point of logic needs some attention right away. It's not clear how the champions of the right brain could possibly win all the conclusions they want. The right hemisphere can't very well be the seat of all intuitive *and* artistic *and* visual *and* divergent capacities because of inconsistencies concerning various disciplines. For example, if verbal capacities resided only in the left brain, while those others remained strictly in the right brain, then the poet couldn't be inventive or intuitive, nor poetry an art. If visual capacities stuck to the right brain and scientific capacities strictly to the left, astronomers, paleontologists, and medical pathologists couldn't make the fine sensory discriminations they need to.

For the rest, I borrow from a critique of the research in this area by Howard Gardner, himself an investigator who has worked extensively with brain-injured patients. Gardner acknowledges that there have been significant findings. He takes it as fairly well established that the left hemisphere has advantages in dealing with language, especially with consonant sounds and rules of grammar, as well as in classifying objects into standard linguistic categories. The right hemisphere seems less strongly specialized, but shows dominance in certain spatial tasks such as mental manipulation of images or finding your way around an unfamiliar environment. Also, the right hemisphere appears to be important for fine sensory discriminations, as in face recognition.

However, Gardner mentions a number of reservations. For example, a wholesale assignment of language functions to the left hemisphere will not do, since processing of vowel sounds and access to the meanings of words appear to be operations performed in both hemispheres. Also, left-handed people often show a different pattern of functioning. Besides qualifications of this sort, the means of investigation have their problems. Correlations between kind of task and the hemisphere supposedly involved often are unimpressively low, even when they reach statistical significance. Many findings come from studies of what tasks have been spared or impaired in different sorts of brain injury, but often, in stroke, particular injuries occur in a brain already ravaged by general physical degeneration. Gardner also cautions that poor performance on a task resulting from a localized brain injury does not imply that the injured portion of the brain performed that task, any more than a radio not working because the plug is pulled proves that the plug did the work of the radio. Finally, efforts to replicate interesting findings often have failed. So only the most robust and repeated findings deserve anything like confident acceptance.

Occasionally, investigators have looked for the seat in the brain of discipline-related skills, such as musical, artistic, or numerical skills. Gardner reports that investigations of this sort have failed to pin down such skills. Sometimes different experiments seem to argue for opposite hemispheres; sometimes individuals show contrasting patterns. Sometimes both hemispheres contribute to the performance under study in distinctive ways. For example, investigations of drawing by brain-injured patients suggest that the right hemisphere dominates in control of overall contour while the left handles recognizing details and internal elements. Since wholesale assignments of musical, numerical or similar abilities to one or the other hemisphere lack justification, all the more absurd are claims that general faculties like intuition or rationality reside on the right or left. Gardner concludes that too often people have played fast and loose with such general faculties, not defining them well enough so that what evidence there is could be weighed.

This could be the end of the matter, since the proposition we began with seems unfounded. However, a better end requires a better understanding of why such notions attract us in the first place.

Ping-Pong

The first reason is the ease with which we map the things of the world onto simple polarities, such as rational versus intuitive or scientific versus artistic. For example, think of several acquaintances or public figures and sort them into two types, the rational and the intuitive. Although a few borderline cases may appear, in general this seems easy to do. Since rational and intuitive are meaningful concepts that provide a ready way of sorting people, it's tempting to suppose that rational versus intuitive is a fundamental dimension of human personality.

But before accepting that, we should try the same exercise using a polarity E. H. Gombrich has toyed with: *ping* versus *pong*. Yes, the words are bizarre. Nonetheless, it's surprisingly easy to sort the things of the world according to them. What, for example, would a fork be? Ping, certainly. What about a spoon? Pong, it seems. What about the ocean? Pong, of course, and a star would be ping. People also fall readily into the ping pile or the pong pile. For example, where would you place Bach, Beethoven, Haydn, or Mozart? If you review some of the acquaintances you brought to mind during the previous paragraph, they too can be tagged as ping or pong.

The moral is simple: ease of classifying means nothing. Most any polarity one can think of, even a silly polarity like ping-pong, gives a way of mapping the world. This is good testimony both to the flexibility of the human mind and to the existence of a conceptual trap. The fact that a polarity like intuitive versus rational maps the world handily is no evidence at all for its special significance or relevance as a polarity, since even a nonsensical polarity will function just about as well.

Let me mention two other factors that make polarities appear more significant than they are. First, there is the ease of treating as a polarity what isn't one. Merely juxtaposing notions like intuitive and rational tends to simplify the meaning of each and to discourage remembering cases with both qualities. Consider what you might miss concerning intuitive versus rational. Whereas having reasons makes a judgment nonintuitive, usually there are no reasons for the reasons. Instead, the backing for the reasons that in turn back a claim is intuitive. The entire claim rests on intuitive judgments one level removed. For another example, highly rational activities like deductive reasoning depend on intuitions about necessity in logic, about what must follow given the premises. In general, understanding how intuitive and rational factors do the work of thinking requires recognizing their pervasive partnership, something an emphasis on polarities obscures.

Also misleading is the way polarities line up with one another. While scientific and rational make a natural-sounding pair opposite artistic and intuitive, scientific and intuitive opposite artistic and rational would sound odd. We tend to read this as deeply significant, inferring that artistic activities are delightfully intuitive and scientific ones doggedly rational. But counterexamples are easy to find. For instance, among the more intuitive scientists one probably would want to list therapists of various stripe along with medical diagnosticians; among the rational artists one might want to list op artists, conceptual artists, and conventional realists. Finally, the mix of intuitive and rational factors in any human activity should be remembered.

In short, the way polarities align often is only skin deep, a superficial feature of the connotations the words bear in our culture. I take this and the earlier points to be a healthy poke at the human love of polar thinking. This is not to say that polarities have no proper role as instruments of thought. Doing completely without them would be difficult. However, it is to plea for a greater critical consciousness.

Revised proposition: The right half of the brain can't with any confidence or cogency be said to house the intuitive, artistic, visual, or divergent faculties. It cannot be called the creative hemisphere. Nor, if it could, would we be very much informed about creativity.

PERSONALITY

There is a Monty Python skit concerning a public accountant who has become profoundly dissatisfied with his profession. He goes to a service that analyzes his capabilities and personality and advises him about what jobs would best fit his potentials. Although he complains that chartered accountancy is a boring profession, he is firmly informed by the agent that all the tests reveal him as an exceptionally boring person. While this would be a drawback for most positions, for chartered public accountancy, he is assured, it is a true asset.

This wry episode is as good a reminder as any that we associate certain personalities with certain professions, professions from chartered public accountancy to automobile assembly line worker to lawyer to politician and so on through the list. Certainly such stereotypes deserve vigorous skepticism, since they often seem little more than cultural myths, supported by hack novels or the characters in TV sitcoms. So stereotypes make a good starting place for considering the personalities of the creative artist or scientist.

Proposition: Creative artists are amoral bohemians. Creative scientists are cold assertive dwellers in ivory towers.

These versions of the artistic and scientific creative personality are not very favorable, but they certainly are familiar. Fortunately, abundant evidence exists to test the stereotypes. It so happens that the kind of personalities associated with creative activities has been one of the best researched matters in the study of

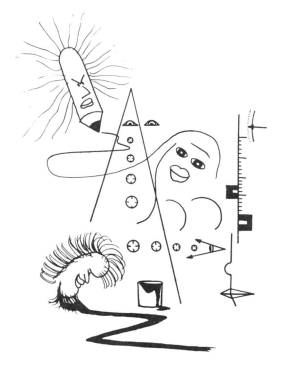

creativity. A number of professions have been investigated. The personality studies for the most part have taken actual creative achievement as their gauge of creativity. The circumstances allow a good appraisal of those cultural stereotypes and a better profile of the creative personality in the arts and the sciences.

Student artists. I've already discussed the study of problem finding conducted by Getzels and Csikszentmihalyi. An earlier phase of their study concerned the personalities, values, and cognitive abilities of art students. The investigators did their work at the School of the Art Institute of Chicago. Although their actual problem-finding experiment involved far fewer students, they initially investigated 179 students representing four areas of concentration – advertising, industrial design, arts education, and fine arts. Through batteries of tests, Getzels and Csikszentmihalyi discovered a personality profile that distinguished the student artists from students in general. The investigators described the contrast this way:

Young artists, while still students, already tend to be reserved, amoral, introspective, imaginative, radical and self-sufficient, and tend to possess attitudes usually associated with the opposite sex. They hold aesthetic values in high regard, and neglect economic and social values – a pattern that contradicts the ethos of the culture in which they live. They do not differ substantially from college students in intelligence as measured by conventional tests, but are far superior to them in spatial and aesthetic perception.

With one important qualification, these same traits sorted out the fine arts majors from the others, and the more from the less successful fine arts majors, as judged by the studio course grades and faculty estimates of originality and potential in each student's file. The fine arts majors, in contrast with commercial and education majors, possessed the listed traits to a greater degree. The more successful males among them were even more extreme. Thus, Getzels and Csikszentmihalyi may have caught the essence of the creative artistic personality, at least as it occurs in our culture.

There is a curious qualification, however. Getzels and Csikszentmihalyi found that women did not display the same traits in association with good studio grades and faculty ratings. Though the general personality profile held for both women and men, in the women, intelligence and tested perceptual abilities, but not more extreme expression of the personality characteristics, related to grades and faculty appraisals. In the men, the pattern reversed. Intelligence and perceptual skills did not relate but the personality factors did. This pattern appeared even more clearly when only the fine arts students were considered. Getzels and Csikszentmihalyi note that the personality profile for the males fits a problem-finding approach to making art, the approach that led to later professional success. For various reasons, Getzels and Csikszentmihalyi restricted their long-term study of problem finding to males. However, they point out, it's plausible that problem finding would help women as artists too, because of the way it figures in creative process generally. If so, it seems that an inappropriate double standard governed the faculty's reaction to men and women in the fine arts programs, the men being rewarded for what really counted and the women for something secondary.

In 1972, Frank Barron, a long-time and vigorous investigator of creativity, reported an extensive study of student artists at the College of the San Francisco Art Institute. This study involved many instruments, among them the Minnesota Multiphasic Personality Inventory. In two words, Barron provided an interesting summary of the personality profile that emerged for the male artists: "gentleman pirates." Barron wrote:

> They are flexible, creative, and spontaneous, and there is a certain flair to their personal style. They move toward life with vigor, seeking experience with a restlessness, expansiveness and enthusiasm that may shade into irritability or quick flashes of anger. This slight swagger to their walk, however, is tempered by a civilized sensitivity to nuance. They see themselves as polite, sensitive, rational, empathic, and fair, with some detachment and capacity for reserve.

Although certainly contrasts appeared, the same general description held for the women subjects. However, Barron found reason not to call them lady pirates. "The main difference between the two profiles," Barron qualified, "seems to be that the female pattern is rather a slightly less flamboyant, more naive, more introverted version of the male." Relationships to grades were not part of Barron's inquiry, so the contrasts between men and women detected by Getzels and Csikszentmihalyi can't be checked here. Although each investigation considered characteristics the other did not, the portraits of the aspiring artist seem essentially the same.

Writers. Frank Barron also conducted a study of creative writers at the Institute of Personality Assessment and Research of the University of California, Berkeley. The general profile of the creative artist applies here, but Barron took particular note of symptoms of psychopathology, such as tending toward schizophrenia, depression, or hysteria. In comparison with less gifted writers, the creative group scored far higher on psychopathology. On the other hand, a provocative counterbalancing factor appeared. Writers in the creative group scored exceptionally high on ego strength, meaning that they possessed the psychological resources to master their tendency toward psychopathologies. Such a pattern runs contrary to the usual one in actual mental disorders, where, while symptoms are high, the resources to resist the tendency are low.

   Architects. Reporting on a 1965 study of architects also carried out at the Institute of Personality Assessment and Research, Donald MacKinnon urged that this of all professional groups seemed most apt for exploring creativity. An architect needed to be both artist and scientist, or at least engineer, as well as something of an entrepreneur. MacKinnon used a panel of experts to identify forty highly creative architects. Two other groups also participated, one made up of randomly selected professionals and the other of professionals who had had at least two years of association and work experience with the original forty. Assessments of the professional work of the architects showed that the associates of the master architects performed somewhat less creatively, and those in the randomly selected group even less so.

   Several findings concerned conformity versus independence. Those in the random group tended to score higher on such measures as abasement, affiliation, and deference, while, on aggression and autonomy, the master group scored more strongly, with the associate group falling between. The top architects saw themselves as guided by some inner artistic standard of excellence, the associates more in terms of efficient and effective work, while the random group emphasized meeting the standards of the profession.

   In measures of psychological richness and complexity, the most creative group appeared more conscious of their psychology, more flexible and feminine, perceptive and intuitive and more valuing of complexity. Finally, MacKinnon made an effort to catch the essence of each group by noting which adjective out of the 300 on the Gough Adjective Check List was most often checked as descriptive of the self. The master group most often checked imaginative, the associates civilized, and the random group conscientious.

Mathematicians. Yet another study conducted at the Institute of Personality Assessment and Research concerned men and women mathematicians identified as highly creative. In a 1971 article, Ravenna Helson reported particularly on the female group. Helson debunked one myth at once: the gifted women mathematicians were not exaggeratedly "masculine," if by this one meant that they scored higher on measures of masculinity-femininity, or of dominance, assertiveness, and analytical ability than did other women with doctorates in mathematics. Instead, Helson characterized the creative women mathematicians this way:

> (a) rebellious independence, narcissism, introversion, and a rejection of outside influence; (b) strong symbolic interests, and a marked ability to find self-expression and self-gratification in directed research activity; (c) flexibility, or lack of constriction, both in general attitudes and in mathematical work.

Helson noted that these traits described creative male mathematicians also, but they appeared more strongly in the women. "Among the creative men," Helson reported, "some were original, flexible, ambitious, but essentially conventional individuals. One may suppose that a conventional women would never develop the concentration, the 'purity of motive,' which seems to be necessary."

Scientists. Anne Roe, a pioneer in the field of relating occupation to personality, studied physical scientists among other groups, and, reviewing her and others' evidence in a 1963 paper, concluded that the findings from different sources proved remarkably parallel. Traits of the creative physical scientist include: very open to experience, highly observant and prone to see things in unusual ways, extremely curious, accepting of unconventional thoughts, ready to recognize and reconcile apparent opposites and tolerant of ambiguities but liking to resolve disorder into order, appreciative of complexity, highly independent in judgment, thought, and action, self-reliant and not responsive to group standards and control. Roe observed that, when circumstances demand, creative scientists can exhibit great perserverance and personal discipline. Their relationships to others reflect their independence and orientation to inquiry. They tend not to be gregarious or talkative, dislike personal aggression, and remain preoccupied with things and ideas much more than with people.

This section began with the problem of cultural stereotypes. Hard evidence was needed to test conventional conceptions.

Affirmed proposition: Creative artists are amoral bohemians. Creative scientists are cold assertive dwellers in ivory towers.

The stereotypes are true. Of course, the characters of creative artists and scientists could be described more positively, but the evidence is there to support the stereotypes, by whatever names one wants. For example, liberal postures and amorality were marked characteristics of the art students studied by Getzels and Csikszentmihalyi, characteristics all the more extreme among the male achievers in fine arts. Barron's investigations of artists found the males to be "gentlemen pirates" with the females leaning in much the same direction. Creative scientists generally have scored low relative to the larger population and their less creative colleagues on gregariousness, and high on assertiveness. Their lives rotate around ideas rather than around other people and their needs and natures.

However, affirming the proposition is not enough. Besides the matter of nothing but the truth, there is the matter of the whole truth. Whatever the contrasts between artist and scientist, there are striking differences within each domain. Whereas Getzels and Csikszentmihalyi found their more creative artists to have less emotional stability, Barron's more creative writers measured high on this dimension. Whereas physical scientists generally prove disinterested in people, social scientists often hold opposite values, as one might expect. Differences associated with sex appear, differences that don't always follow the same pattern. Getzels and Csikszentmihalyi found that the women fine arts majors showed a less extreme version of the traits displayed by the males, but Helson found that women mathematicians outdid males on the traits of creative mathematicians. Even within a particular discipline and within the same sex, wide variations can occur. William Michael, in a 1977 article, warns that the range of variation within such groups usually far exceeds the mean difference between groups. So whatever trends emerge, exceptions are exceptionally easy to find.

Then does any common portrait of the creative person emerge which goes beyond simply affirming that the person is creative? For the most part, no. Those traits that recur again and again appear closely linked to the fact of being creative. A person can't be very creative without seeing things in unusual ways, accepting unconventional thoughts, or exhibiting independence of judgment. Other traits, while less logically necessary, seem to play clear supporting roles in creative effort. Being highly observant or tolerant of ambiguities or appreciative of complexity all would contribute fairly directly to the process of creating. In short, it's fair to complain that, if one cancels contrasts from discipline to discipline, such studies reveal few surprises about the creative personality.

However, our complaint should not be too loud. The studies do reveal some interesting differences from field to field. They also demonstrate that there *is* such a thing as a creative personality . It might have turned out that creativity involved only inventiveness in a profession, rather than qualities pervading the whole person. Perhaps of most interest, the efforts to relate creativity to personality have been more successful than the efforts to relate it to abilities. This affirms the importance of matters other than ability in creativity.

A COMBINATION OF INGREDIENTS

TV commercials have given the world two paradigms for analyzing phenomena. One of them is the "purity" paradigm: power derives from purity – pure aspirin, pure soap, pure whatever. The other paradigm is the "combination of ingredients." Here, power comes from pooling the vigor of several things. Perhaps because one is simpler than several, most thinking about creativity has leaned toward the purity paradigm. Creativity comes from a – not several but a – creative ability such as ease of making remote associations, or from the right side of the brain, or from that restless unity, the creative personality.

None of these approaches has turned out to be satisfying. No specifically creative ability wholly stands up, although Westcott's intuition comes close. The left brain, right brain approach falls down altogether. The personality approach goes in circles, a person with a creative personality turning out to mean about the same thing as a person who behaves creatively. Maybe it's time the combination-of-ingredients approach had a chance. In fact, it makes some sense to think of creativity as a trait made up of five sorts of ingredients: abilities, style, values, beliefs, and tactics. The results of the personality research can be recast in these terms, and a good deal more said besides.

Abilities. If these turn out to be specifically creative abilities, this category makes room for them.

Style. What psychologists call "cognitive style" is important here. Cognitive style refers to recurrent patterns in the way a person approaches problems and, more generally, processes information. Some patterns of thinking promote creativity. The problem-finding approach to tasks identified by Getzels and Csiksentmihalyi is one. Donald MacKinnon, in his investigations of creativity in science, has singled out another. He found that the more creative individuals were more reluctant to judge whatever they encountered. Instead, there was a strong tendency to try to apprehend the thing or situation objectively and penetrate its nature. Less creative people seemed more prone to evaluate quickly and turn to other matters. Albert Rothenberg reports a tendency of creative people to think in terms of opposites or contraries and unite them in inventive ways. He calls this pattern of thought Janusian thinking, after the Roman God Janus, who had faces on both sides of his head and looked two ways at once.

Not to be forgotten here is the style of products. Even when a maker does not produce in a novel way each time around, an unusual style brings with it an abiding originality. For example, one Jackson Pollock dribble painting is not that much of an innovation over another, although each has its individual qualities, but the style as a whole has great freshness. Also, sometimes each product involves blatant invention. Then inventiveness is part of the style. The paintings of Magritte, for example, find way after way to pull the rug out from under our complacency with the everyday things of this world.

Values. The evidence is that creative people value originality quite directly, cherishing their own independence of judgment, responding to originality in the work of others and desiring originality in their own output. One could hardly ask for a trait that supports creativity more directly. However, highly creative people do not limit themselves by the kind of arrogant originality that loses touch with standards. In a 1962 study of student artists, Robert Burkhart identified two important personality types, the spontaneous and the deliberate. Deliberate students gained direction mostly from outside themselves, producing works sometimes technically very skilled but works that mostly reflected the standards of the community and the instructor. Spontaneous students were more imaginative and inner-directed. Within each type, Burkhart observed a range of competence. The low spontaneous type would produce erratic although imaginative works and remain closed to criticism and lacking in perspective. The high spontaneous type, the type he found most creative, would rely on an inner vision while at the same time accepting helpful guidance from others. It's worth recalling that openness to advice also was characteristic of the better poets in my study.

Besides valuing originality, creative people are strongly oriented toward general fundamental problems, problems that may carry great personal meaning also. It is easy to see why this would be so in the sciences, since fundamental explanation for physical and other phenomena is the whole point. Moreover, the importance of fundamentalness may be broader, according to an analysis by George Welsh. Welsh argues that creativity arises from dimensions he calls origence and intellectance. Origence, roughly speaking, is originality. Intellectance does not mean intelligence as such, but refers to the tendency of the person to view things in generic, highly symbolic ways rather than in terms of concrete and pragmatic particulars. Welsh presents evidence that creative individuals are those who rate high on both counts. Finally, Getzels and Csikszentmihalyi report that, in the arts, a concern with fundamentals fosters creative activity. The investigators discovered that the high problem finders in their sample, the ones who indeed turned out to be the best artists, tended to base their works on matters of deep personal concern which involved some of the grand dimensions of human existence – life and death, male and female, and so on. This was so even when such a theme might not be apparent in the final product.

Finally, besides what people value in products, what people value in themselves ought to be mentioned. The ideal self-image a person cherishes obviously will influence the directions in which the person develops. Marie Curie's doctrine of disinterestedness certainly is a case in point. Concerning creativity specifically, people who *want* to be creative, who deeply value such a characteristic in themselves, are more likely to make themselves creative and keep themselves that way.

Beliefs. A person's beliefs concern what the person takes to be real. Mention of reality inevitably recalls the familiar physical reality of bricks, automobiles, and icicles, but I have in mind two realities quite different from this everyday one. The first is simply people's apprehensions of themselves, their self-concepts, so to speak. Do you perceive yourself to be creative? What avenues and attainments of a creative sort do you believe are personally possible? Certainly, what an individual tries to do will grow out of his or her conceptions of personal actualities and potentialities.

Second, somewhat separable, and just as important, is a person's beliefs about what might be called the *problem space* in which the work gets done. This doesn't mean the physical environment of studios or desks, but the conceptual space of alternative discoveries "there" awaiting the discoverer and of the paths to them, the sort of space Newell and Simon have written about. The maker's understanding of this space and how to navigate in it mostly will be specific to the maker's discipline. However, some beliefs may cut across disciplines and constitute part of the person's orientation toward invention in general. For example, creative people might believe that multiple approaches and multiple solutions are there waiting to be caught at. The space of opportunities is well rather than sparsely populated. Such perceptions foster creativity by vouching for its possibility and convenience.

Tactics. This final category of the five concerns the maker's conscious lore about managing a creative activity. As usual, most of this lore will involve matters specific to the discipline. However, also relevant are general heuristics that bridge disciplines and assist invention in any domain. Tactics of this sort include such familiar moves as setting a work aside for a while, or sleeping on an idea.

"What makes the difference?" has been the guiding question of this chapter. I've tried to say what makes some people more creative than others who appear just as able. Although what a person accomplishes will be somewhat limited by a person's abilities, it will have much to do with whether a person uses those abilities in ways and to ends that favor creative results. I've tried to name traits that make that difference, suggesting that only such traits are properly a part of creativity.

All this may seem plausible enough for modest degrees of creativity. However, you might ask whether it really explains the furthest reaches of creative achievement. My answer is yes. Consider for a moment how we usually feel about explaining extraordinary creativity. We feel, quite naturally, that something in the explanation has to capture the extremity of the creator's achievement. Because such creators are so immensely able, we attribute their success to extraordinary abilities. Because we think of those abilities as so extraordinary, we imagine them to be different in kind from the sorts of mental abilities that get us through the day. Because those abilities are different in kind, we insist that the explanation for creativity must define what those abilities are and how they work.

But consider again one of my favorite comparison cases: athletics. We are much less troubled by understanding extraordinary athletic achievement. First of all, we don't attribute such success solely to abilities. Instead, we recognize the importance of style, values, beliefs, tactics. Second, we don't view whatever extraordinary abilities are involved as different in kind from those that get us through the day. Strength, coordination, and so on are all in lesser measure familiar aspects of everyday action. Third, since the abilities aren't seen as different in kind, we don't feel the need for special explanations of them. Rather, we understand such extraordinary abilities as more of the same. The weightlifter's strength is ours, only stronger. The sprinter's speed is ours, only faster.

My argument off and on throughout this book has been that creativity really allows much the same sort of explanation we readily accept for athletic excellence, if only we look at it carefully. Much besides ability is involved. In fact, there may not be any specifically creative abilities that cut across fields. The extraordinary, if not specifically creative, abilities involved in extraordinary creating are not different in kind. They can be understood as exceptional versions of familiar mental operations such as remembering, understanding, and recognizing. They are more of the same. Creativity has to be understood as the combination of traits which fosters the creative use of that *more* – the mind's best work.

10

THE SHAPE OF MAKING

How can we understand the creative process? Not just by understanding creativity, because creativity and creating are different matters. Whereas creativity involves traits that make a person creative, creating calls upon many resources not intrinsically creative. The ordinary acts of recognition that warn us away from open manholes can, in the right situation, warn us away from pitfalls in problem solving. Acts of recollection that tell us where we last used the pen with the blue cap can, in different circumstances, give us a word of poetry. Such resources are not what makes people creative, but they are what does much of the work of creating. And some of the factors that do make people creative do not do the work. Understanding that creative ideas are there to be found sets the stage for the inquirer to seek them but does nothing to find them.

To understand creating is to understand how the originality and other qualities get into the product. So far, I've dealt with this piecemeal. We've seen the maker using moments of recognition that sometimes make for insight, the schemata that both limit and enable invention, problem finding and heuristics of problem solving, the patterns of search that lead the maker to a final product, critical judgment with its reasons that paradoxically often are not reasoned out. Variety, yes, but this sprawling carnival of strategies and capacities needs to be put together into a single show under a single tent.

So now let us look at the shape of making, the logic behind the complexity of our mental resources and their best work. Viewed in the right way, the logic turns out to be simple, the shape an elegant one. For a preview, creating can be seen as a process of gradually selecting from an infinity of possibilities an actual product. The properties the maker selects for include originality and other kinds of quality. The process of selecting is roundabout, because of limits on human mental resources and the human will to push those resources to their limits. Creating goes beyond what a person can simply, straightforwardly and effortlessly do because of four fundamental moves.

Planning: instead of producing the work directly, the maker produces a plan for it, or for part of it. Abstracting: instead of always working from general intent to particulars, the maker abstracts new ideas from the particulars of the work in progress or other sources. Undoing: instead of getting everything right the first time, the maker undoes and redoes parts of the work. Making means into ends: instead of always being preoccupied with the final product, the maker often addresses a means as an end in itself.

The guiding force that puts these moves together and gets something worthwhile out of them is purpose – the purpose to create or to resolve problems that require invention. This is the teleological view of creating I've emphasized before. Such a view does not mean that the maker knows at some level just what the product will be before making it. On the contrary, products are vaguely and tentatively conceived, groped for, caught at, discovered in process. However, all this is part of the teleology, part of the purposeful striving toward something that will become increasingly specified and realized. Now for the details.

CREATING AS SELECTING

Imagine a monkey sitting at a typewriter and poking randomly at the keys. Eventually, just by chance, this monkey will type *Hamlet*. The only further requirement for a literature factory is a sharp critic, someone to select *Hamlet* or something just as good when it comes along. The catch, of course, lies in how long the critic would have to wait and the monkey would have to type. In fact, if the monkey had been typing since the beginning of the universe, at, say, one character per second, the chances of his having hammered out a single line anywhere in *Hamlet* are essentially zero. This simply reflects the vast number of typographical sequences the keys can make and the very small number of those, comparatively speaking, that are even meaningful, much less a part of Shakespeare's play.

The trouble with the monkey, of course, is that he doesn't have enough teleology. Beyond operating at the typewriter, his actions are not channeled by conditions that favor a literary product. The literary critic who does the selecting does most of the work of creating, while the monkey merely supplies very raw material. This artificial division of labor demonstrates how a creative product can be thought of as a very special selection out of a chaos of possibilities. A mathematical proof, like *Hamlet*, is a selection from the possible sequences of typographical characters. A painting is a selection from the possible distributions of pigment on a surface. A physical invention, the pilot model of a new engine, say, is one choice from among the infinity of ways that matter could be arranged into an object.

Admittedly, this is an odd way of describing what a creator does. After all, neither poet nor mathematician would be likely to think about that infinity of character sequences they could be said to select from. Even if we took a narrower field of possibilities, ones the mathematician might come close to considering, the mathematician certainly would not arrive at a proof by lining up candidate proofs and choosing. Likewise, Shakespeare did not choose *Hamlet* from a large set of alternative dramas, like pulling out the best chocolate from an assortment. Makers build up their products rather than pick them out.

One could say, of course, that makers select *by* building up. This is what I will say. But why should the notion of selecting be stretched so far? The answer is that, pursued persistently and artfully enough, the notion begins to pay off in an integrated picture of the way creating works.

One immediate gain is a sense of perspective on how special something like a good play or a good proof is. By seeing a play or proof as a choice from a chaos of possibilities, we remind ourselves how remote these products of human genius are from the mere anarchy of particles and radiation in a vacuum, where it all began. We remind ourselves that behind the building up the mathematician and poet do on a particular occasion lies a whole saga of preselection – years of training and striving for the individual maker, centuries of history in the discipline, millennia of general cultural evolution, billions of years of biological evolution, and, behind all that, the physical evolution of the universe. Taking this long perspective, we discover that the maker's work on the occasion is the least part of the work. The language, the symbols, the concepts, the cultural and personal style, even the particular task, already have been chosen. The maker of the moment merely puts the last block on the top of a pyramid of selection, a tower of ever higher and narrower ranges of possibility which finally finds its summit in a particular creative product.

There's a seeming paradox here. Is it right that so much credit go to preselecting, that is, to the selection already implicit or explicit when the maker begins? After all, we are talking about creating, where the maker ought not be hampered by conditions that limit the work of hacks. Challenging the preselection ought to be business as usual for the genuinely creative person.

That is true, but not entirely true. Yes, along the way to proving one theorem, a mathematician may depart from his or her preselection by discovering another theorem more worthy of attention, or perhaps some insight will lead the mathematician to challenging the axioms that so far have guided the work. However, the fact remains that no one can depart from much of the preselection at once and expect to make progress. The mathematician cannot discard the familiar axioms *and* conventional notation *and* traditions about which sorts of questions are worthwhile *and* the usual format for proofs. People in such a position would find themselves trapped by the self-made vacuum around them as much as if they had been frozen in blocks of ice. Such radical assaults on preselection simply don't occur. What we perceive as revolutionary innovation in a field always challenges only a little of the preselection. Only because we focus on the contrast rather than the continuity does innovation seem so much of a departure.

THE NECESSITY OF COMPLEXITY

Imagine that a time machine takes us to the far future, where we could walk among our descendants, evolved a million years beyond us. We are glad to find that this difficult business of creating is easier for them. They talk in perfect poetry, or with the rigor of mathematical proofs, quite as easily as you or I remember our phone numbers. Whatever strains our brains they carry off handily. Too bad things aren't that easy for us. But why aren't they? Some tasks, like holding an informal conversation, we accomplish readily. Why does creating get so complicated? The simple answer is that we do what we have to.

Planning is one of those necessities. When we cannot simply write out our poems or proofs – as we usually can't – we rely on an inbetween step, a plan. Then we try to go the rest of the way. Here I want to use the word plan very broadly. Included are painstakingly developed overt plans like outlines or blueprints. But also included is the sudden conjecture that points toward the complex experiment, the fleeting intention that guides a poet to the next word, the spontaneous idea for an image almost as quickly added to the painting in progress.

All these plans share an interesting feature: they all amount to selection. None selects its outcome yet – the article, the building, the experiment, the word, the image. Even less does any select the completed work – the article as finally revised, the building with paint job, the experiment plus results, the finished poem or painting. But each one delimits the range of the final result, narrowing down its possibilities. In short, a plan is a kind of divide-and-conquer strategy applied to the work of selection. Part of the selecting is done by making the plan, and then we try to continue with the guidance of the plan. Probably we need another plan, a little more specific than the first, that divides up the work of selection even more finely. So we proceed, from the first initial idea vaguely grasped to the final product, narrowing down and narrowing down through a chain of plans for the whole work and its parts.

Abstracting is another necessity. It would be most convenient if we could just narrow down until the work of selection were done. But expecting matters to be so neat ignores the way that selections already made can have unanticipated impact. One equation requires another, one part of a mechanical invention demands that another keep out of its way, one stroke of pigment calls for a neighbor with contrasting color. Besides requirements, opportunities appear. Such requirements and opportunities are plans we didn't think of, until the work in progress or some other situation suggested them. So plans arise not only by narrowing down more general plans, but by abstracting from particulars. In fact, often whole works grow from the first particulars, the plans arising mostly by abstraction. The initial words or brushstrokes suggest a plan for the next, and so on. Part way through, the maker abstracts a unifying conception, a plan which guides the completion of the work. This may happen quite spontaneously. Again, as with plans, I'm using "abstract" in a very broad sense to include simple and complex, spontaneous and deliberate, low-level and high-level abstractions.

Thus we narrow down toward the final work, translating plans into more particular plans or parts of the work and getting more plans by abstracting from the work or prior plans. Eventually we get there – but only if we're lucky. Allowance has to be made for mistakes, and that introduces the third necessity – undoing. We have to be able to undo parts of the work and redo them, as well as undo plans that don't turn out well in favor of new plans. Such acts are the opposite of selection. They open up possibilities again, after we thought things were suitably narrowed down. At first thought, this seems only a regretable consequence of human error, but not so. Often there simply is no reasonable way to detect difficulties other than by working through a situation until they appear. For instance, a mathematician may set out to prove a theorem that in fact is false. Only by attempting to prove it, failing, and searching long and hard for a counterexample can the mathematician finally discover that the mission is futile. Trial and error permeates human thought not just because people are less alert than they might be but because a trial selection often is the only way to give an error a chance to show itself.

Planning, abstracting, and undoing might seem to provide enough flexibility to get anything done. But there is one more complication. In narrowing down, the maker often encounters problems that really don't concern the final product. Rather, a means is needed to overcome an obstacle along the way. So the maker addresses the means as an end. For instance, a writer may have to check the meaning of a word in a dictionary, a physicist may seek the exact formula in a book, a painter may mix pigments to get the right hue. Such minor detours get more interesting as they snowball. A writer may decide a dictionary has to be written, a physicist try to derive a formula that would illuminate many problems besides the one at hand, a painter invent the pigment that will have the flexibility and durability desired. Sometimes means may become entirely detached from their ends. Sculpture has its origins in religion and ritual, but has become a worthwhile pursuit in its own right. Mechanics began with the practical tools of moving things about – the wheel, the lever, the ramp – but has become a sophisticated theoretical discipline concerned with the motions of planets and atoms.

Planning, abstracting, undoing, and making means into ends are the basic organizing tactics of selection. They are what we compose our actions out of when we cannot narrow down to the result we want in a single fluent motion of mind and hand. In a superficial sense, the four all are symptoms of the limited maker, roundabout ways of doing what the maker would rather accomplish directly. But this disgruntled view is also misguided. It makes more sense to see the roundabout tactics as symptoms of a refusal to settle for what can be done directly. If creating were limited by the convenience of the process, convenience and not excellence would shape its nature. But the teleological view implies that the excellence of the results dominates. Inevitably and appropriately, behavior is pushed toward its complicated limits to achieve such results.

Remember our descendants a million years hence rattling off poems and proofs? Serious creating for these far evolved beings would not be those easy poems or proofs. It would be something grander and more subtle, something we could not even imagine, something that makes them plan, abstract, undo, and convert means into ends – something that keeps them as roundabout as we are.

SELECTING FOR WHAT?

With all this talk of teleology, I've said little about what makes a course of selection creative. The question is crucial, since the general description of creating as selecting could apply just as well to uncreative activities, such as building an ordinary bird feeder or a picket fence. For example, room appears for undoing as a measurement taken earlier turns out to be wrong or a nail bends over in the driving.

What, then, makes creating special among other courses of selection? Simply, what is selected *for*. The maker selects for creative products, meaning original high-quality products. Sometimes originality gets into the creative product by being selected for directly. Over the last decades visual artists have doggedly sought innovative modes of expression. On the other hand, sometimes originality is not selected for – it's a spinoff from other characteristics closer to the maker's intent. As I said several chapters ago, originality often results when people put "unreasonable" demands on themselves and their products, demands that have to be met with originality if at all.

However, let's not overestimate the significance of originality. Although necessary by definition for a creative product, originality is one of the most dispensable ingredients for a simply worthwhile product. Cleverly building a bird feeder out of a tin can or a milk carton may be original, but hardly very worthwhile if the tin can sizzles the birds under the summer sun or the milk carton turns soggy with the first rain. The mundane bird feeder that works outdoes the original one that doesn't. The same can be said for paintings, poems, mathematical proofs, and theories in physics. In essence, originality only counts for much when the product achieves quality in other respects.

Furthermore, although any field will have its individual standards, those "other respects" include some general ones for substantial creative achievement. Products judged highly creative by the society will have such features as scope and significance. Qualities of these sorts, in addition to originality, imbue creative products with value. Anything but easy to achieve, such qualities impose demands that push the person seeking them toward originality even if the person does not strive for originality as such.

THE IMPORTANCE OF ACCIDENT

James Austin's encounters with chance remind us that accident has much to do with invention. There is no guaranteed pattern to the problems or the opportunities noticed in a developing work. Where the maker's eye falls, at what particular time, with what particular mind set, may send the maker in a wholly unforeseen direction. At first thought, this much room for accident seems at odds with the teleological view of creating. But not so.

First of all, accident realizes purpose. The plans that constrain the work to come don't usually determine it. Rarely is a range of alternatives well enough defined or small enough for the maker to survey them all and somehow choose the best. Satisficing rather than maximizing is the mainstay of creating. This means that most narrowings down are acts of commitment rather than wholly calculation. They are taken not because the conditions allow only that selection, but because the only effective way to proceed is to settle for something. Such chance selections are a way of fulfilling the plan and carrying forward the teleological process.

Also, accident arises out of purpose or, as Pasteur said, chance favors the prepared mind. The accidents that carry the work along because the maker encounters an opportunity in the work so far, or in another experience altogether, are not mere accidents. The opportunity would never have been recognized had the maker not been saturated in the subject. So accidents are reflections of the teleology of the maker and the making.

Finally, accident is assimilated to purpose. A naive view would have accidents directing the maker down utterly new paths to utterly unexpected consequences. This can happen, of course. However, much more often accident deflects, enlarges, sharpens, simplifies, rather than radically altering. This is not because accidents always fit the context, but because the maker makes them fit.

HOW SELECTION HAPPENS

Chapter after chapter, we've looked at psychological processes that do the work of creating. We pondered everything from a poet capturing the essence of her poem in a few seconds of insight to Darwin remaking his problem over many months. Doing the work of creating means doing the work of selection that leads toward a creative result. In fact, most of the processes relate to the basic selective moves I've outlined – planning, abstracting, undoing, and making means into ends. To understand how this is so is to understand how the splendidly varied resources of the human creature fit together, a mosaic of potentials out of which creative products appear. A few cases in point:

Noticing opportunities. Noticing meant detecting relevant features spontaneously, without having to seek them out. Noticing an opportunity is a kind of abstracting, which adds to the plan another direction to be pursued.

Noticing flaws. This too is abstracting, but the result also is an undoing. The flaw must be removed and something better put in its place.

Directed remembering. This named the everyday ability to retrieve information from memory satisfying several constraints at once. Directed remembering often realizes plans, providing the poet with the word to match the need, for instance.

Reasons in judgment. Critical reactions to a work underway typically come with reasons. The reasons amount to plans for what to undo, better plans than if the maker experienced a vague pro or con reaction without reasons.

Looking harder. This meant evaluating a work with certain features or categories in mind. The maker has taken the trouble to think out what to look for, and so that "what" is an example of a means that temporarily was made into an end. The usual result of looking harder is new plans abstracted from the work.

Setting a work aside. This does no selecting by itself, of course. However, it contributes to later selecting because the flaws and opportunities of the work may prove more obvious when the maker returns to it.

Long searches. These reflected the maker's high standards, not chronic fluency. In its simplest form, a long search amounts to a chain of selections and undoings, as the maker generates and rejects option after option until one proves sound.

Hill climbing. The entire process of selecting can be seen as hill climbing. A narrowing down is a step up the hill, an undoing a step backwards in hopes of finding a way up an even higher hill nearby.

Schemata. The schemata that stand behind a creative effort are part of the maker's preselection. Some schemata appear in a final product with little variation, as with a word in a writer's vocabulary, a standard scientific formula, or a stock image a painter uses again and again. These provide a repertoire of specific selections; the maker need only plug them in. Many schemata have a much more open structure, one filled out in context-dependent ways. The schemata of English syntax are an example. These schemata provide a repertoire of plans that, often quite quickly and unconsciously, guide the making of more specific selections. Schemata do the work of selecting by having it already done. Schemata substitute preselected units and structures for selecting the maker otherwise would have to do at the time.

Problem finding. This is an example of a means temporarily becoming an end. What problem to address is itself taken as the problem.

THE SUM OF IT ALL

Let me attempt a terse summary of the points in this chapter and the general view of creating they offer. Those who like to think from generalizations to particulars might well have started here and read the book backwards. Here is what creating seems to be all about.

*Creating is the process by which a maker achieves a creative product.

*The process is a teleological one, governed by plans restricting the final product that exist at the outset and plans that arise during the course of creating. The plans lead to the marshalling of the maker's resources to realize them. Accident occurs abundantly, but realizes, arises out of, or is assimilated to purpose.

*Understanding how creating occurs requires understanding how originality and other qualities that make a product creative get put into the developing product.

*To explain this, it is useful to view creating as a process of selecting from among the many possible outcomes – arrays of words, formulas, pigments on a surface, and so on.

*The preselections of the maker's personal history and the histories of the culture, the species, and the physical world channel what the maker will attempt and equip the maker with skills and schemata to attempt it.

*Although the simplest sort of making would involve a direct jump from preselection to a final selection, makers, by adopting roundabout tactics of selection, can drastically increase the reach of their efforts. The basic roundabout tactics are planning, abstracting, undoing, and making means into ends.

*The resources of mind discussed throughout the book – noticing, realizing, directed remembering, problem finding, schemata, hill climbing, critical reasons, and many more – each contribute to creating by helping to accomplish selection.

*These same resources of selection explain masterly and more ordinary creating. The master will notice more, remember more, exercise better critical judgment, and so on, but the processes involved are the same in kind.

*The creative quality gets put into a work primarily through skillful selecting for it or selecting for features that favor it. The selective processes involved need not be intrinsically creative, but simply responsive to what is being selected for.

*Originality may occur through direct selecting for it or as a spinoff, a side effect of selecting for other qualities.

*In any case, selecting for originality cannot dominate the selective process, because originality adds little worth to the product unless the product achieves competence in other respects.

*Creativity involves a style, values, beliefs, and tactics that specifically favor selecting for a creative product.

*Creating at an extraordinary level depends on superior learned and inborn abilities to do the relevant work of selection. However, for the most part, these abilities shouldn't be considered a part of the maker's creativity, since other persons equally able may function quite uncreatively. Creativity concerns what we do with our abilities. Any normal person can be creative in terms of whatever abilities he or she has or can acquire.

*To understand creating as a process of selection, to understand how various psychological phenomena contribute to the work of selection, and to understand that products become creative because that is what is selected for, to understand all this is to grasp, in one way at least, the nature of creating.

AN IMAGE OF WIDE SCOPE

Of course, a neat description is not everything. It may not provide something the mind can grasp as a whole and entertain as essence. In fact, we know a way to do that job better – Howard Gruber's notion of images of wide scope. Such images, remember, included Darwin's tree of nature which guided him to his theory of natural selection, and, I suggested, the glow of radium with its puzzle of energy resident in matter. Then why not an image of wide scope for creating?

The image comes with a story. A couple of years ago, my oldest son accosted me with news from kindergarten as I came home from the office. He had learned something about apples and wanted to demonstrate. Out of the drawer came a knife, one of those he was not supposed to handle, and out of the refrigerator a McIntosh. "Dad," he said, "Let me show you what's inside an apple."

"I know what's inside an apple," I said, riding for a fall.

"C'mon, just let me show you."

"Listen, I've cut open lots of apples. Why ruin an apple just to show me something I already know?"

"Just take a look."

Ungracefully, I gave in. He cut the apple in half, the wrong way. We all know the right way to cut apples. One starts at the stem and slices through to the dimple on the bottom. However, he turned the apple on its side, sliced the apple in half perpendicular to the stem, and displayed the result. "See Dad. There's a star inside."

Sure enough, there was. In cross-section, the core of the apple made a distinct five-pointed star. How many apples I had eaten in my life, cutting them in half the right way and never suspecting the hidden pattern waiting for me until one day my child brought news of it home, out to convert the infidel – and he did.

I have not tried to find out, but I'm sure this star-shaped structure is common knowledge in botany, where no doubt there are students of apples who do dissections of McIntosh and Golden Delicious, nibbling the scraps as they go. Whoever first sliced an apple the wrong way may well have had a good reason to do so, curiosity being one good reason. Or it might have been one of those fruitful – I choose the word carefully – mistakes all of us make sometimes. Whatever the case, no matter. The occasion and process of discovery are not my concerns at this moment. What struck me then and still impresses me now is that this hidden pattern fascinated enough to make its way around. The knowledge of it traveled from unknown origins to my son's kindergarten class and so to me and you. Its very survival and vigor as something to know about vouches for the engagement we find in discovery.

So, if you want to know what creating is for, in part it's for an apple – sliced the wrong way.

NOTES
SOURCES
INDEX

NOTES

Author (date) entries refer to the complete references under Sources.

A Parable

Easter Island: Heyerdahl (1958) von Dänikan (1970)
Quote from Plato: Ion, 534, Cooper (1961)

Chapter 1.   Witnesses to Invention

Introduction
Coleridge quote: Lowes (1927), p.356
Coleridge's sources: Lowes (1927)
On composition: Poe (1945)
"Most writers": p. 551
"The sound": p. 556

Kubla Khan and The Raven
The writing of "Kubla Khan": Schneider (1953)

The writing of "The Raven": Allen (1926), Bonaparte (1949), Porges (1963), Woodberry (1909)
"The raven too": quoted in Porges (1963), p. 137
Quotes from Chivers' verse: Allen (1926), p. 611

Hard Evidence
Arnheim (1954)
"An interplay": p. 131
"are always more than formal": p. 133
"The gain": p. 124
"Guernica is not": p. 24
"the bulls body": p. 27
"Did the need": p. 124
"there can be no real": p. 14

A Voice for the Mind
Valéry quote: Arnheim (1954), p.1
Introspection: Boring (1953)
Eyewitness testimony: Buckhout (1974)
Problems of introspection: Nisbett and Wilson (1977)

Two-string problem: Maier (1931)

Stages of thought: Wallas (1926)

Think-aloud studies of poet and artists: Patrick (1935, 1937)

Of chess: de Groot (1965)

Of problem solving: Newell and Simon (1972)

Of medical diagnosis: Elstein, Shulman, and Sprafka (1978)

Articles of mine drawing on think aloud-techniques: Perkins (1977a, b, 1978, 1979a, in press a)

No disruption by think-aloud techniques

With poets and artists: Patrick (1935, 1937)

In discrimination learning: Karpf (1973)

In mental arithmetic: Dansereau and Gregg (1966)

In formal reasoning: Newell and Simon (1972), pp. 473-475

Critique of Nisbett and Wilson: Smith and Miller (1978)

Chapter 2.   Creative Moments

Introduction

Poincaré quote: Ghiselin (1952), p. 37

Darwin's discovery: Darwin (1911), p. 68

Archimedes' discovery: Vitruvius (Loeb ed.)

The Still-Waters Theory

Poincaré quote: Ghiselin (1952), p. 38

On incubation: Olton (1979), Olton and Johnson (1976)

Incubation on a chess problem: Olton (1979)

Darwin quote: Darwin (1911), p. 68

Wallace quote: Wallace (1905), pp. 361-362

The Blitzkrieg Theory

Research on story understanding: e.g., Schank and Abelson (1977)

Beyond the information given: Bruner (1973)

Humor as insight: Koestler (1964), part one.

The Better-Mousetrap Theory

Bisociation: Koestler (1964)

Paleologic: Arieti (1976)

Lateral thinking: de Bono (1970)

Janusian thinking and homospatial thinking: Rothenberg (1979)

Chapter 3.   Ways of the Mind

Directed Remembering

Directed remembering of words: Nickerson (1977)

Noticing

Visual search: Henderson (1978), Neisser (1963), Neisser, Novick, and Lazar (1963)

Noticing in mathematical problem solving: Perkins (1975)

Contrary Recognition

"Seeing as" and metaphor: Hester (1966)

Contrary recognition: Perkins (1978)

Beckett as buzzard: Levine (1969)

Discovery of the benzene ring: Koestler (1964), p. 118

Synectics as Gordon described it (current practices of Synectics Incorporated differ): Gordon (1961)

Face recognition and contrary recognition, Perkins and Hagen (1980).

The child's drawing: My son Ted, five at the time, found me doing the drawings for this chapter, wanted to try, and, upon my supplying him with several pages of umbrellas, produced a couple of dozen transformed umbrellas in short order, illustrating how even a child can perform contrary recognitions readily.

Visual likenesses in poetry: Perkins (1978)

Examples of discovery by metaphor: Koestler (1964), chap. 8, and Schon (1963)

Reservations about the role of analogy in discovery: Perkins (in press a)

Analogy in acquiring skills: Howard (1977, in press)

The Trouble with Bisociation
Bisociation: Koestler (1964)
Koestler's table: pp. 659-660
"The essence of discovery": p. 201

The Essence of Invention
Mozart's musical memory: Bombet (1817)

Chapter 4.   Critical Moments

Introduction
"Two soaps" anecdote about Einstein and his commitment to simplicity: Holton (1971-72)

Playing dice with the universe, Einstein and Bohr: "The Year of Dr. Einstein," *Time Magazine*, February 19, 1979, p. 79.

Analysis and Intuition
On the limits of intuition: Perkins (1977b)

Looking Harder
Standards for diving: Walker (1974)

Feeling as Knowing
Self-perception of emotions experiment: Schachter and Singer (1962)

Cognitive emotions: Scheffler (1977)

Expression: Goodman (1976), chap. 2.

"the *emotions function cognitively*": p. 248

Twins experiment: Hess (1965, 1975)

Being Sure and Being Right
On "right" aesthetic judgments: Perkins (1979a), Beardsley (1970)

Chapter 5.   Searching For

Something for Nothing
"Don't know" judgments: Kolers and Palef (1976)

Searching Longer

The chickens-next-door puzzle is adapted from: Parnes, Noller, and Biondi (1977), pp. 272-273

Beethoven's fluent improvising: Thayer (1921) vol. 1, p. 199, vol. 2, pp. 15, 44, 90-91

Slow composing: Diehl (1908), p. 70; Thayer (1921) vol. 1, pp. 258-261, vol. 3, pp. 76, 126

Experiments on searching longer: see the thoughtful review by Johnson (1972), pp. 300-338

Getting General, Specific, Concrete, and Abstract

Flexibility: Guilford and Hoepfner (1971)

Hill Climbing

The seductive orchid: Bristow (1978)

Innovation as variation and selection: Campbell (1960, 1974)

Perceptual hill climbing: Perkins (in press b), Perkins and Cooper (1980)

Reversals not always discovered: Girgus, Rock, and Egatz (1977)

Perception trapped by early hypotheses: Wyatt and Campbell (1951)

Maximizing and Satisficing

Satisficing: Simon (1969)

Footracing: Ryder, Carr, and Herget (1976)

How settled do artists consider their works?: Getzels and Csikszentmihalyi, (1976), chap. 6

Search in Summary

Search: Simon (1969), Newell and Simon (1972)

Chapter 6.   Plans Down Deep

Introduction

A. C. Aitken: Hunter (1977)

Fluency and Mastery

Mozart: Bombet (1817), pp. 384-385 and in general

On fluency in poets: Bartlett (1951), chaps. 5 and 6

Fluency estimates made from: Packard (1974)

How Fluency Happens

L. E. Sissman: Gordon (1972)

Lord Byron: Bartlett (1951), chap. 5

Allen Ginsberg: Merrill (1969)

Oral poetry: Lord (1974)

Psychologists who have relied on the schema concept in some form include: Bartlett (1932), Bregman (1977), Minsky (1975), Neisser (1976), Schank and Abelson (1977)

Schemata in chess: Simon and Chase (1973)

Schemata in art: Gombrich (1961, 1979)

Quote on feeling in acting: Benedetti (1976), p. 214

Rostropovich's metaphors: *Time Magazine*, October 24, 1977, p. 85

Invention and Stereotype

Scientific innovation: Kuhn (1962)

"to suggest that": p. 10

New theories are weak at first: Feyerabend (1975)

Qualifications about schemata as traps: Scheffler (1967)

Self-refuting argument of subjectivists: pp. 21-22, 53

"Our expectations": p. 44

"Novelty emerges": Kuhn (1962), p. 65

More on schemata as traps: Perkins (1979b)

A Plan for Invention?

Four phases of inventive thinking: Wallas (1926)

Phases sought empirically: Patrick (1935, 1937, 1938)

Study of artists: Getzels and Csikszentmihalyi (1976)

How Down Deep?

On A. C. Aitken: Hunter (1977)

Chapter 7.   Plans Up Front

Introduction

Four-color-map theorem: Appel and Haken (1977)

Big Plans

Heuristics in mathematical problem solving: Polya (1954, 1957)

Managerial strategies also needed: Schoenfeld (1978, 1979a, b)

The calculus experiment: Schoenfeld (1978)

The experiment with seven students: Schoenfeld (1979b)

SQ3R method: Higbee (1977), Robinson (1970)

What People Learn from Heuristics

The five-step plan: Noller, Parnes, and Biondi (1976)

142 investigations reviewed: Torrance (1972)

Effectiveness of creativity training questioned: Mansfield, Busse, and Krepelka (1978)

Creativity tests criticized: Crockenberg (1972), Wallach (1976a, b)

No Substitute for Knowledge

Critique of psychology's "significant difference" approach: Simon (1974)

Zen koans: Hoffman (1977)

Particular koans: A. p. 57; B. p. 94-95, #3; C. p. 97, #10; D. p. 59, #11; E. p. 59, #12; F. p. 98, #13; G. p. 99, #15; H. p. 101, #21.

Teaching Invention

The LOGO project: Papert (1980)

Philosophy in the classroom: Lipman (1974), Lipman and Sharp (1975), Lipman, Sharp, and Oscanyan (1977)

Learning to monitor others' understanding: Korzenik (1977)

Chapter 8.   Lives of Inquiry

Charles Darwin: The Transformation of a Problem
Darwin's discovery of natural selection: Gruber (1974)
"Saw in Loddiges garden": p. 159
"One invisible animalcule": p. 161
"Three principles": p. 459

Marie Curie: Discovery as Dedication
On Marie Curie: Reid (1974)
"All my mind": p. 49
"If sometimes": p. 50
"Its glass roof": p. 95
"It was a cross": p. 95
"with my own eyes": p. 96
"I would be broken": p. 96
"best and happiest": p. 97
"stirred us": p. 98
"What a terrible shock": p. 151
"the celebration of a victory": p. 156

James Austin: Time and Chance
Chance in invention: Austin (1978)
Fleming's discovery of penicillin: Koestler (1964), p. 194
Roentgen's discovery of X rays: Koestler (1964), p. 195

Regulating Inquiry
How people regulate their careers: Gruber (1978a, b)
"I made thin frozen": Austin (1978), p. 19

Sense of the discipline: Parsons (1978)

Chapter 9.   Having It

Introduction
More on the meaning of "creativity": Howard (in press)

Talent and Creativity
Problem finding: Getzels and Csikszentmihalyi (1976)
Bisociation: Koestler (1964)
Ideational fluency: Johnson (1972), pp. 300-338, Wallach (1970)
Ideational fluency and creative achievement: Crockenberg (1972), Hudson (1966, 1968), Wallach (1976a, b)
Remote associates: Mednick (1962), Wallach (1970)
The RAT, test takers' strategies, and creative achievement: reviews in Blooberg (1973), Mendelsohn (1976)
IQ and achievement in a discipline: Barron (1969), Wallach (1976a, b)
Insight: Westcott (1968)

Left Brain, Right Brain
Numbers but not words: Gardner (1975), p. 16
Critique of left-brain, right-brain findings: Gardner (1978)
Ping versus pong: Gombrich (1961), pp. 370-371

Personality
Student artists: Getzels and

Csikszentmihalyi (1976), Barron (1972)

"Young artists": Getzels and Csikszentmihalyi (1976), p. 45

"They are flexible": Barron (1972), p. 45

"The main difference": p. 45

Creative writers: Barron (1969)

Creative architects: MacKinnon (1965)

Mathematicians: Helson (1971)

"rebellious independence": p. 217

"Among the creative men": p. 217

Scientists: Roe (1963)

Within group variation far exceeds across group: Michael (1977)

A Combination of Ingredients

Cognitive style generally: Kagan and Kogan (1970), Messick et al. (1976)

Deferred judgment: MacKinnon (1962)

Janusian thinking: Rothenberg (1979)

Spontaneous and deliberate personalities: Burkhart (1962). See also Beittel (1972)

Origence and intellectance: Welsh (1977)

Problem space: Newell and Simon (1972)

SOURCES

Allen, Hervey. *Israfel: The Life and Times of Edgar Allan Poe*, vol. 2. New York: George H. Doran, 1926.

Appel, Kenneth, and Wolfgan Haken. "The Solution of the Four-Color-Map Problem." *Scientific American*, 1977, *237(4)*, 108-121.

Arieti, Silvano. *Creativity: The Magic Synthesis*. New York: Basic Books, 1976.

Arnheim, Rudolf. *Picasso's Guernica: The Genesis of a Painting*. Berkeley: University of California Press, 1962.

Austin, James H. *Chase, Chance, and Creativity*. New York: Columbia University Press, 1978.

Barron, Frank. *Creative Person and Creative Process*. New York: Holt, Rinehart and Winston, 1969.

_____ *Artists in the Making*. New York. Seminar Press, 1972.

Bartlett, F. C. *Remembering*. Cambridge, Eng.: Cambridge University Press, 1932.

Bartlett, Phyllis. *Poems in Process*. New York: Oxford University Press, 1951.

Beardsley, Monroe C. *The Possibility of Criticism*. Detroit: Wayne State University Press, 1970.

Beittel, Kenneth. *Mind and Context in the Art of Drawing*. New York: Holt, Rinehart and Winston, 1972.

Benedetti, Robert L. *The Actor at Work*. Englewood Cliffs: Prentice-Hall, 1976.

Blooberg, Morton. Introduction: Approaches to Creativity. In Morton Blooberg, ed., *Creativity: Theory and Research*. New Haven: College and University Press, 1973.

Bombet, L. A. C. *The Life of Haydn and the Life of Mozart*. London: John Murray, 1817.

Bonaparte, Marie. *The Life and Works of Edgar Allan Poe*. London: Imago Publishing Co., 1949.

de Bono, Edward. *Lateral Thinking: Creativity Step by Step*. New York: Harper and Row, 1970.

Boring, E. G. "A History of Introspection." *Psychological Bulletin*, 1953, *50*, 169-189.

Bregman, Albert S. "Perception and Behavior as Compositions of Ideals." *Cognitive Psychology*, 1977, *9*, 250-292.

Bristow, Alex. *The Sex Life of Plants*. New York: Holt, Rinehart and Winston, 1978.

Bruner, Jerome S. *Beyond the Information Given*. New York: Norton, 1973.

Buckhout, R. "Eyewitness Testimony." *Scientific American,* 1974, *231(6),* 23-31.

Burkhart, Robert C. *Spontaneous and Deliberate Ways of Learning*. Scranton: International Textbook, 1962.

Campbell, Donald. "Blind Variation and Selective Retention in Creative Thought as in Other Knowledge Processes." *Psychological Review*, 1960, *67(6),* 380-400.

———"Evolutionary Epistemology." In P. A. Schilpp, ed., *The Philosophy of Karl Popper*, vol. 14, I and II. LaSalle: Open Court Publishing Co., 1974.

Cooper, Lane, trans. Ion, 534. In Edith Hamilton and Huntington Cairns, eds. *The Collected Dialogues of Plato*. Princeton: Princeton University Press, 1961.

Crockenberg, Susan B. "Creativity Tests: A Boon or Boondoggle for Education?" *Review of Educational Research*, 1972, *42(1),* 27-45.

Däniken, Erich von. Chariots of the Gods? Unsolved Mysteries of the Past. New York: G. P. Putnam, 1970.

Dansereau, D., and L. W. Gregg. "An Information Processing Model of Mental Multiplication." *Psychonomic Science.* 1966, *6,* 71-72.

Darwin, Charles. *The Life and Letters of Charles Darwin*, vol. 1. Francis Darwin, ed., New York: D. Appleton, 1911.

Diehl, Alice M. *The Life of Beethoven*. London: Hodder and Stoughton, 1908.

Elstein, Arthur S., Lee S. Shulman, and Sarah A. Sprafka. *Medical Problem Solving: An Analysis of Clinical Reasoning*. Cambridge: Harvard University Press, 1978.

Feyerabend, Paul. *Against Method: Outline of an Anarchistic Theory of Knowledge*. London: New Left Books, 1975.

Gardner, Howard. *The Shattered Mind*. New York: Alfred A. Knopf, 1975.

_____"What We Do and Don't Know about the Two Halves of the Brain." *Harvard Magazine,* March-April 1978, 24-27.

Getzels, Jacob, and Mihaly Csikszentmihalyi. *The Creative Vision: A Longitudinal Study of Problem Finding in Art.* New York: John Wiley, 1976.

Ghiselin, Brewster, ed. *The Creative Process.* Berkeley: University of California Press, 1952.

Girgus, J. J., I. Rock, and R. Egatz. The Effect of Knowledge on Reversibility of Ambiguous Figures. *Perception and Psychophysics,* 1977, *22(6),* 550-556.

Gombrich, Ernst H. *Art and Illusion: A Study in the Psychology of Pictorial Representation.* Princeton: Princeton University Press, 1961.

_____The Sense of Order: A Study in the Psychology of Decorative Art. Ithaca: Cornell University Press, 1979.

Goodman, Nelson. *Languages of Art.* Indianapolis: Hackett, 1976.

Gordon, John. "Never Trust a Guy Whose First Name is a Letter." *Boston Review of the Arts,* July 1972, *2(4),* 11-17; 77-78.

Gordon, William J. *Synectics: The Development of Creative Capacity.* New York: Harper, 1961.

de Groot, Adriaan. *Thought and Choice in Chess.* The Hague: Mouton, 1965.

Gruber, Howard E. *Darwin on Man: A Psychological Study of Scientific Creativity.* Together with Darwin's early and unpublished notebooks, ed. Paul H. Barrett. New York: E. P. Dutton, 1974.

_____"Darwin's 'Tree of Nature' and Other Images of Wide Scope." In J. Wechsler, ed., *On Aesthetics in Science.* Cambridge, Massachusetts Institute of Technology Press, 1978a.

_____ Emotion and cognition: "Aesthetics and Science." In Stanley S. Madeja, ed., *The Arts, Cognition, and Basic Skills.* St. Louis: CEMREL, 1978b.

Guilford, J. P., and Ralph Hoepfner. *The Analysis of Intelligence.* New York: McGraw-Hill, 1971.

Helson, Ravenna. "Women Mathematicians and the Creative Personality." *Journal of Consulting and Clinical Psychology,* 1971, *36,* 210-220.

Henderson, Leslie, "Pandemonium and Visual Search." *Perception,* 1978, *7,* 97-104.

Hess, Eckhard Heinrich. "Attitude and Pupil Size." *Scientific American,* 1965, *218(18),* 46-54.

_____"The Role of Pupil Size in Communication." *Scientific American,* 1975, *233(20),* 110-119.

Hester, Marcus B. "Metaphor and Aspect Seeing." *Journal of Aesthetics and Art Criticism,* 1966, *25(2),* 205-212.

Heyerdahl, Thor. *Aku-Aku.* New York: Rand McNally, 1958.

Higbee, Kenneth L. *Your Memory: How It Works and How to Improve it.* Englewood Cliffs: Prentice-Hall, 1977.

Hoffman, Yoel, trans. *The Sound of the One Hand.* New York: Bantam Books, 1977.

Holton, Gerald, "On trying to Understand Scientific Genius." *American Scholar,* Winter 1971-72, *41,* 95-110.

Howard, Vernon A. "Artistic Practice and Skills." In David Perkins and Barbara Leondar, eds., *The Arts and Cognition.* Baltimore: Johns Hopkins University Press, 1977.

_____ *Artistry: The Work of Artists,* Indianapolis: Hackett Publishing Co., in press.

Hudson, Liam. *Contrary Imaginations: A Psychological Study of the English Schoolboy.* London: Methuen, 1966.

_____ *Frames of Mind.* London: Methuen, 1968.

Hunter, I. M. L. "Mental Calculation." In P. N. Johnson-Laird and P.C. Wason, eds., *Thinking.* Cambridge, Eng.: Cambridge University Press, 1977.

Johnson, Donald M. *A Systematic Introduction to the Psychology of Thinking.* New York: Harper and Row, 1972.

Kagan, Jerome and Nathan Kogan. "Individuality and Cognitive Performance." In P. Mussen, ed., *Carmichael's Manual of Child Psychology,* vol. 1. New York: John Wiley, 1970.

Karpf, D. A. "Thinking Aloud in Human Discrimination Learning." Dissertation, State University of New York at Stony Brook, 1972. *Dissertation Abstracts International,* 1973, *33,* 6111B.

Koestler, Arthur. *The Act of Creation.* New York: Dell, 1964.

Kolers, Paul A., and Sandra R. Palef. "Knowing Not." *Memory and Cognition,* 1976 *4(5),* 553-558.

Korzenik, Diana. "Saying It with Pictures." In David Perkins and Barbara Leondar, eds., *The Arts and Cognition.* Baltimore: Johns Hopkins University Press, 1977.

Kuhn, Thomas. *The Structure of Scientific Revolutions.* Chicago: University of Chicago Press, 1962.

Levine, D. *Pens and Needles.* Boston: Gambit, 1969.

Lipman, Matthew. *Harry Stottlemeier's Discovery.* Upper Montclair: Montclair State College Press, 1974.

Lipman, Matthew, and Ann Margart Sharp, eds. *Instructional Manual to Accompany "Harry Stottlemeier's Discovery."* Upper Montclair: Montclair State College, Institute for the Advancement of

Philosophy for Children, 1975.

Lipman, Matthew, Ann Margaret Sharp, and Frederick S. Oscanyan. *Philosophy in the Classroom.* Upper Montclair: Institute for the Advancement of Philosophy for Children, 1977.

Lord, Albert B. *The Singer of Tales.* Cambridge: Harvard University Press, 1960.

Lowes, John Livingstone. *The Road to Xanadu.* Boston: Houghton Mifflin, 1927.

MacKinnon, Donald W. "The Nature and Nurture of Creative Talent." *American Psychologist,* 1962, *17,* 484-495.

_____"Personality and the Realization of Creative Potential." *American Psychologist,* 1965, *20,* 273-281.

Maier, Norman R. F. "Reasoning in Humans: II. The Solution of a Problem and Its Appearance in Consciousness." *Journal of Comparative Psychology,* 1931, 12, 181-194.

Mansfield, Richard S., Thomas V. Busse, and Ernest J. Krepelka. "The Effectiveness of Creativity Training." *Review of Educational Research,* 1978, *48(4),* 517-536.

Mednick, Sarnoff A. "The Associative Basis of the Creative Process." *Psychological Review,* 1962, *69,* 220-232.

Mendelsohn, Gerald A. "Associative and Attentional Processes in Creative Performance." *Journal of Personality,* 1976, *44,* 341-369.

Merrill, Thomas F. *Allen Ginsberg.* New York: Twayne Publishers, 1969.

Messick, Samuel, et al. *Individuality in Learning.* San Francisco: Jossey-Bass, 1976.

Michael, William B. "Cognitive and Affective Components of Creativity in Mathematics and the Physical Sciences." In Julian C. Stanley, William C. George, and Cecilia H. Solano, eds., *The Gifted and the Creative.* Baltimore: Johns Hopkins University Press, 1977.

Minsky, Marvin, "A Framework for Representing Knowledge." In P. H. Winston, ed., *The Psychology of Computer Vision.* New York: McGraw-Hill, 1975.

Neisser, Ulric. *Cognition and Reality: Principles and Implications of Cognitive Psychology.* San Francisco: Freeman, 1976.

_____"Decision-Time Without Reaction-Time: Experiments in Visual Scanning." *American Journal of Psychology,* 1963, *76(3),* 376-385.

Neisser, Ulric, Robert Novick, and Robert Lazar. "Searching for Ten Targets Simultaneously." *Perceptual and Motor Skills,* 1963, *17,* 955-961.

Newell, Allen, and Herbert Simon. *Human Problem Solving.* Englewood Cliffs: Prentice-Hall, 1972.

Nickerson, Raymond S. "Crossword Puzzles and Lexical Memory." In S. Dornic, ed., *Attention and Performance, VI.* Hillsdale: Erlbaum, 1977.

Nisbett, R. E., and T. D. Wilson, "Telling More Than We Can Know: Verbal Reports on Mental Process." *Psychological Review,* 1977, *84,* 231-259.

Noller, R. B., S. J. Parnes, and A. M. Biondi. *Creative Actionbook.* New York: Scribner, 1976.

Olton, Robert M. "Experimental Studies of Incubation: Searching for the Elusive." *Journal of Creative Behavior,* 1979, *13 (1),* 9-22.

Olton, Robert M., and David M. Johnson. "Mechanisms of Incubation in Creative Problem Solving." *American Journal of Psychology,* 1976, *89(4),* 617-630.

Packard, William, ed., *The Craft of Poetry.* Garden City: Doubleday, 1974.

Papert, Seymour. *Mindstorms: Children, Computers, and Powerful Ideas.* New York: Basic Books, 1980.

Parnes, S. J., R. B. Noller, and A. M. Biondi. *Guide to Creative Action.* New York: Scribner, 1977.

Parsons, Michael J. "A Discussion of 'Emotion and Cognition: Aesthetics and Science'." In Stanley S. Madeja, ed., *The Arts, Cognition, and Basic Skills.* St. Louis: CEMREL, 1978.

Patrick, Catherine. "Creative Thought in Poets." In R. Woodworth, ed., *Archives of Psychology,* 1935, *178.*

_____"Creative Thought in Artists." *Journal of Psychology,* 1937, *4,* 35-73.

_____"Scientific Thought." *Journal of Psychology,* 1938, *6,* 55-83.

Perkins, D. N. "Noticing: An Aspect of Skill." In *Conference on Basic Mathematical Skills and Learning, I: Contributed Position Papers.* Washington, D. C.: National Institute of Education, 1975.

_____"A Better Word: Studies of Poetry Editing." In David Perkins and Barbara Leondar, eds., *The Arts and Cognition.* Baltimore: Johns Hopkins University Press, 1977a.

_____"The Limits of Intuition." *Leonardo,* 1977b, *10,* 119-125.

_____"Metaphorical Perception." In E. Eisner, ed., *Reading, the Arts and the Creation of Meaning.* Reston: National Art Education Association, 1978.

_____"Are Matters of Value Matters of Fact?" In C. Nodine and D. Fisher, eds., *Perception and Pictorial Representation.* New York:

Praeger, 1979a.

_____"Schemata, Stereotype and Invention in the Arts." In E. Sacca and J. Victoria, eds., *Presentations on Art Education Research*, vol. 4. Montreal: Concordia University, 1979b.

_____"Novel Remote Analogies Seldom Contribute to Discovery." *Journal of Creative Behavior*, in press a.

_____"The Perceiver as Organizer and Geometer." In J. Beck, ed., *Representation and Organization in Perception*. Hillsdale: Earlbaum, in press b.

_____ and R. Cooper. "How the Eye Makes Up What the Light Leaves Out." In M. Hagen, ed., *The Perception of Pictures, II. Durer's Devices: Beyond the Projective Model*. New York: Academic Press, 1980.

_____ and M. Hagen. "Convention, Context and Caricature." In M. Hagen, ed., *The Perception of Pictures, I. Alberti's Window: The Projective Model of Pictorial Information*. New York: Academic Press, 1980.

Poe, Edgar Allan. "The Philosophy of Composition." In Phillip Van Doren, ed., *The Portable Edgar Allan Poe*. New York: Viking Press, 1945.

Polya, Gyorgy. *Mathematics and Plausible Reasoning*, 2 vols. Princeton: Princeton Unversity Press, 1954.

_____ *How To Solve It: A New Aspect of Mathematical Method*, 2nd ed. Garden City: Doubleday, 1957.

Porges, Irwin. *Edgar Allan Poe*. New York: Chilton Books, 1963.

Reid, Robert. *Marie Curie*. New York: Saturday Review Press, 1974.

Robinson, Francis P. *Effective Study*. New York: Harper and Row, 1970.

Roe, A. "Psychological Approaches to Creativity in Science." In M. A. Coler and H. K. Hughes, eds., *Essays on Creativity in the Sciences*. New York: New York University Press, 1963.

Rothenberg, Albert. *The Emerging Goddess: The Creative Process in Art, Science, and Other Fields*. Chicago: University of Chicago Press, 1979.

Ryder, Henry W., Harry Jay Carr, and Paul Herget. "Future Performance in Footracing." *Scientific American*, 1976, *234(6)*, 109-119.

Schachter, Stanley, and Jerome Singer. "Cognitive, Social, and Physiological Determinants of Emotional State." *Psychological Review*, 1962, *69*, 379-399.

Schank, R., and R. P. Abelson. *Scripts, Plans, Goals and Understand-*

ing: An Inquiry into Human Knowledge Structures. Hillsdale: Erlbaum, 1977

Scheffler, Israel. *Science and Subjectivity.* Indianapolis: Bobbs-Merrill, 1967.

_____"In Praise of the Cognitive Emotions." *Teachers College Record,* December 1977, *79(2),* 171-186.

Schneider, Elisabeth. *Coleridge, Opium and Kubla Khan.* Chicago: University of Chicago Press, 1953.

Schoenfeld, Alan H. "Presenting a Strategy for Indefinite Integration." *American Mathematical Monthly,* 1978, *85(8),* 673-678.

_____"Can Heuristics Be Taught?" In Jack Lochhead and John Clement, eds., *Cognitive Process Instruction.* Philadelphia: Franklin Institute, 1979a.

_____"Explicit Heuristic Training as a Variable in Problem Solving Performance." *Journal for Research in Mathematics Education,* 1979b *10(3),* 173-187.

Schon, Donald A. *Displacement of Concepts.* London: Tavistock, 1963.

Simon, Herbert A. *The Sciences of the Artificial.* Cambridge: Massachusetts Institute of Technology Press, 1969.

_____"How Big is a Chunk?" *Science,* 1974, *183(4124),* 482-488.

Simon, Herbert, and William Chase. "Skill in Chess." *American Scientist, 1973, 61,* 394-403.

Smith, E. R., and F. D. Miller. "Limits on Perception of Cognitive Processes: A Reply to Nisbett and Wilson." *Psychological Review,* 1978, *85,* 355-362.

Thayer, Alexander W. *The Life of Ludwig van Beethoven.* New York: The Beethovan Society, 1921.

Torrance, E. Paul. "Can We Teach Children To Think Creatively?" *Journal of Creative Behavior,* 1972, *6(2)* 114-143.

Vitruvius. *On Architecture,* 2 vols. Morris Hicky Morgan, trans. Loeb Classical Library. Cambridge: Harvard University Press, 1914.

Walker, John S. (chairman). *Official AAU Diving Rules for 1974.* Indianapolis: Amateur Athletic Union of the United States, 1974.

Wallace, Alfred Russell. *My Life,* vol. 1. New York: Dodd, Mead, 1905.

Wallach, Michael A. "Creativity." In Paul Mussen, ed., *Carmichael's Manual of Child Psychology,* vol. 1. New York: John Wiley, 1970.

_____"Psychology of Talent and Graduate Education." In Samuel Messick et al., eds., *Individuality in Learning.* San Francisco: Jossey-Bass, 1976a.

_____"Tests Tell Us Little About Talent." *American Scientist,* 1976b, *64,* 57-63.

Wallas, G. *The Art of Thought.* New York: Harcourt, Brace, 1926.

Welsh, George S. *Creativity and Intelligence: A Personality Approach.* Chapel Hill: Institute for Research in Social Science, 1977.

Westcott, M. R. *Toward a Contemporary Psychology of Intuition.* New York: Holt, Rinehart, and Winston, 1968.

Woodberry, George E. *The Life of Edgar Allan Poe,* vol. 2. Boston: Houghton Mifflin, 1909.

Wyatt, D. F., and D. T. Campbell. "On the Liability of Stereotype or Hypothesis." *Journal of Abnormal Social Psychology,* 1951, *46,* 496-500.

INDEX